Connected *for* Development

Information Kiosks and Sustainability

Edited by:
Akhtar Badshah
Sarbuland Khan
Maria Garrido

United Nations

United Nations
Information
and
Communication
Technologies
Task Force

4N2
ST/ESA/ICT
2004504

Table of Contents

SECTION II
Characteristics for Determining Success

Raising the Bar - Empowerment through Knowledge Transfer and Capacity Building

Leaving No One Behind - Developing an Inclusive Approach

Entrepreneurship and Innovation - Models for Financial Sustainability

SECTION III
Measuring Impact - Methodological Challenges and Evaluation Tools

Acknowledgements

I would like to express my deepest gratitude to both Mr. Sarbuland Khan, Director of the Division of ECOSOC Support and Coordination and Executive Coordinator of the United Nations ICT Task Force and Mr. Sergei Kambalov, Deputy Executive Coordinator of the United Nations ICT Task Force without whose contributions and guidance this book would not have been possible.

I would also like to thank the authors featured in this volume who so graciously contributed their time and energies to making this publication a success. Representing the corporate, government, development, academic, and NGO sectors, these authors have collectively produced a body of work that can provide valuable insight into the use of information kiosks for development.

Finally, I would like to thank all of those who worked tirelessly behind the scenes to prepare this book for publicaiton. Ms. Enrica Murmura of the United Nations ICT Task Force Secretariat provided invaluable and unconditional support to make this publication a reality. Special thanks are due to Martin Samaan of the Department of Public Information, United Nations for the cover design. Osama Manzar and Shaifali Chikermane, the copy and design editors respectively, slept little to meet tight deadlines and demanding requirements. Additional thanks go to Jennifer Beaston, Thomas Bell and Justin Thumler of Digital Partners whose dedication and hard work contributed enormously to the design and fulfillment of this project. I would also like to thank Digital Partners Board member Paul Maritz who funded the initial research that ultimately led to this book. Lastly, this publication was built upon initial research conducted by Maria Garrido whose unwavering commitment and continuous oversight throughout the production process saw this project through.

Akhtar Badshah
CEO and President
Digital Partners

Preface

Jose Maria Figueres
Chairman, United Nations ICT Task Force

On behalf of the members of the United Nations Information and Communication Technologies (ICT) Task Force, I am delighted to present, "Connected for Development - Information Kiosks and Sustainability." The UN ICT Task Force is charged with lending "a truly global dimension to the multitude of efforts to bridge the global digital divide, foster digital opportunity and thus firmly put ICT at the service of development for all." An integral component of meeting this mandate is learning from experience and collecting best practices to offer useful examples of sustainable progress. This effort helps ensure that field programs are based on a continuously evolving foundation of knowledge.

Information kiosks can be a timely model based on lessons learned from Internet Cafes and other community access points that have been deployed to expand opportunities for communication. While the aim of Internet Cafes is to provide market based points of access to the World Wide Web and communication applications, Information Kiosks shift the thinking from the objective being access to computers and places the focus on using the technology as a tool to deliver information and services to the underserved. Thus, the rural and disenfranchised of the world are given a voice. With that voice comes the prospect for expanded self-determination and the pursuit of a better life, as well as the possibility for a power shift from an elite few to a broadly engaged majority.

The historical challenge of offering services to rural populations has been well documented. Whether it was extremely expensive to provide roads, electricity, telephone service, or broadband connectivity - the problem was always rooted in sparse population density and heavy infrastructure costs. However, new modes of connectivity are emerging and the prices continue to drop. So whether a linkage is created through satellite, wireless loop, WI-FI or other technology, the need no longer exists for thousand of miles of wires, pipes or pavement to connect the rural population to their urban cousins. Healthcare, financial, agricultural, and economic information and services can now be delivered through a portal supported by limited fixed expenditures and rapidly decreasing marginal costs. If the world recognizes that knowledge is power, and there is no excuse for the enormous costs associated with providing access to information, then we now have an obligation to use these information kiosks as a tool for advancement.

This publication is a compilation of the various models of information kiosks being tested and deployed around the world, as well as insight from experts in this field about the different key components necessary for success. While this is not meant to act as an instruction manual, we do hope this publication will be a resource for individuals and organizations embarking on the mission of providing universal access and services. The sharing of ideas and best practices across continents has the potential to spur international cross-pollination, and more rapid innovation and success.

Foreword

Bruno Lanvin
Manager, Information for Development Program (infoDev), World Bank

The World Bank is not an institution specializing in information technology or tele-communications. If it has become a major player in that area, it is only because evidence is now sufficient to affirm that information technology, telecommunications and connectivity in general are significant contributors (and in some regards pre-requisites) to poverty reduction.

In year 2000, the international community adopted a set of quantified objec-tives and targets generally referred to as the 'Millennium Development Goals' (MDGs). By giving itself the objective of halving the number of people living in absolute poverty by 2015, it has also provided a common policy framework and an array of sectoral directions in which international organizations, governments and civil society can now work with a higher degree of synergy and efficacy.

For the first time ever in an effort of this breadth and scope, ICTs have been mentioned as a tool for development, and connectivity has been described as an indicator of development. The digital divide is now seen and recognized as a sig-nificant component of the development divide. For the poor, digital opportunities then become not only a response to new challenges (e.g. globalization) but also a tool to address longstanding (and unanswered) issues such as inequality, and lack of access to basic education or health services.

However, available evidence and experience (such as those emanating from the several hundreds of projects financed by infoDev over the last eight years) suggest that efforts initiated at the higher levels of central governments and international fora seldom reach their objectives unless they are fully endorsed, nurtured, reinvented and eventually carried out at the local level. The involvement and empowerment of local (especially rural) communities is hence the lynchpin of successful efforts to turn ICTs , telecommunications and connectivity into efficient instruments of development, job creation and poverty reduction.

This is why telecommunications community centers and information kiosks have been so instrumental in generating sustainable efforts to bring communication to the poor. The time has now come to gather, compare and combine the many successful experiences of such centers and kiosks around the world, to identify best practices, and to encourage and support their replication and their dissemination.

By looking at ways in which traditional technologies (such as community radios) and more advanced ones (such as WiFi) can be used to reach and empower local communities, this book can help all of us to identify and promote new ways of using ICT for development. By considering various possible business models and sustainability strategies for information kiosks, it can also help all of us to instill new energy and imagination in waging the fight against poverty.

It is still too early to say what the most successful will be among the approaches identified here or those that will emerge in the near future. One thing is certain however: the more local communities will be involved in applying and designing ICTs to address their immediate daily needs, the more we shall all learn on the way. By involving and empowering young people, women and individuals who had formerly no access to knowledge and education, information kiosks will inevitably play a major role in this process.

It has been said that any long march starts with a single step. The true success of the information revolution in making our world more equal and sustainable may very well start with the 'last mile'. May this book help decision makers and practitioners to identify ways in which old and new technologies, as well as global and local knowledge can contribute to blacksmith this missing link.

Introduction

Akhtar Badshah and Sarbuland Khan

Since the invention of the telegraph, communication technologies have played a determinant role in societies. The exchange of information through different medium of mass communication among nations - through newspapers, radio, television, etc. - have influenced human development by drawing economic geographies, shaping national identities and rebalancing the distribution of power within societies and among countries.

Nowhere is this influence more evident that in the current information revolution. In the sweep of a decade, the expònential growth of Information and Communication Technologies (ICT), particularly the Internet, has transformed the scale and speed at which the world does business and the ways we interact with one another. Every aspect of society has been impacted, ranging from development of public policy, gaining an education or even receiving medical care.

Perhaps the most surprising development of this revolution is the search for new solutions to alleviation of the debilitating poverty that permeates many parts of the world. New ICT technologies are facilitating the acquisition and absorption of knowledge, offering developing countries unprecedented opportunities to enhance educational systems, improve policy formulation and execution, and expand the range of opportunities for social change in even the poorest communities.

Departing from the premise that knowledge and information exchange is becoming an increasingly determinantal competitive factor for developing economies, different actors from development institutions, primarily NGOs, Multilateral organizations, and Governments, have conceived ICT as an engine for economic and social development in marginalized and poor communities. Among these actors, it is widely recognized that these technologies open unparalleled windows of opportunity to bring the benefits of information and ICT-enabled services to the developing world.

Along these lines, telecenters, defined as "shared premises where the pu-blic can access information and communication technologies" (Colle and Roman

1999:1), have been widely promoted as a vehicle to provide access to information especially for low-income communities in the developing world. During the decade since the telecenter movement started, development institutions have experimented with different models and generated a growing body of literature[1] aimed at researching these initiatives, their sustainability and their impact on the communities.

Building upon this valuable literature, the overarching objective of this book is to understand the preconditions and critical components necessary for the successful use of Information Kiosks for development and to learn lessons and practices generally instructive to the field from leaders of promising initiatives. The term "Information Kiosks" (IK) is used instead of "Telecenters" to connote, not a paradigm change in the field of development communication, but rather the transition to another phase in the evolution of the telecenter movement. For the purpose of this book, "Information Kiosks" is defined as public access points where information and communication technologies are used as a tool to deliver a basket of services to the underserved communities.

This transition in terms focuses the emphasis not so much on the type of technologies made available, but the ways in which these technologies can help meet the demand for social services and localized information. The contributing authors to this book explore the key factors influencing this transition. They are generally described below:

Governments in developing countries are orchestrating market-oriented reforms, deregulating and privatizing the telecommunications sector.
The influence of transparent regulatory frameworks in the development of information kiosks is two fold: First, these regulatory regimes allow governments in developing countries to establish telecommunications development funds aimed at expanding network infrastructure and connectivity into previously underserved areas. These funds, allocated under different schemes, are fuelling the growth of many information kiosks initiatives (See Proenza in Section I, and El Salvador case study of this publication).

Second, these regimes are building an enabling environment for the participation of the private sector in the development of information kiosks. A marquee example is the exponential growth of commercially oriented cybercafés in many urban areas in developing countries. These public access points are providing ICT access and connectivity to low-income segments of societies at an affordable price and in a sustainable manner; a market that had largely been ignored by the private sector (See Proenza in Section I and Fernandez-Maldonado in Section II).

The development of national e-strategies that are bringing much needed social services and information into an electronic form.
Thus, the relevance of orchestrating public e-initiatives with information kiosks services to meet the need of the poor and underserved. This trend is of particular relevance since governments are turning to information kiosks as mechanisms to

deliver social services, escalating not only the participation of kiosks in development, but also increasing the chances for them to achieve some sort of financial sustainability (See Proenza, Schware in Section II and Drishtee, Indonesia, and Peru in Section V).

The use of networks as a form of organization to build partnerships among different actors for the exchange of information and resources.
Facilitated by ICT-enabled technology, a multiplicity of actors representing NGOs, governments, international organizations and the private sector are building ad hoc networks of communication to foster dialogue, the efficient use of ICT resources for development and the flow of resources - financial and non-financial - among members. The shift toward building partnerships, signalled by the increasing growth of these networks, underlies one of the most fundamental premises behind the transition to information kiosks: the understanding that ICT for development is a multilayer process in which trust and collaboration enhance the role that information kiosks play in meeting the needs of the poor (See Proenza, Sherry et al. and Stoll in Section I and Hungary, Chile, and Peru in Section V of this publication).

New models of information kiosks are being developed that look to achieve economic sustainability while being more responsive to local needs.
Information kiosks that rely entirely on donors' funds for their operation have less chances of becoming viable mechanisms for development. Instead, the trend is shifting develop financially sustainable and commercially viable kiosks with clear business models. The more promising models rely on domestic entrepreneurs with supporting networks for their design and management assistance. From this perspective, nourishing capacity building at the local level ensures that information kiosks become more responsive to local demands providing services to the communities that are socially and culturally sensitive (See Kusakabe, Jensen, Proenza, and Schware in Section II of this publication).

There is a rising awareness of the need for systematic, multidisciplinary and cross-national research and mechanisms to share, diffuse and exchange the knowledge generated.
The dynamic nature of ICT and the diversity of projects - in terms of the cultural, social and economic contexts of the communities served - make imperative the reliance on systematic and cross-national research to guide the development of information kiosks as a tool for global development.

As seen from this perspective, comparative and systematic research can become a valuable mechanism to promote participation by the communities being served, which in turn, will help the information kiosks become more responsive to local needs[2] while fostering the crosspollination of ideas at a global level.

Current global knowledge-sharing systems can be adapted to nourish international cooperation and dialogue among different actors interested in development. Universities,[3] which have not played a key role in research during the first decade of the telecenter movement, can serve a particularly valuable role (See Colle & Roman, Wisner and Peizer in Section III of this publication)

Country-level ICT assessments are guiding strategic public policy and investment decisions including how these technologies can be used to promote social development
International organizations are supporting a variety of initiatives to create comprehensive assessments regarding the status of information and communication technologies in different countries. These assessments gather key data regarding ICT infrastructure, penetration of ICT in society, business climate for investing in the ICT sector, and the appropriateness of the policy frameworks that guide ICT initiatives for the purpose of social and economic development. Among the programs are, E-Readiness by InfoDev; Networked Readiness Index by the Centre for International Development at Harvard and e-ForAll by Francisco J. Proenza.[4] These assessments are becoming a valuable tool to guide public policy and investment in ICT initiatives that have as a core principle the fight against poverty.

"Connected for Development: Information Kiosks and Sustainability" offers the reader an initial analysis of these main factor influencing the development and performance of information kiosks as tools for economic empowerment. The authors represent a diversity of backgrounds and expertise and provide a valuable and enriching perspective on ICT and development.

In Section I, **Building an Enabling Environment for the Development of Successful Information Kiosks,** the authors address the way in which public policy frameworks and partnerships among different actors increase the probabillity that information kiosk will achieve sustainability while generating greater social and economic benefits for the communities they serve.

In Section II, **Characteristics for Determining Success,** the authors offer a deep analysis of the specific characteristics of information kiosks that influence their performance and impact. They address the importance of generating a participatory process in which community members, local entrepreneurs and public authorities are involved in every phase of the project development. The contributors underscore the need for developing inclusive approaches that engender capacity building, knowledge transfer and social and economic sustainability at the local level. An underlying theme is the need to lessen the dependence on external donors by considering models that combine private-sector investment, government subsidies, and local entrepreneurship.

In Section III, **Measuring Impact - Methodological Challenges and Evaluation Tools,** the authors present valuable insights regarding the challenges that development practitioners and researchers face when designing methodologies to measure the social and economic impacts of ICT Kiosks. The authors offer some alternative frameworks for evaluating information kiosks and address strategies that can help researches overcome some of the methodological challenges.

In Section IV, **New Approaches to ICT for Development**, the authors suggest that a number of innovative information kiosk models, spanning most core development sectors, are emerging at the enterprise level. They investigate in depth some of these ground-breaking initiatives in different regions and offer a preliminary scenario of the next stage in the information kiosks movement.

In Section V, **Analysis of Selected Case Studies: Lessons from the field**, Projects in Asia, Africa and Latin America are presented to understand regional best practices as well as the potential for cross-regional application. This section includes a wide variety of information kiosks including commercial, government and NGO-led initiatives, with the purposes of sharing lessons from the field, discerning the best models across sectors and regions and understanding the limitations and potential that these models offer for possible scaling or replication.

Notes

1. See for example [Colle & Roman 1999; Schware 2000; Proenza 2001, 2003; Roman & Blattman 2001; Latchem & Walker (eds) 2001; Wellenius 2001].

2. See [Colle & Roman 2001] and [Roman & Blattman 2001].

3. See [Colle & Roman 2001].

4. Proenza, F. (2003) "e-ForAll: A poverty Reduction Strategy for the Information Age" pre-sents a comparative analysis of two of the most prominent e-readiness methodologies and offers a more inclusive methodology to guide public policy.. This document can be found at: http://communication.utexas.edu/college/digital_divide_symposium/papers/e-ForAll.pdf

SECTION I

Building an Enabling Environment for the Development of Successful Information Kiosks

The Role of the Government and Development Agencies - How Can Policies Help?

A Public Sector Support Strategy for Telecenter Development: Emerging Lessons from Latin America and the Caribbean
Francisco J. Proenza

The Power of Networking - Building Partnerships among NGOs, Governments and the Private Sector.

ICT-Enabled Networks, Public Sector Performance and the Development of ICTs
Francisco J. Proenza

Navigating Multiple Networks: ICTs, Multinationals and Development
John Sherry, Tony Salvador and Hsain Ilahiane

Somos@Telecentros: Networking in Action
Klaus Stoll

Overcoming Unreliability of Telecom and Energy Infrastructure

Connecting Rural India Towards Prosperity
Ashok Jhunjhunwala

Information Kiosks and Sustainability: Key Components for Success
Mike Jensen

A Public Sector Support Strategy for Telecenter Development:
Emerging Lessons from Latin America and the Caribbean

Francisco J. Proenza*
Food and Agricultural Organization (UN)

Abstract

The author examines the main schemes used by governments in Latin America and the Caribbean to support the establishment of telecenters. He proposes a framework for a public support strategy during the two major phases in the evolution of telecenters - establishment and consolidation - and emphasizes the need for research and independent evaluation of these programs.

Telecenters are a way of providing connectivity and computer services to the low-income sector of the population. They enable low-cost access to information and communication technologies (ICTs), by offering shared services within the same premises to the public at large. This report focuses on those telecenters that provide Internet services, since it is this technology that offers new opportunities for distance telecommunication services and applications, and because the management and operation of telecenters that provide Internet connectivity is a more complex undertaking.

If kiosks and small telecenters with only one computer are included in the count, Latin American and Caribbean governments sponsored the installation of over 5,000 telecenters in the past few years. Plans for 2003-2004 include the installation of an additional 10,000 state sponsored telecenters, requiring an investment of over USD 250 million. Argentina has had the most ambitious program, but may soon be overtaken by Brazil and Mexico.

Not all the centers that have been established are still in operation. In Argentina, for example, between August 1999 and June 2000 a total of 1,281 Community Technology Centres (Centros Tecnológicos Communitarios or CTCs) were installed. A year later, only about 72 per cent of these CTCs were still wor-

---

*The views presented in this paper are those of the author and do not necessarily represent the official position of the FAO.

king, and no one knows how many CTCs remain open today. Anecdotal evidence of remarkable achievements under very difficult conditions abounds; but very little is known about the impact that CTCs are having on the communities they serve.

Telecenters are a highly visible, powerful and inexpensive political tool. They generate much fanfare during the early planning and inauguration stages of the programs, but interest in their operation and effectiveness wanes shortly afterwards. Most of the programs that have been established are still young, and this limits data availability. More troubling, however, is that very few programs provide for parallel efforts to collect and analyze data on costs and development impact. From 1994 through 2001, Canada's Community Access Program funded the establishment of over 8,000 telecenters, yet today we know very little about what happened to these centers. The successes or failures of past programs remain undocumented, and politicians tend to start from scratch, hurriedly moving towards the inauguration of the next center.

Notwithstanding data limitations, quite a deal is already known about what works and what doesn't. Ideally a telecenter should increase the welfare of a low-income target population, be relatively easy to replicate and have good prospects of being sustainable. All of these three objectives are important and are covered in this brief note, but it is the last one that is most challenging. The annual operating costs of a telecenter are similar to or even higher than investment costs. Installing a telecenter is easy; the hard part is to keep it running.

Emerging lessons

Most State sponsored telecenter initiatives in Latin America and the Caribbean are primarily targeted at inhabitants of small towns in rural areas and represent a governmental response to the market's inability to serve rural communities on a purely commercial basis. The urban lowest-income population is the target of a few of these programs. This is the case of the telecenters sponsored by the Prefeitura de Sào Paulo in Brazil and of the Amic@s in Asunción, Paraguay. Two other programs - one in Brazil and another one in Chile - aim to serve small and micro-enterprises. State programs have used three main schemes to support telecenter establishment:

- direct selection of site and operating institution by the State (e.g., CTC Program in Argentina and Telecentros de Prefeitura de São Paulo in Brazil).
- minimum subsidy programs, commonly used by Telecommunication Development Funds (e.g., Subtel in Chile, COMPARTEL in Colombia, FITEL in Peru).
- investment funds where small local entities compete directly for the subsidies provided by the government (e.g., Chile - Sercotec - Ministry of Economy; and Brazil - SEBRAE-MDIC-CDI).

Direct selection entails a risk of political meddling in the process, as well as the potential for bureaucratization and squandering of scarce fiscal resources.

Minimum subsidy schemes are appropriate wherever connectivity infrastructure development is required, but are limited in their ability to meet the needs of low-income groups. Investment Funds rely more on local institutions and are therefore in principle more suitable to provide for poor populations, but they are difficult to apply where important infrastructure developments are needed. They also call for careful design and implementation arrangements, in order to avoid political interference from compromising the effectiveness of the process of selecting sites and awarding subsidies.

In South America, there are several noteworthy efforts to increase the impact of telecenters on the needy, including:

- establishment of telecenters with the dual purpose of serving the school and the community at large (Chile, Guyana);

- support to micro and small entrepreneurs as part of a new Telecenter Development Program (Brazil, Chile) or by expanding the services provided by existing centers (Peru);

- sponsorship of community projects applying ICTc (Brazil, Colombia);

- promotion of community networks to encourage social change (many countries);

- use of open source software by the telecenter program of the Prefeitura de São Paulo, and the recently reformulated GESAC[1] program that will cover all of Brazil;

- sponsorship of network formation through the minimum subsidy selection scheme, as applied by Subtel in Chile, to encourage alliances between different sectors of society;

- use of community radio stations, in conjunction with telecenters and with Internet-aided information exchange networks, as a means of extending services to remote rural communities that are very needy but also expensive and difficult to serve (e.g. in Brazil).

Basic Features of a Telecenter Support Strategy

There are two major phases in the evolution of telecenters in which the State can and should provide support, always with a view to achieving sustainability and high social impact. The first one refers to the initial establishment period and the second one to the consolidation of centers and the enhancement of their social impact. These two phases are not necessarily sequential; they may be implemented in parallel. But, of course, without telecenters in place, the second phase cannot take effect. The main features of public support strategy are outlined in the accompanying table and briefly described below.

Establishment

- In urban areas with good infrastructure, it generally makes no sense to promote the establishment of State-subsidized telecenters. A powerful educational and dissemination campaign on the possibilities offered by the Internet could instead be a very effective means of encouraging the installation of privately run telecenters (e.g. cyber cafés, cabinas publicas, locutorios).

- It is in rural areas and small towns where State support becomes critical during the initial set up phase. Where the sustainability of a telecenter is questionable, as would be the case of very small, remote, low productivity communities, a support strategy should focus on viable alternatives, including for example the support of rural radio stations. In somewhat larger, more prosperous rural communities, where the chances of telecenter sustainability are greater, the kinds of telecenters that can be established will for the most part be small (e.g. say 1 to 3 computers). State support should be based on merit contests, either following a minimum subsidy scheme or the kind of competitive funding more commonly used by community investment funds.

- At the local level, the institutions responsible for these centers may be small businesses, NGOs or educational institutions. Local governments can also potentially perform well as administrators, but in practice they are often compromised by political interference to the detriment of sustainability, particularly in poor communities where telecenters have a high profile.

- The installation of rural telecenters must also envisage the development of inter-institutional alliances to enable: i) the sharing of connectivity and costs, in order to maximize use and impact, and ii) an increase in the customer base of the center, as the various institutions participating in the alliance encourage their members to make use of the facilities. The State can encourage and nurture these partnerships, but cannot force them into existence. Instead, they will have to be formed voluntarily at the local level by the local partners on their own initiative.

Consolidation

The second phase, during which telecenter consolidation takes place, may be launched simultaneously or shortly after the installation of the centers. We know less about what works for this phase, in part because the programs are new, but also on account of the paucity of data and serious studies on what goes on after the centers have been established.

The kinds of activities that governments may support during this phase - for the benefit of both rural and urban communities - include efforts to reach out to communities and to low income groups, and the provision of government content and services online (see Table 1).

Conclusion

Connectivity and policies favoring access to marginal areas and an expansion in services to low-income populations are a hot topic. The numerous international

Table 1. Telecenters: State Support Mechanisms Recommended by Setting

		Urban		Rural	
Phase	**Intervention Type**	Good Telecom infrastructure			Poor Telecom infrastructure
		Many Telecenters	Some Telecenters	No Telecenters	
Establishment	**ICT Literacy Campaigns**		X	X	X
	State-Sponsored Telecenter Establishment				X
	Minumum subsidy schemes			X	
	Investment fund approach		X	X	X
	Partnerships				
	Local sharing of connectivity		X	X	X
	Sponsorship of local partnerships to enable the provision of public services		X	X	X
Consolidation Enhancement of Social Impact	**Outreach to Community and Low-Income Groups**				
	Training grants	X	X	X	X
	Proficiency grants	X	X	X	X
	Funding of applications and content wth high social impact	X	X	X	X
	Government Content and Services				
	Microenterprise support	X	X	X	X
	Online transactions geared to the specific needs of telecenters	X	X	X	X
	Efforts to increase share of government purchases supplied by microenterprises	X	X	X	X
	Information on project funding opportunities and initiatives	X	X	X	X

gatherings that take place tend to be used by each country to promote their own model and, for the most part, focus on general policy concerns. They are seldom used for deliberate consideration of sound analytical studies, or well-documented best practices and lessons of experience, or to discuss options for concerted action on practical matters of common concern.

Many experiments and innovations presently underway in Latin America and the Caribbean are in general well conceived and have good prospects of successful replication throughout the region and even worldwide. Regretfully, there is little dialogue and discussion among countries and these experiences are not well known.

What looks promising on paper may turn sour in practice. Only a few of these programs are providing for serious independent evaluation. They deserve more careful professional scrutiny regarding their impact and sustainability, as an input to an open debate focused on very practical program design and operational issues, with full participation of government agencies, academia, private companies and civil society institutions.

Notes

[1] GESAC - Governo Eletrônico - Serviço de Atendimento ao Cidadão

ICT-Enabled Networks, Public Sector Performance and the Development
of Information and Communication Technologies

Francisco J. Proenza*

Food and Agricultural Organization

Abstract

The author argues that the participation and interaction of a broad range of stake-holders in networks that provide for the exchange of experiences and up to date information on ICTs, will facilitate the updating of State institutions by upgrading the proficiency and knowledge of public officials regarding innovations, analytical tools and best practices.

CT enhance the productivity and competitiveness of firms, as enterprises find it is less costly and more profitable to automate and link up computers for purchasing and sale operations, to form part of industrial clusters, and to set up alliances and short term business deals with other firms. ICTs are giving new vitality to civil society, as they give communities, not for profit organizations and informal groups, an enhanced capability to share information, ideas, activities, and assets. ICT can also enhance public sector effectiveness, accountability and transparency, by enabling increased cooperation and communications across agencies, and between agencies and enterprises and ordinary citizens. To profit from ICT-enabled networks institutions need to reorganize their operational and governance structures. This is trying for any organization, but is a major challenge for public sector agencies. This challenge needs to be urgently addressed to help expand ICTs in developing countries. It is also a challenge that ICTs can help overcome.

Networks are a key feature of human interaction. Networks are founded on trust, and trust is built up through personal often informal communication, frequent contact, and the practical experience by participants that their connection to other network members are advantageous and address their particular concerns.

*The views presented in this paper are those of the author and do not necessarily represent the official position of the FAO.

Information and communication technologies do not change the basic character of networks. What they bring that is new, is that they enable the expansion of networks, even worldwide, at minimal cost. In so doing, they enable the diversification of the actors that can become part of the network and thus significantly change network dynamics and power relationships.

ICT-Enabled Networks

In the modern world, administrative structures need to be light and agile, strategic alliances take on added significance, and an institution's ability to respond swiftly is a key determinant of performance. These three features - decentralization, cooperation, and rapid response - underlie ICT-based increases in productivity and institutional effectiveness. They are key attributes of ICT-enabled networks and give rise to a new institutional paradigm.

Widespread decentralization in the organizational structure of firms has been made possible by increased information flows between management, field workers, customers and suppliers. Field workers are closer to the customer and in the best position to make decisions that are in tune with changes in market demand. But field workers cannot be in the fringes of the firm's procedures and organizational culture. To be responsive to increasingly frequent changes in technology and markets while keeping its separate identity, the modern firm adopts an agile decision-making structure with few hierarchical levels that encourages interaction and swift communication - using ICTs - between workers at all levels of the enterprise.

Strategic alliances allow companies to take advantage of complementarities with other producers that do not compete in the same market, and to profit from an enhanced ability to coordinate input supply through ICT-enabled low-cost outsourcing. Agricultural and agroindustrial export ventures frequently aggregate supply from many producers within a region or locality, to jointly compete with the rest of the world to serve far away markets. Industrial clusters develop between enterprises that support each other while forming part of interlinked supply chains.

Rapid response is made possible by ICT, and is at the same time indispensable in today's markets. The Internet, the mobile phone, computers interconnected across enterprises, all enable firms to remain open for business and service clients 24 hours a day, 7 days a week. And beware the firm unwilling or unable to adapt!

Non profit private organizations are also seeing their organizational structures and operating procedures radically changed by ICT-enabled networks. Their outreach has dramatically increased,[1] and their effectiveness and prospects for success have become conditional on their ability to adapt in much the same way as private firms. Their organizational structures need to be decentralized, their ability to network with other NGOs with shared objectives has become paramount, and opportune fund raising and rapid service capabilities are key determinants of survival.

Whereas the ICT-enabled Network paradigm calls for organizational changes on all kinds of institutions, public agencies are particularly ill suited to make the necessary adjustments. By tradition, incentive structure and at times even mandate, public organizations have vertical structures with multiple hierarchical layers.[2] Their efficiency and response capacity are subject to various levels of consultation, to complex formal representational protocols, and to strict functional demarcations of "turf"; all of which make interdisciplinary networking with other agencies and civil society difficult to realize.[3]

The main difference between public organizations, and private companies and NGOs, lies in the consequences of delays in adjusting to the new paradigm (see Table 1 below). Whereas a firm or NGO that does not adapt its strategies and structures will perish, a public agency can in most cases languish endlessly, no matter how irrelevant or ineffective its actions.

Table 1. Organization type and relative capacity to adjust to new instituional paradigm

	Private Sector	NGO	Public Sector
Decentralization	Decentralization is indespensable to satisfy a clientele that is ever more demanding and facing increasing number of options.	Decentralization and informal relationships are dominant. These attributes give strength to NGOs but are also a major source of weakness; especially for long term sustained effort.	By tradition, public agencies have hierarchical multilayer structures. Political considerations are paramount and delegation of authority is risky and unrewarding.
Partnerships	Increasing specialization of knowledge and the need for multidisciplinary work effort, give added importnace to partnerships, **B2B = ICT aided enterprise networks**	The more effective NGOs have many partners and share information and resources enhanced by electronic networks.	Partnerships are difficult to achieve. Demarcation and protection of turf is the dominant concern. Duplication of effort is commonplace.
Capacity to Respond to Stakeholder Demands	Swift response and quality of service is rewarded through profits and higher worker earnings.	Rapid response and effectiveness is rewarded through achievement of objectives and, frequently, also highter staff salaries.	Loyalty and respect for hierarchy is rewarded. Rapid response obeys political considerations - often at the expense of technical wisdom. The "client" can wait.
Consequences	The enterprise that adapts to the new paradigm prospers. The firm that does not adapt loses money and sooner or later is forced to close down.	The NGO that adjusts is successful - achieves objectives and raises funds. The one that does not adapt, disappears.	A public agency that adjusts becomes effective and complies with an ever changing mandate. The one that does not, becomes irrelevant, but lingers along indefinitely.

ICT Development and Governance

Modernization of the telecommunications sector and universalization of ICT use is necessarily a multidisciplinary undertaking that calls for cooperation and concerted action with other organizations and economic and social agents.

- State support is needed to foster competition in the telecommunications sector and to provide a transparent, stable and independent regulatory framework that protects incentives for private investors as well as the rights of consumers. These could be by developing public services and content online on a wide range of economic and social spheres; by providing affordable subsidies that enable the expansion of connectivity to rural areas; and by developing applications that help combat poverty and redress inequality in opportunities (employment, education, health services, etc.).

- Private enterprise is indispensable, to invest risk capital to develop infrastructure and help further technological innovation, and to operate complex telecommunications and private service networks.

- NGOs are an important source of innovation in the design and implementation of initiatives that benefit low-income communities and marginalized groups, and may play an important advocacy role in support of fairness in opportunities and a more equitable development.

The participation and interaction of a broad range of stakeholders - entrepreneurs, researchers, NGOs and public administration authorities - in networks that provide for the exchange of experiences and up to date information on ICT, will facilitate the updating of State institutions by upgrading the proficiency and knowledge of public officials regarding innovations, analytical tools and best practices.

More importantly, if such networks are structured so that they bring about critical, open discussion and analysis of political decisions and negotiations of national interest, or if they enable the participation of a wide range of sectors of society in the supervision of the implementation of specific projects, they can also modify the incentive structure that public officials face and thus contribute to making State action more effective. Seen from this perspective, the formation and strengthening of public-private-civil society alliances is a key element in any strategy that aims to provide for universal access and the development of ICT in developing countries.

Sample Practical Applications

Consider three areas of prime importance to developing countries.[4]

1) Rural telecenter establishment,
2) School-based telecenters,
3) Business development services online in support of microenterprise.

Rural Telecenter Establishment

Argentina's experience with the establishment of its *Centros Tecnológicos Comunitarios* (CTCs) exemplifies a traditional bureaucratic approach and reads like a set of guidelines for disappointment.[5]

First, assume that the Government will be able to service all telecenter users for free. In the case of the CTCs, time proved that the Government simply could not afford to continue the subsidies required. The unknown number of centers that are still operational find a way to pay for operating costs by charging for services under the guise of "voluntary contributions" from users. **Second**, set them up in a hurry. The CTC program was implemented during the last year of a Government's term in office in a politically charged transitional setting. The **third** guideline is a corollary of a rush job: When you are in a hurry, it is more expedient to determine site locations following political as opposed to technical criteria.[6] The end result: no buy-in from local telecenter administrators (government pays for everything, and center managers had little say in the program); no transparency (everything is done under the directive of "authorities") and no accountability (it was all done by a departing government).[7]

The experience of Chile and Perú with Telecommunications Development Funds is more encouraging.[8] Their reverse auction programs award subsidies on a competitive basis to operators that establish and run telecenters in low profit rural areas. Even if a poor country cannot afford to serve all rural towns, these schemes enable Governments to control how much of a subsidy they are willing and able to spend in order to serve rural communities. A suitable auction design is vital, not just to assure accountability, transparency and sustainability, but to increase competitive pressures by encouraging a large number of bidders to participate.

Neither OSIPTEL in Peru nor Subtel in Chile[9] are impervious to political pressures. Nevertheless, both of these agencies have considerable operational independence. Both agencies have adopted a policy of open dialogue - making extensive use of ICT networking - through several rounds of consultation with a broad range of stakeholders. The selection of sites and the design of the telecenter programs are determined by a government agency, but only after considerable consultation (networking) with civil society and private enterprise organizations.[10] Under these institutional arrangements, stakeholder buy-in is easier to achieve, public officials are under greater pressure from the public to address technical issues in a fair, transparent and efficient way, and in association with other agencies as required.

School-based Telecenters

Commercial telecenters everywhere get very little business in the morning, which is when most schools can make use of connectivity services. It is common to find commercial telecenters serving private schools during the daytime under private terms. Public school systems present a greater challenge.

Although in principle an ideal way to share scarce connectivity resources, public school telecenters have in practice proven to be quite difficult to implement. Public school systems are usually run under highly centralized authority, whereas telecenters thrive under local management and decision-making. National school administrators are weary of sharing their school's equipment and connectivity, and they discourage the charging of fees by local school officials. Without the means to pay for operation and maintenance - be it through fees or direct support if governments can afford it - telecenter sustainability is compromised.

Chile has put together a workable program that is opening up public school labs to serve the community at large after school hours. The program aims for a total coverage of 5,000 schools and hopes to provide ICT training to a total of about one million people between 2002 and 2005. The first set of 500 schools opened for service to the public in 2002. In exchange for a service agreement and sustainable operational plan from the school, the program offers financial support to participating schools, to help them cover the administrative costs including the salary of the teacher in charge of the program.

The program is run by a Subtel staff member, a systems engineer who was previously in charge of Subtel's Telecommunications Development Fund, and is now under secondment working for the Ministry of Education. Herein is a prime example of cooperation across agencies and disciplines, in support of ICT development. The program was established only after practically all schools in the country were connected to the Internet. Since schools are connected, the program is advertised and operated through ICT-enabled networks that engage target schools in a consultative and training process during program design and implementation.

Business Development Services Online

The past couple of years have witnessed a dramatic surge in business development services offerings online, mostly geared to small and microenterprise development, many provided under government sponsorship. What is the impact of these "services"? It is impossible to tell because practically no monitoring is taking place, but with so much duplication it is safe to say that many of these websites are used infrequently and yield little that is of practical value.

Chile's "Advice online" service provided by its small and microenterprise su-pport agency, Sercotec, stands apart for its brilliant use of ICT-enabled networks to provide public services online.[11] Chilean entrepreneurs registered in the site (www.redsercotec.cl) may send specific queries to any one of 80 specialists covering 40 different fields of expertise. These messages are answered within 48 hours. For each advice category, the site gives the user a choice of several specialists, providing for each of them his or her picture, location, summary cu-rriculum vitae, and a record of the responses that the specialist has already given to date. Since its inception in March 2002, a total of 2,000 queries have been answered and recorded and may be read online. Over 20 private and public institutions have allied with Sercotec to support the service. Queries related to agriculture may, for instance, be addressed to the National Institute of Agricultural Development (INDAP); legal queries may be directed to upper class students of the University of Chile's Law School; and so on.

Think of the impact on public service incentives, and of the implications for public agency efficiency, accountability and transparency. Imagine you are a public servant and that every question you are asked, you are obliged to answer within 48 hours, in the understanding that your response will be placed on record, identifying you as the author, and made available for everyone in the world to read!

Conclusion

Countries worldwide are gearing up to be part of the information society. Many are recognizing the importance of governmental leadership and inter-agency cooperation for the implementation of comprehensive e-government programs.[12] There is less awareness of the high risks associated with investments in ICT, of the urgency of improving public sector efficiency, accountability and transparency, and of the possibilities for relying on ICT-enabled networks to change institutional incentives and develop mechanisms that provide for coordination, control, monitoring and consultation with full participation of civil society.

International cooperation can contribute to fill this gap, mainly through thorough and careful detailed studies that provide rigorous examinations of best practices, benchmarking initiatives that let governments know where they stand and helps them identify the obstacles they face and need to overcome, and through a comprehensive worldwide network of knowledge exchange on e-government best practices.

Notes

1   "Jody Williams won the Nobel Peace Prize in 1997 for her contribution to the international ban on landmines. She achieved that ban not only without much government help, but in the face of opposition from all the major powers. And what did she say was her secret weapon for organizing 1,000 different human rights and arms control groups on six continents? 'E-mail'." [Friedman 2000, page 14].

   See also [Garrido and Halavais 2003].

2   "The clash between the vertical structure of government and the trend towards horizontal networks, no fan of hierarchy, is one of the main problems facing government (governance) in the information society." (Curtin [2001], page 7.) "One of the basic reasons for public-sector inefficiency-"bureaucracy"-is that, whereas departments are vertically organized, many of the services that they have to deliver require complex collaboration between employees across departments. The British government has for several years been preaching the need for "joined-up government", but has found that the underlying structures of government conspire against it." The Economist [2000].

3   Stiglitz, Orzag and Orzag [2001, pág. 35-36] give the following list of reasons why failures of the State occur: i) lack of bankruptcy treat; ii) weak incentives for workers who are difficult to dismiss, and for managers aware of these difficulties; iii) misaligned incentives which may, for example, induce a manager to maximize the size of a public agency as opposed to maximizing social be-

nefits; iv) risk aversion, since the cost of a mistake may be high, whereas the benefits of a good decision are only perceived indirectly; and v) "dynamic inconsistency" because no one can enforce the State into complying a contract agreement, and therefore public agency managers can not make credible long term commitments.

4   In the US, the enactment of the E-Government Act of 2002 [US Congress 2002] and the establishment of a site specifically dedicated to e-rulemaking (www.regulations.gov) has stimulated considerable interest and research on the applications of ICTs to public sector governance (Coglianese 2003a,b, Brandon and Carlitz [2003], Carlitz and Gunn [2002]). Visit also the Harvard's Regulatory Policy Program papers e-rulemaking: www.ksg.harvard.edu/cbg/rpp/papers.htm. Similar discussions in Europe (e.g. Curtin 2001], were stimulated by the publication of the European Commission's White Paper on Governance [EC 2001].

For developing countries, Schware [2000] has given concrete examples of the application of ICTs to improve public sector performance. Here we focus on the use of ICTs in developing countries to strengthen public sector performance in the development of ICT infrastructure and online public services.

5   We know that a number of measures adopted by Argentina undermined its Centros Tecnológicos Comunitarios (CTC) program. Whether in fact these measures will lead to failure in a different country context is difficult to anticipate; but the Argentinean experience should, at least, serve as a warning.

6   Center locations and equipment allocations "were in many cases determined solely according to the will of project authorities". Ruffa and Zubieta [2000], page 52.

7   There is nothing atypical or special about the Argentinean case. It is only a recent and well documented example of a telecenter establishment program that followed a traditional public organization's approach. According to the Performance Institute [2002], page 8, "Of the $48 billion spent on information technology in FY 2002, this survey indicates that most of those expenditures were not justified by mission-aligned performance measures. This practice represents a "high risk" business practice that could result in failed IT projects and losses to the taxpayer."

8   The mechanisms involved in telecenter establishment are described in detail by Wellenius [2001]. Here we wish to emphasize some key institutional features involved.

9   OSIPTEL is Peru's Organismo Supervisor de Inversión Privada en Telecomunicaciones. Subtel is Chile's Telecommunications Subsecretariat. Both institutions are highly reputable telecommunications regulators. They were recently nominated by Pyramid Research as candidates for its first "Regulator of the year" Annual Telecommunications Award (along with Brazil's Anatel and El Salvador's Siget). According to Pyramid, its nominees for regulator of the year using the following criteria: innovation (25%), autonomy (25%), credibility (20%), transparency (20%) and efficiency (10%).(www.pyramidresearch.com/conf/lasum03/votepyr.asp)

10   The consultative process that has been followed by OSIPTEL may be appreciated with respect to their latest project in the pipeline, that will provide for the establishment of about 800 cabinas públicas in the country's District capitals. The project's descriptions and public comments may be downloaded from: http://www.fitel.gob.pe/contenido.php?ID=13

11   That Chile keeps coming up in examples of best e-Government practices is not an accident. According to the World Economic Forum's ranking of 80 countries with respect to the quality of public institutions, Chile (along with Uruguay) comes ahead of more industrialized nations like Belgium, France, Italy, Japan, Korea, Portugal, Spain, Taiwan. Public sector reform has been a governmental priority for over ten years now; and the application of ICTs as an input to enhancing

public sector performance is well recognized. See Gobierno de Chile-INAP [2003], Gobierno de Chile-Universidad de Chile [2003], Comité Inerministerial de Modernización de la Gestión Pública [2000], and visit www.gestionpublica.gov.cl and www.modernizacion.cl/.

12 According to Accenture [2002] the figure of Chief Information Officer, with responsibility for inter-agency coordination of e-Government initiatives, is now well established in many countries.

References

Accenture, "e-Government Leadership - Realizing the Vision", April 2002. (www.accenture.com/xd/xd.asp?it=enWeb&xd=industries%5Cgovernment%5Cgove_welcome.xml).

Brandon, Barbara and Carlitz, Robert, Online Rulemaking and Other Tools for Strengthening our Civil Infrastructure, Administrative Law Review, 2003 (www.ksg.harvard.edu/cbg/Conferences/rpp_rulemaking/Brandon_Carlitz_Online_Rulemaking.pdf)

Carlitz, Robert D. and Gunn, Rosemary W., "Online Rulemaking: A Step Toward E-Governance", June 15, 2002. (www.info-ren.org/publications/giq_2002/giq_2002.html)

Coglianese 2003a "The Internet and Public Participation in Rule Making" 2003, (www.ksg.harvard.edu/cbg/research/rpp/RPP-2003-05.pdf)

Coglianese 2003b "Information Technology and Regulatory Policy: New Directions for Digital Government Research" 2003b, (www.ksg.harvard.edu/cbg/research/rpp/RPP-2003-12.pdf)

Commission of the European Communities (EC) "Enhancing democracy: A White Paper on Governance in the European Union", 2001. (http://europa.eu.int/eur-lex/en/com/cnc/2001/com2001_0428en01.pdf).

Cornelius, Peter and Klaus Schwab, ed, The Global Competitiveness Report 2002-2003, World Economic Forum, Oxford University Press 2003 (www.weforum.org/).

Curtin, Deirdre, The Commission as Sorcerer's Apprentice? Reflections on EU Public Administration and the Role of Information Technology in Holding Bureaucracy Accountable, 2001. (www.jeanmonnetprogram.org/papers/01/011801.html)

Davidziuk, María Alejandra, "Las TIC como instrumento de inclusión comunitaria y desarrollo social. El caso del Proyecto CTC.", student thesis, Universidad de Buenos Aires, February 2002. (www.links.org.ar/infoteca/otros/tesinactc.html)

The Economist, "Government and the Internet", 22 June 2000. (www.economist.com/surveys/showsurvey.cfm?issue=20000624)

Friedman, Thomas L., The Lexus and the Olive Tree, Anchor Books (de Random House), April 2000.

Garrido, Maria and Halavais, Alexander, "Mapping Networks of Support for the Zapatista Movement: Applying Social-Networks Analysis to Study Contemporary Social Movements, Chapter 8 in: Cyberactivism: Online Activism in Theory and Practice Edited by Martha McCaughey and Michael D. Ayers. Routledge:NY 2003

Gobierno de Chile and Instituto de Asuntos Públicos de la Universidad de Chile, Buenas Prácticas de Gestión Pública en Chile, April 2003 (www.gestionpublica..gov.cl).

Gobierno de Chile y Universidad de Chile, Gobierno Electrónico en Chile: Estado del Arte, April 2003 (www.modernizacion.gov.cl).

Performance Institute, Creating a Performance Based Electronic Government, October 30, 2002. (www.performanceweb.org/pi/research/egovernment.htm)

Proenza, Francisco J. Argentina: Establecimiento y experiencia inicial de los Centros Tecnológicos Comunitarios 2003 (forthcoming).

Rabadán, Silvia and Roxana Bassi, "Proyecto CTC: La experiencia argentina", paper presented at the workshop Apropiación Social de Tecnologías de la Información y la Comunicación, in Cajamarca, Perú, 17 al 24 de marzo del 2002. (www.edutic.org.ar/documentos/proyecto_ctc.pdf).

Ruffa, Adriana, y Roberto Zubieta, "Análisis de la Encuesta de Uso de los Telecentros instalados en la Argentina", febrero 2002.

Schware, Robert, "Information Technology and Public Sector Management in Developing Countries: Present Status and Future Prospects", Indian Journal of Public Administration, October 2000. (www1.worldbank.org/publicsector/egov/Schware.pdf)

Stiglitz, Joseph E., Peter R. Orszag y Jonathan M. Orszag, The Role of Government in a Digital Age, documento comisionado por la Computer and Communications Industry Association, October 2000 (www.ccianet.org/digital_age/report.pdf).

United States Congress, E-Government Act of 2002, December 2002. (http://frwebgate.access.gpo.gov/cgibin/getdoc.cgi?dbname=107_cong_public_laws&docid=f:publ347.107.pdf).

Wellenius, Björn, "Closing the Gap in Access to Rural Communication: 1995-2002", November 2001 (www.infodev.org/library/chile_rural/Chile%20-%20final%2017%20december%2001%20-%20revised.pdf)

Navigating Multiple Networks: ICTs, Multinationals and Development

John Sherry, Tony Salvador
Intel Corporation

Hsain Ilahiane
Iowa State University

Abstract
The authors discuss the biggest challenge facing multinational corporations (MNC) hoping to provide technologies and services to developing nations. The authors identify four different networks where the presence of MNC could be vital for the provision of ICT to the developing world. Furthermore, they argue that corporations must establish different kinds of partnerships in order to achieve legitimate positions in these "other" networks.

C urrent estimates suggest that over one billion people use cell phones, and roughly 700 million have access to the Internet.[1] While these are impressive numbers, it is also true that the vast majority of the world's population still has no access to such information and communications technologies (ICTs). Partly as a result of this situation, and partly out of recognition that ICTs bring efficiencies to the transfer of information, an increasing number of researchers and practitioners have begun to turn to ICTs as tools for international development.

The thinking is that by lowering the costs of access to information (indeed by simply making it possible in some cases), ICTs will enable those in marginalized communities to better accomplish their own economic goals, and possibly better achieve some modest prosperity. Associated with this approach is a shift in development thinking from "top-down" intervention by states or foreign NGOs to an emphasis on market forces, regarded as necessary for ICTs "to gain wide, robust and long-lived usage" (Best and Maclay, 2002). This shift has also entailed new ways of imagining the participation of multinational corporations (MNCs). Prahalad and Hammond (2002), assert that "prosperity can come to the poorest regions only through the direct and sustained involvement of multinational companies." Markets that were once either too difficult to reach or too poor to be of interest can, so the thinking goes, be made accessible and profitably addressed through the use of information technology.

But for all the infusion of interest, the path by which ICTs will lead to economic prosperity is vague, indeed, not without controversy. As Prahalad and Hammond assert, for MNCs to approach the "bottom of the pyramid" they must come up with new ways of thinking about products, business practices and perhaps most importantly, the people are supposed to benefit from this transformation. This paper is a tentative first step in that direction. We propose that among these new ways of thinking, firms will have to expose virtually all aspects of their business (e.g., products, infrastructures, supply chains and distribution channels) to renewed scrutiny. One way to begin to do this is to look more closely at the various networks of relations and processes that operate in these challenging new environments.

For roughly seven years authors Sherry and Salvador have been part of a small research staff within Intel Corporation employed to develop accounts of potential "new uses and new users" of computing power. Our work has involved ethnographic research, shadowing, participant observation and nondirective, situated interviews across a wide variety of domains aimed at a richer understanding of technology users (or potential ones). Joined by co-author Ilahiane, and drawing on prior research experience (Sherry, 2002; Ilahiane, 2001), we more recently began a collaboration examining the possibilities and challenges for deployment of information technologies in developing economies. Our fieldwork has taken us to both North and South America, southern Asia, central Europe and North Africa.

These investigations have produced insights (and additional questions) in a number of areas. To provide the briefest possible overview, we organize some high level results into a framework that explores four types of networks that MNCs might do well to consider when thinking about intervention in these untapped or emerging markets. While technology firms are most likely to think of networks largely in terms of the physical and technological connectivity, we use the term here to refer to a more general notion of the term, involving constellations of actors and objects, and the important relations among them. Our framing draws on a well-established anthropological tradition of looking holistically at both the production and use of technology (e.g., Suchman, 1987; Traweek, 1988; Miller and Slater, 2000). As other analyses have shown (e.g., Bijker, Hughes and Pinch 1987) any artifact is merely the touch point for entire (often largely invisible) systems of infrastructure, labor, capital, the natural environment, social networks and many other dimensions; entire ecosystems must be in alignment for the viability of any offering. Any product or service must not only fit within economic systems of production, supply chains, maintenance, financing and the like, but will also affect and be affected by social and cultural systems of daily practice, relations of power, the construction of meaning and value, and many other, hard-to-measure systems and processes.

Among the various networks that might be considered, we focus on the following four: Networks of provisioning and support, that is, social networks whereby technological goods and services are both introduced to and maintained in communities; networks of access, that is, constellations of technologies and people that allow those with limited means to access these technologies or their products; networks of value, those various forms of resources and socially valued goods that govern people's evaluations of new technologies; and networks of places, the locations, media and modes of interaction by which information is shared, and relationships and knowledge are created.

Networks of Provisioning and Support
As any user knows, computing technology requires considerable product support, including component and software installation, upgrades, troubleshooting, repairs, maintenance, or simply assisting users with arcane operations and user interfaces. In developed economies where such technologies have some history of presence, users rely on populations of both formal and informal support, from the corporate IT department to "mom and pop" PC shop owners to the proverbial "geeky kid next door." Even in large firms, users rely heavily on "local informal experts" to help with a wide variety of problems, from quick advice to troubleshooting (George, Iacono and Kling,1992).

The same may not be said of computing technology in other environments. Official statistics (e-readiness indicators,[2] for instance) may overestimate the availability of expertise within a country by using too gross a resolution. India's thriving IT sector, which is primarily focused in Bangalore and Hyderabad, may belie large regional gaps in poorer states. Simple issues of geographical distance and human transportation can thus severely limit the normal operations of technology.

Scarcities in the availability of expertise may render otherwise "breakthrough" technologies less valuable. Consider, for example, the case of delivering broadband connectivity in India. As a result of an initiative by the federal government, the Indian state of Jaipur enjoyed the ostensive advantage of optical fiber covering much of its territory. This did have advantages: That fiber backbone has provided some opportunities for the delivery of cable TV services, etc. At the same time, these networks may ultimately prove less useful than copper - simply because outages are more catastrophic. When a line is (inevitably) cut, the greater technical skill required for its repair has meant much longer periods without any form of access. This has resulted in several cases of extended service outages there.[3]

Perhaps an even greater challenge facing MNCs is the fact that in many cases the networks of provisioning and support that do exist are outside the formal, accepted channels. Among the large and ever growing population of informal economy workers are those who will play a role in the provisioning and support of technologies to an increasing number of users worldwide. In the streets of the old market districts of Rabat or Casablanca in Morocco, for instance, thriving markets for European and North American technology goods service a large swath of North Africa. The entrepreneurs who operate these street-side deals are the face of the technology to a large number of customers who cannot afford to visit (and in fact are intimidated by) the glass-windowed shops of the "official" telecoms and computer companies. They provide not only equipment but advice, technical support and services of various kinds. And yet, it is safe to say (and our own data suggests) that those in the corporations regard these street vendors with disdain. If one looks beyond the easy label of "gray market dealers", one finds motivated, intelligent and skilled workers whose primary offense is a lack of means to establish a more formal relationship with branded product and service providers. Tapping into such networks, though challenging in many ways, may provide firms with a considerable competitive advantage.

Networks of Access

In many places individual ownership of ICTs may be, if not impossible, at least suboptimal. As discussed above, ownership carries with it burdens in addition to privilege. As a result, a wide variety of types of shared access have developed around the world. Telecenters, cyber-cafés, kiosks, and various other constellations of people and technology provide users with access to the benefits of technology without the burdens. In this section we examine three aspects of why shared access may be considered preferable to individual ownership.

1) **Community-wide benefits.** In several poor districts of Santiago, Chile a network of telecenters known as El Encuentro provide people of limited means not only with points of Internet access, but rather focal points for community development. El Encuentro focuses its operations on building assets for the community as a whole. It features a community radio station, a college preparatory instructional center, a volunteer staff of young people eager to gain experience with digital and networking technologies, and a community leadership-training program, among other community-oriented services. Access to the Internet is primarily in service of these broader community-based agendas. Details such as the layout, staffing and daily operations of the center are designed to intensify community participation among those who frequent the centers (of El Encuentro, more below).

2) **Economic sustainability.** In many situations, the costs of computing (e.g., capital outlays, operating and maintenance costs) outweigh the value of owning the technology. If the technology actually produces income for the owner, however, the calculations obviously change. In many places, an individual willingly shoulders and offsets the burden of ownership by charging affordable rates to others for access. Such is the case, for instance, with Grameen's "village phone" project, as well as with many of the shared access sites we've visited in our own research. The cabinas publicas of Peru, for instance, represent an attractive entrepreneurial opportunity in a place where unemployment is high and prospects are limited. Cabinas typically remain small, family owned businesses, and while any individual cabina may not be a long-term enterprise, the model itself has proven remarkably persistent.

There may be several reasons for this. First, initial investment is not small, but it is limited. Entrepreneurs able to invest about USD10,000 can obtain a "contained" business (including 10 machines, connectivity and a well-developed "cookbook" for how to operate the business). Second, time to money is relatively short, with most cabinas recuperating their entire investment within roughly a year. Third, services offered in the cabinas - primarily communications such as e-mail and voice over Internet - competed favorably with extant telephone services, (in particular satisfying an unmet need for cheap long distance communication with émigré loved ones). Fourth, cabinas also offer additional services that essentially "come for free" with access to the Internet, e.g., access to "free" software, movies, music and pornography were and are among the most popular items (and the reason why the cabinas operate as mostly smallscale, informal economy enterprises).

3) **Leverage Effects.** In a number of places, the issue is not so much shared access to technology, per se, but rather access to technology's benefits. Economic advantages may obtain to entrepreneurs who can offer services by virtue of ownership of technology. In India, a corporation called Drishtee is attempting to build a network of village kiosks, run by local entrepreneurs, who collectively benefit from Drishtee's access not only to portions of the Indian government, but also to various large private firms hoping to reach the rural Indian market. In the case of Drishtee's e-government services, individual rural villagers who submit applications, complaints or other government business via the kiosks benefit from reduced travel and other costs, and are assured of greater government responsiveness. Such villagers never actually touch the technology themselves. The value here derives from the effects and efficiencies of aggregating demand across villages (in the case of the e-government services) and across the entire Drishtee network (in the case of private sector services). No individual villager could generate enough value to justify personal ownership of the technologies needed to access these services.

Understanding shared access therefore requires a more thorough understanding of the constellations of actors, technologies and services involved in such systems, from government representatives to staff on site to modes of acquiring and operating software. Variability among the sites all glossed as "shared access" is quite high.

Networks of Capital
For most high tech firms, the familiar networks of capital are constituted in and among a relatively limited number of "global cities" (Sassen, 2002). A spectacular volume of capital flows through these networks, made possible by the "dematerialized and hypermobile" nature of financial products - the ability to trade in representations of assets (and derivatives thereof), not material assets themselves.

The resulting flows of capital are enabled by and in turn provide the fuel for the continuous expansion of technology. Counterintuitively, however, the decentralizing effects of new technological networks has made these global cities even more important as centers of coordination and consolidation. As these global centers become more integrated, they become less attached to their own geographical, political and cultural roots.

Those outside such networks face entirely different challenges. It is unclear whether it is possible, through the use of technology, to simply integrate ever more users (that is, the types of users we are particularly interested in for this paper) into the systems Sassen describes. As she puts it, the "edges are sharper" between the corporate centers and what is exterior, "which comes to be read as marginal." Various regimes, as de Soto (2000) and others have pointed out, erect barriers that prevent individuals from productively representing their assets (e.g., one's residence) to raise capital and participate legitimately in formal economic systems. No one in the favelas of Rio, for example, has a mortgage, nor are deeds clear. Their houses are thus not potentially representable as capital. Their participation in formal economy pursuits is thereby restricted. This pattern is repeated the world over.

In many marginalized communities, the scarcity of financial capital raises the importance of other forms of capital. From familial obligations to the bonds of mutual trust and concern, a variety of alternate resources have been labeled "social capital." Researchers such as Putnam (2000) and Bourdieu (1986) have - from admittedly fairly different perspectives - focused on the functioning of these alternate forms of capital within communities.[4] Part of this functioning is evident as very different judgments about the value of technologies or of various economic opportunities. Attachment to place and community, desire to protect traditional culture and local natural resources, local empowerment, or simply the bonds of mutual obligation all rank as values competitive with - and in many cases outweighing - the value of individual economic gain. From a logical perspective, it is perhaps not difficult to understand: in places where resources have historically been scarce, it does not behoove one to forego the social relationships on which one depends in hard times for what may be viewed as dubious or short term personal financial gains. "We have seen what computers can do," we were told by one indigenous man, a modestly successful entrepreneur from southern Ecuador, "but we need to acquire these technologies on our own terms, in ways that fit with the needs of our community." Ignoring these relations of value may result in failures that outside firms regard as "inexplicable." Many cases of technology adoption are direct political or cultural responses to the unwanted effects of globalization, rather than economic pursuits (Bird, 1995; Sherry, 2002).

In our own research, a number of experiments involving ICTs were conducted with the explicit goal of creating or building social capital. El Encuentro, for example (described above) illustrates how this agenda may influence operating decisions. "El Encuentro is about building social capital," its founder stated to us explicitly. At the time of our visit, gaming and pirated content were not seen as a legitimate means of deriving operating revenues for the centers (compare this to the Cabinas Publicas in Peru, for instance, where these are key revenue sources for operators). A collaboratively operated entrepreneurial development center, however, was considered very valuable. Entrepreneurs who have completed training and successfully set up sites in turn are asked to help educate other potential entrepreneurs. The viability and deployment of ICTs may thus depend as much on their ability to handle the exchange and development of these alternative forms of capital as they do on simple economic viability.

Networks of Places

Closely related to the notion of "social capital" is the need to understand the means by which it is constructed and deployed. Here our focus turns to networks of places. Townsend (2000) has argued that the decentralized nature of current mobile communications systems (cell phones, etc.) results in a more responsive allocation of resources to productive uses - an increase in the urban metabolism. This intensification seems to offer potential for economic development. Our studies suggest that such intensification may ultimately depend on networks of physical places - locations where the preparations for such intensification are made possible.

Consider the example of a plumber from a shantytown in Casablanca. This plumber exists at the hub of an entire network of carpenters, plumbers, electricians, masons, roofers, tile makers, and others. The mobile phone, as per Townsend's insight, enables the plumber and his contacts to rapidly mobilize in response to a need or opportunity. Note, however, that the effectiveness of the mobile network rests on a somewhat more complex network of places where the "work" of preparing this network of providers is carried out.

The plumber himself occupies a privileged position within the network by virtue of his modest physical store-front. It represents a known "first stop" for people who don't know where else to turn for help with their household building plans or improvement needs. It serves as a physical anchoring, a touch point into a trus-ted, accountable network of providers. The very presence of the store explicitly or inadvertently communicates to customers the plumber's willing accountability in this system of referrals. "Trust me," his store says, "I will find you the right person. And you know where to find me if he turns out bad."

The plumber's own network of relations, in turn, is built up through a series of places - the café, the soccer field, job sites - where working relationships and bonds of trust are formed, where information about opportunities is exchanged, along with verbal banter and teasing, discussions about the relative merits of techniques and tools, and discussions about other workers and various clients. This network of places provides a kind substrate on which the plumber, and many members of his own social network, assemble and pursue the relations that govern their modest economic livelihood. In essence, these physical places provide the location for the creation of the alternate forms of capital described above.

It's not that the mobile phone is unimportant. It provides the plumber's customer an instant connection into this network of trusted and "vouched-for" contacts. For the plumber: a chance to make another sale (he becomes the supplier to the contacted workman). It also provides the opportunity to enhance his social capital - his prestige within the network and stronger reciprocal bonds with those whom he has referred. For the lucky recipient of the plumber's call, it provides a chance for much desired work. Mobile phones thus enhance, rather than displace, other places in the network, and the "work" of relationship building across these other places pays off with the phone call.

In contrast to such technological concepts as the virtual marketplace, the present example suggests that new technologies do not necessarily succeed by "rationalizing" the operations of a given system. The plumber's modest storefront, now augmented with the cell phone, symbolizes the way that new technologies might better succeed by adding to, rather than attempting to replace, existing systems and networks. The network of store front / work site / football pitch / café, and the work carried on at these places, is rendered more valuable by the presence of the mobile phone.

Conclusion

Perhaps the biggest challenge facing multinational corporations hoping to provide technologies and services to developing nations is that they have no place in these networks. Alternatively, their presence may be out of their control, through channels they themselves do not approve of (as in the gray market example). Non-local firms will have to find ways of legitimately engaging networks or promoting new ones by offering sustainable benefits to these networks and their constituent actors. We are thus not arguing that firms must preserve existing networks, but rather those firms that have an understanding of how these networks operate will be in the best position to make informed decisions about where and how to engage them, leverage them, or even disrupt them.

Among other implications, this means that corporations must identify new kinds of partnerships, including those, which may not directly resemble those with which global firms are currently most familiar and comfortable. It also may mean that the standards by which global firms operate - their methods of assuring trust, providing accountability, or simply negotiating prices - may be less useful in these new environments. It is not that these are not values in any business transaction, but rather that the means of providing these values may be different. Finally, firms may need to be much more open not just to new product and service innovations, but to how that innovation happens. Whether firms engage in the delivery of end-to-end services or the creation of open, modular and modifiable platforms, it seems almost certain that entrepreneurs with ideas (and backgrounds) far different from our own will need to be part of the development process.

To achieve any of this, firms will need to start by identifying how they can achieve legitimate positions in these "other" networks.

Notes

1. Mobile phone estimates from the International Telecommunications Union; Internet Estimates from International Data Corporation.

2. For instance those developed by the Information Technology Group in the Center for International Development at Harvard University. See http://www.readinessguide.org/index.html .

3. These insights courtesy of consultants at Catalyst India, Priya Viswanath and Surya Prakash, via personal communication.

4. The rather different treatments of "social capital" in Bourdieu and Putnam can be seen, for our purposes, as a difference in perspective: Bourdieu viewing it from the perspective of an individual within a community, Putnam, from the perspective of the collective action of such resources on the community as a whole.

References

Best, Michael and Colin Maclay (2002) "Community Internet access in rural areas: solving the economic sustainability puzzle." The Global Information Technology Report: Readiness for the Networked World. G. Kirkman, ed. Oxford: Oxford University Press

Bijker, W., Hughes, T., Pinch, T., eds. (1987). The Social Construction of Technological Systems. Cambridge, MA: MIT Press.

Bird, B. (1995) The EAGLE Project: re-mapping Canada from an indigenous perspective. Cultural Survival Quarterly 18(4): 23-24.

Bourdieu, P. (1986). The Forms of Capital. In John Richardson, Ed. Handbook of Theory and Research for the Sociology of Education. New York: Greenwood Press, pp. 241-258

George, Joey F, Suzanne Iacono & Rob Kling (1992) "How Do Office Workers Learn About Computing?" Information Technology & People 6(4).

Ilahiane, Hsain (2001) The Social Mobility of the Haratine and the Re-working of Bourdieu's Habitus on the Saharan Frontier, Morocco. American Anthropologist 103 (2): 380-394.

Miller, Daniel and Donald Slater (2000) The Internet: An Ethnographic Approach. Oxford: Berg.

Prahalad, CK and Allen Hammond (2002) "Serving the world's poor, profitably." Harvard Business Review, September, 2002.

Putnam, R. (2000) Bowling Alone: The Collapse and Revival of American Community. NY: Simon and Schuster.

Sassen, S., ed. (2002) Global Networks, Linked Cities. Routledge.

Sherry, J (2002) Land, Wind and Hard Words. Albuquerque, UNM Press.

de Soto, Hernando (2000) The Mystery of Capital: Why capitalism triumphs in the West and fails everywhere else. NY: Basic Books.

Townsend, A (2000) "Life in the real-time city: mobile telephones and urban metabolism." Journal of Urban Technology 7(2): 85-104.

Suchman, Lucy (1987) Plans and Situated Actions: The Problem of Human-Machine Communication. Cambridge: Cambridge University Press.

Traweek, Sharon (1988) Beamtimes and Lifetimes: The World of High Energy Physicists. Cambridge: Harvard University Press.

Somos@Telecentros: Networking in Action

Klaus Stoll
Fundacion Chasquinet

Abstract
The author discusses the importance of building cooperative networks among NGOs, governments and the private sector for facilitating efficient exchange of information and resources and fostering coordination within the development community. He illustrates the advantages of a network form of organization with lessons learned from Somos@Telecentros, and underscores the need for having a dialectic relationship between self interest and common goals in order to exert the power of networking.

N etworking as a concept, has become an integral process in any society, culture, organisation and institution. All segments of societies, over the ages have established various patterns of communication/interaction, within the same society segment, or with other segments within a society or with segments of other societies. Contemporary ICT policies are no exception, emphasizing on networking and partnerships between social, private and governmental sectors, also known as the 'SPG partnerships'.

Networking and SPG partnerships are often seen as crucial factors in the process of achieving specific ICT policy goals like digital inclusion and the strategic use of ICTs for development. The experiences in this field show clearly that networks and partnerships require large investments of time, resources and human understanding. Success in this case is, most certainly, not always assured.

Somos@Telecentros (S@T), the Network of Telecenters in Latin America and the Caribbean[1] (TELELAC) is a showcase of networking inside one sector that actively seeks SPG partnerships. In 1999 the TELELAC project was established for a two-year period.[2] The principal aim of the project was to investigate the current status of the Telecenters in the region, compile data about their dimensions and needs, collect their stories, to produce a number of online resources and initiate a "network" among these telecenters.

The S@T network quickly grew in strength and relevance by responding directly to the practical day-to-day problems diagnosed among Telecenters. The ICT applications provided by Telecenters helped the S@T network to provide a forum on social change, by letting Telecenters voice out their relations and dealings with the other sectors of society, for example in relation to ICT policy decisions.

The Telecenter Network uses numerous methods for internal communication and to fulfill its mission. For the communication purposes, the best usage has been S@T email Discussion Forum. Besides the general S@T discussion list, there exists a wide range of e-mail forums, on topics like, gender, open source, policies, training, and many more.

Another focal point of the work is the Somos@Telecentros Resource Centre.[3] The Resource Centre is a virtual library providing regional telecenters with access to an organised, growing collection of about 200 training courses, software, reports and articles, evaluations, web sites, and proceedings of workshops and meetings. It also have resources of Telecenters' stories, researchers' analyses, advices and contacts with other telecenters doing similar work. The resource center works as a meeting place to share, preserve and download information for free.

The Somos@Telecentros Network is a constantly growing body, which consists of over 200 active members located throughout Latin America and the Caribbean, and lists over 1,500 Telecenters in its directory.

Telecentres are subject to various pressures, and are especially vulnerable to isolation, intense demand for digital services, competition from commercial cybercafes, and lack of supportive policy environments. Being part of a network provides them with much needed scalability and the subsequent support to cope with these constraints.

The main lessons learned by S@T in its development can be summed up simply by saying that: The S@T network cannot exist as a simple platform for a group of like-minded people but S@T exists in order to leverage the advantages that co-operation and economy of scale offer. Its members receive direct and measurable advantages for the day-to-day running of a Telecenter operation through:

1) *Reducing the running costs of a Telecenter*
   This is achieved through sharing experiences and resources, collective evaluation and learning, collaborating on the production of appropriate tools and information resources, joint development of training materials and the direct support of Telecenter operators and users.

2) *Giving Telecenters a strong role to play in local, national, and international policy and decisionmaking*
   ICT-related policy and legislation in the LAC region is at a stage of extreme

fermentation. Every government in the region now realizes the importance of information and communication technologies, and is making important choices. Industry regulation, public policy, universal access programs and e-government initiatives are being continuously announced, often debated, but may not always fully implemented. Large IT product and services companies are already lobbying for securing their interests. Local businesses and special interests are also pushing to ensure their wish lists on the agenda.

ICT policies are therefore of vital interest and importance, but a Telecenter, due to its size and limitations of resources, is unable to participate effectively in the policy decision-making process. A regional network like S@T is able to give the individual Telecenter a voice and due to its grassroots outreach in every country in the region, is uniquely positioned to speak for people who would otherwise be voiceless in the debate. This can be achieved through:

- Having an effective communication platform in place inside the network. This platform enables a wide ranging, open and transparent discussion, the identification of needs and the formulation and dissemination of joint policies.

- The monitoring, documentation, evaluation and dissemination of policy discussions and developments related to the area of the new information technology and in particular focused on new innovations in connectivity technologies.

- Holding regular workshops and training events and publishing frequent reports. Telecenter practitioners need to understand the issues that are under development in their countries and across the region only then they can participate in a competent and informed manner in the policy decision making process.

- Engaging regional policy makers and other stakeholders in active discussions. In order to represent these views to the politicians, policymakers and other stakeholders in each area, the network needs to actively participate in relevant conferences, forums, meetings, and public consultations. The issues also need to be communicated to public through media, such as editorial pages in newspapers across regions.

3) Opening up new income streams
Sustainability is not something that tends to happen by accident, either for individual telecenters, or for an umbrella organization. Strategic plans for revenue generation have to be developed and implemented. The network has a good potential to generate revenue for its own maintenance and the benefit of its members and partners, because the network has accumulated expertise, knowledge and research that is attractive to the private and governmental sectors.

A number of approaches have been made from these sectors towards the network to seek its assistance in their digital inclusion projects. The network and its scope in itself represent a value that can be used for the testing, evaluation and marketing of products. The experiences in this field show that this is not restricted to technology-related products, but includes a surprising range of products. Network members, for example, are involved in product testing and the network has developed a number of marketable products.

.The S@T network possesses characteristics that would make it a useful partner/supplier/customer of private sector and this is why S@T is focusing on private sector partnerships as one of the most promising sources of revenue and long-term sustainability for the network itself and its individual members.Therefore, it becomes clear that each sector of society has its own strengths and weaknesses and the problems in hand can only be solved when all sectors co-operate in a concerted effort.

It is interesting to note that because of the different background of each of the SPG partners, often most used words like "sustainability" has different connotations for each of the partners. The representative of the private sector will define sustainability foremost as "financial" sustainability and s/he has every reason to do so from his/her perspective. The government representative will agree with the private sector representative but s/he will put emphasis on "political and technological" sustainability whilst at the same time the representative of an NGO will stress "social and cultural" sustainability. In addition, some donor agencies see "sustainability" as a code word for their own exit strategy from ongoing support of a project. Only when the SPG partners have learned to understand the legitimate needs, motives and concepts of each partner involved, will the SPG partnership be able to look creatively for win-win solutions and to implement them.

In other words the SPG partners will discover that networking and partnership is based on finding a common ground where the conflicting interests and values can positively combine for as long as is required to achieve the mutual beneficial outcomes. Networks and partnerships require more than trust and goodwill. They are dialectic between self-interest and common goals, and require the ability to arbitrate and bring about a decision among partners, by partners, in partnership.[4]

Notes

1. wwww.tele-centros.org

2. http://www.chasquinet.org/telelac The project is coordinated by a non-governmental organization, Fundación Chasquinet (www.chasquinet.org) based in Quito, Ecuador and funded by the International Development Research Council, IDRC, www.idrc.ca, Canada.

3. http://www.chasquinet.org/telecentros/recursos/contenido.php3

4. I would like to acknowledge with gratitude the valuable contributions Prof. Michel Menou and Mr. Steve Cisler have made to this article.

Connecting Rural India Towards Prosperity

Ashok Jhunjhunwala
IIT Madras (India)

Abstract

The lack of telecommunications infrastructure remains one of the biggest obstacles to providing access to information and communication technologies in rural areas. In this article, the author offers an alternative technological solution, currently being used by n-Logue Communications - a company incubated by professors at IIT Madras in India, that has the potential to bring access and connectivity to underserved areas.

It is widely recognized today that the Internet is not just a communication medium but is Power. Yet, most rural areas of developing countries have no access to the Internet. The problem is that most rural homes can afford to spend very little (not more than $2 per month) on Communications and Internet. Can villages be provided computers and connectivity that is financially sustainable at this low income? Further, will there be power in the villages to drive such computers and connections? Finally, what would be the applications that would be available with such a connection? These questions have not found satisfactory answers despite several efforts all around the world.

n-Logue Communications, Chennai, India is a company incubated by professors of IIT Madras in India with a goal of commercially providing and operating Internet connections in rural areas of India. By charter, the company is barred to operate in urban areas. The question now is how does n-Logue run an Internet connectivity business exclusively in rural areas, and tackle the multi-fold problem of low-affordability, connectivity and lack of power in the villages and make the business venture commercially viable?

A Model for Reference

In the mid-eighties most of the middle and lower middle class families in Indian urban areas did not have access to a telephone. A unique business model aggregated the demand of all such people living in a street and attempted to service this demand by using an entrepreneur operated Public Call Office (referred to as STD-PCOs in India). The entrepreneur kept this place open for 16 hours a day, 365 days a year and got 20 per cent commission on all the calls made. Today there are 950,000 STD-PCOs in India generating about 25 per cent of the total telecom revenue of the country and providing service to about 300 million people who do not have telephones at home.

n-Logue uses the same "aggregation of demand to serve low-income groups" model to provide Internet connection in rural areas. But how does it provide the connectivity? Fortunately BSNL (Bharat Sanchar Nigam Limited), the state-owned incumbent operator in India, has already provided optical fibre drop at most taluka (county) towns. If one provides wireless connectivity in a 15-20 km radius around these towns, one can connect almost 85 per cent of Indian villages. n-Logue uses a technology called CorDECT Wireless in Local Loop, a system developed at IIT Madras in India, to provide wireless connectivity in about a 30-km radius around these fibre points.

At each village, a subscriber wall-set connected on wireless to the base station at taluka town, provides a telephone connection as well as a 35 / 70 kbps Internet connection at a deployed cost of under $300 per connection.

The Local Entrepreneur

All it requires in each village is a small entrepreneur, who is assisted by n-Logue to set up a kiosk. The kiosk is equipped with a CorDECT wireless connection, a PC with Multimedia, Web camera, printer, power back-up and a suite of Local Language Applications and a low bit rate video-conferencing application in addition to a telephone. It is made available to the kiosk operator at a total cost of $1000, which includes training and maintenance for a year. Bank loans are available to the operator to pool in the business investment.

n-Logue installs the CorDECT wireless exchange and base station at the taluka town and provides service to about 300 villages in the surrounding area. Co-located with the exchange is an Internet server using an innovative product called "Minnow" which is an ISP Server in a Linux box developed by Nilgiri Networks and IIT Madras. All the equipment at taluka town operates at 55° C and the total power requirement to provide 1000 connections in the area is only 1 KVA. A low-cost diesel generator provides the power back up at the site. n-Logue takes a local partner (referred to as a Local Service Partner or LSP) to operate the service in the town and provide complete support to the kiosks in the villages.

The key to the business model is that each kiosk, set up with an investment of $1000 needs to earn at least $70 per month to break even. n-Logue and the LSP help the Kiosk Operator to offer a variety of services to the villagers, thus helping him generate the break-even figure within the first six months of business.

Besides providing telephony service, the Kiosk Operator provides several stand-alone computer services. The first usage of the computer starts within days of its installation and these are usually stand-alone computer services like learning basic typing, word-processing and even "CAD-CAM". The computer is also used for a variety of educational services including several online courses for school children, complementary to their school learning, and courses 'open' for all like Spoken English Courses, using both audio and visual techniques. The Kiosk computer is also used for photography as the camera is used to take pictures, a photo-editor used to edit it before printing the picture locally or even remotely. The picture can be delivered at a cost of around 10 cents.

It is however, the Internet that is making a huge impact. A local language Office package called CK-Shakthi developed by Chennai Kavigal, a company incubated by IIT Madras at Chennai is included with the kiosk. This is especially useful for the villagers as they can now send emails in their local language. But more popular are the voice mails and video mails as a means to communicate, especially since a significant percentage of the population in villages work in urban areas. Similarly, the computer is used to access all kinds of services provided by the local government offices in the district. But above all, it is the multi-party video conferencing on Internet, which has enabled a great variety of applications. Using a package called "iSee" developed by IITM and a Chennai based company Object Oriented Programming Services Pvt. Ltd. (OOPS), it is possible for multiple kiosks to have multi-party video-conferencing with each other and any one else on the Internet even at low bit-rates. The villagers take their agricultural and veterinary problems to experts in the respective fields via the video-conferencing facility and get them sorted online. Similarly even doctors are consulted for online medical checkups. Government officers and extension workers to simultaneously meet people from several villages also use the multi-party video-conferencing.

n-Logue is now working with banks to extend financial and insurance services on Internet to villages. It is working with rural development departments of the government to provide a variety of online training courses towards entrepreneurship development.

The discussions above dealt with solutions for the two issues of affordability and connectivity. The focus now is on the problem of power. n-Logue provides about a 24-hour back-up for telephones and a 4-hour back-up for Personal Computers in the kiosk. This will work if power supply is available in the village for about 16 hours a day. But, this is really not so in several parts of India. Even if the back-up is increased to 8 hours, the village must have power for 8-12 hours. n-Logue and IITM are examining the use of solar power; however, today this is an expensive alternative. They are also examining the development of a low-cost 250 W diesel or kerosene generator. A solution to this problem is a must if n-Logue is to succeed in connecting villages in certain parts of India.

Today n-Logue has started service in about 20 districts in different states of India and has kiosks in over 600 villages. Over the next one year it will expand its service in 75 districts and connect about 10,000 villages. Once the Kiosk numbers cross 10,000, it would become commercially feasible for a number of small companies to develop applications especially relevant to rural areas; with much smaller number of kiosks, the application development largely remains in the voluntary sector. As the 10,000 kiosks start making money, n-Logue will not find it difficult to expand its services to about 500,000 villages in the plains of India in the next few years.

The problem of connectivity and commercial viability in setting up Internet Kiosks in the hilly and sparsely populated areas of India is more complicated. IIT Madras is currently working with the Indian Space Research Organization (ISRO) to develop a dual-hop system, combining a satellite back-haul wireless system with a terrestrial CorDECT like wireless system to connect villages in such areas. Costs will be slightly higher than what n-Logue is using today in the plains and special efforts may be required to make such connections commercially viable. But the solution to the problem will not only solve the connectivity problem for hilly areas, but may also be applicable in many sparsely populated areas of Africa and Latin America.

Information Kiosks and Sustainability: Key Components for Success

Mike Jensen
Independent Consultant

Abstract
The author discusses some of the main factors that affect the performance and sustainability of information kiosks: 1) knowledge of the technology options available; and 2) understanding the strategies to effectively meet the needs of users. He presents a thorough overview of a broad range of technologies and value-added services that can be considered under different conditions and demands from users.

The success of public access information service providers is mainly affected by two factors: 1) knowledge of the technology options available and 2) understanding of strategies to effectively meet the needs of users.

Technology Options
The provision of low-cost public access requires an understanding of the broad range of technologies that are needed to meet the varied conditions and demands from users. At the infrastructure and access level this will usually involve both fixed and mobile solutions using wired, satellite, and wireless connectivity along with a mix of low cost access devices.

WiFi is a particularly promising technology for the provision of low cost access services. Providers in North America, Europe and Asia are already extensively using WiFi 'hotspots' to provide public access connectivity and are currently amongst the fastest-growing segment of Internet services. With prices now less than $100 for shared access points, and less than $40 for user equipment, WiFi networks are rapidly emerging in most urban areas worldwide. Similarly, handheld/PDA access is becoming increasingly popular following the introduction of wireless handhelds, smartphones, and other devices capable of connecting to the Internet. A recent study[1] by the World Bank's Development Gateway sites 802.11 WiFi and handhelds as critical emerging technologies for developing countries.

For areas in close proximity to each other, wired connections can also be adopted. Experience elsewhere in high density areas such as in Indonesia has shown that use of wireline connectivity via standard 10/100-BaseT Ethernet cable is a lower-cost and more effective solution than WiFi for short distances - up to 250 meters, which can be augmented with daisy-chained switches. Another alternative wireline technology adopted could be to use the existing electric power grid within a substation, usually called HomePlug or Digital Powerline technology. Siemens manufactures a HomePlug router for $199.

The use of 'hybrid' connectivity options also plays an important role in the solutions-mix to maximize accessibility while minimizing costs. These range from using digital satellite television and radio receivers[2] for downloading data at high speed, to supporting GSM-SMS requests for data, and delivery of hard-copy e-mail printouts and voice e-mail. Overall, operators need to provide a varied mix and continuously evolving set of solutions for providing the underlying connectivity which allow for the emergence of new options in the future, such as CDMA/3G, PHS[3], OFDM[4] and UWB.[5] The technologies available for these services are still in flux, with several new but as yet not fully tested solutions likely to emerge shortly, such as those by Flarion, Navini and Soma.

In the area of access equipment, new and refurbished desktop PCs are usually required. These should be sourced in bulk, preconfigured and loaded with appropriate software. In many cases a thin-client configuration with server will be the preferred solution to minimize cost and maintenance requirements.

While traditional access via desktop PCs will continue to be important for many operators, handheld connectivity solutions are becoming increasingly popular. This can actually start in the backoffice area initially, providing access, information and applications to mobile phones via GSM/WAP/GPRS/SMS, but also information providers are able to provide these services via WiFi, Bluetooth and Infrared access to a broader range of handheld /devices. These can range from portable PC solutions (and Tablet/notebook PCs), to GSM and CDMA2000-1x based 'Smartphone/PDAs'[6], through to refurbished low-end Palm handhelds costing less than $50. New devices especially designed for a developing country environment, such as the Simputer[7] and the VillagePDA[8] can also be adopted, as they become available.

Aside from the low price and portability features of handheld devices, another important attraction is that these devices can be more easily shared amongst a group or household. A group's wealthiest member or the head of the household will likely be the first to own a handheld device, but will be able to pass it around to his/her peers or family for their use too. In addition, the success of the mobile phone model will be emulated in which small individual entrepreneurs who sit at street corners or walk around with the device and sell services to others who can not afford their own equipment.

Many GSM phones, handhelds and laptops are already equipped with an Infrared Port so there is likely to be an immediate demand to provide connectivity services to existing devices, particularly for backup of GSM phone and handheld data. With appropriate software, smartphones and handheld/PDAs will be able to quickly synchronise data, update stock lists and prices, receive news[9] and use store-and-forward e-mail, voicemail etc.

Service Strategies
At the applications or value-added service level, a comprehensive and attractive range of bundled services for users needs to be made available. Connectivity related services should include web browsing, e-mail and other related public access Internet services such as instant messaging and VoIP. The latter service is of high importance for many reasons, in particular, due to the familiarity of the average person with telephony, the unmet demand for voice services, the potential for reducing the cost of voice communications and because of the revenue generating possibilities for the providers.

Aside from basic Internet access and voice communications, services should also include voice-mail and unified messaging, news and market information, trade matching/e-procurement, funds transfer and other financial services. Also, demand for SMS and WAP-based market price information and other transaction-oriented facilities have been demonstrated where these services have been launched.

A vital step in establishing public access services is to develop its links with the local community - this means making the community aware of the facility and obtaining their feedback to define what sort of information services are required. The service provider will need to call public meetings and invite as many different sectors of the community as possible. Target groups will normally include a number of the following:

- Individuals (local community members, tourists and passing professionals such as truck drivers and engineers)
- Small businesses
- Schools
- Youth
- Disabled people
- Farmers
- Women's groups
- Churches
- Clinics, hospitals and healthcare workers
- Police
- NGOs
- Trade unions

- Civic organisations
- Political parties
- Government departments

Small and informal businesses are a key user group and are often concen-
trated (clustered) in small geographic areas where they can obtain access to a
wide range of resources. In this respect operators providing integrated business-
support services and facilities provision will help to foster business incubators in
these locations, including by leveraging their infrastructure to improve processes
for the support of small businesses by SME and micro investment funds. This not
only reduces the cost of entry and operational costs for SMEs in the traditional
industries, but also for new businesses in the ICT sector, such as IT equipment
distribution, assembly and refurbishment, programming, teleworking, information
gathering and supply, training, education and entertainment.

Policy Recommendations

The quality of the environment in which information kiosks can flourish is determined by four main factors - a) access to telecommunications, b) electricity, c)·
finance and d) skills. These in turn are to a great extent affected by national policies, particularly in the area of communications - if telecommunication services
are not available at competitive rates there is little that can be done in the other
areas that will ensure the sustainability of these services. Cross-subsidisation has
been promoted in the form of universal access funds (which take a percentage
of the profits from operators in restricted competition, most often in duopolies or
triopolies). But as an alternative to open markets and user-provisioned infrastructure using wireless and satellite technologies, the importance of these funds has
yet to be proven.

In the other areas, access to electricity in rural areas is a key constraint. Solar
power is an alternative but is costly unless Independent Power Producer policies
are in place and finance is available. Import duties also add to the cost of solar
equipment in many countries, as it does for ICT equipment. Although import tariffs
have come down in many countries for fully assembled PCs, they usually remain
high for satellite equipment, components and peripherals.

Access to finance is a particularly severe problem because of the generally
deficient capital markets in most countries and because the relatively small needs
of kiosk operators fall in the gap between traditional micro-finance and larger venture and investment capital funds. Medium-sized funds need to be created for this
sector, most likely by combining private funds with government or development
agency guarantees and human resource support.

Access to skills and experience will need to be addressed due to the general
lack of technical and managerial capacity, especially in the rural areas, a feature that is even more extreme in the area of ICTs. Investment in improved and
more widespread training facilities (including using ICTs for distance training) is

necessary at all levels, from schools to the workplace and in the informal sector, particularly outside the major urban areas.

Notes

1. The Future of Information and Communication Technologies for Development. http://www.development gateway.org/node/133831/sdm/docview?docid=551153

2. Such as the DSTV-based services providing 400kbps downloads, and Worldspace's multi-media service providing 128Kbps downloads.

3. PHS is the Personal Handifone System from Japan now deployed in Africa by UTStarcom.com and others. It provides wireless telephony (including a low-cost walkie-talkie mode) as well as 64kbps data channel in an inexpensive handheld costing only $40.

4. OFDM stands for Orthogonal Frequency Division Multiplexing and is an advanced protocol for maximising data throughput over radio links developed by Wi-Lan.

5. UWB is the name for various new broadband wireless connectivity solutions being developed which use signals across a broad section of the radio spectrum to transmit data more efficiently.

6. Such as the Sony Ericsson P800 and the O2 (GSM), and the Audiovox Thera or Blackberry 6750 (CDMA2000 1x).

7. The Simputer is a sophisticated handheld device produced in India for developing country environments. www.simputer.org

8. The VillagePDA or ePDA is a low-cost ($25-50) Bluetooth powered handheld reference design developed by US-based company Mediasolv. www.mediasolv.com

9. Allafrica already provides news formatted for handhelds - http://allafrica.com/mobile

SECTION II

Characteristics for Determining Success

Raising the Bar - Empowerment through Knowledge Transfer and Capacity Building

Knowledge Sharing and Capacity Building: Scaling up Information Kiosks
Motoo Kusakabe

Satisfying the Demand for ICT Connectivity of Low-Income Groups
Ana Maria Fernandez-Maldonado

Leaving No One Behind - Developing an Inclusive Approach

Basic Principles of Community Public Internet Access Point's Sustainability
Klaus Stoll

Digital Innovation in Communities: The Diffusion Effect
Richard Fuchs

Entrepreneurship and Innovation - Models for Financial Sustainability

Private Sector Kiosks and Government Incentives: What Works and What is Sustainable?
Robert Schware

Expanding State Purchases from Micro and Small Enterprises: A Promising Approach from Peru
Francisco J. Proenza

Knowledge Sharing and Capacity Building: Scaling up Information Kiosks

Motoo Kusakabe
E-community Link

Abstract
The author recognizes the challenge of scaling up sustainable models of Information Kiosks and discusses the main elements that need to be considered in order for this scalability to become viable. He argues that financially sustainable and commercially viable models that are driven by domestic entrepreneurs, responsive to community needs and sensitive to local languages, are key for sustainable kiosks.

Information Kiosks are being increasingly recognised as key instruments for providing economic opportunities and empowering undeserved people in urban and rural communities. There are numerous pilot projects and some commercial franchise activities to create information kiosks. Some of these pilots provide valuable lessons for operational and financial sustainability and social developmental impacts. However, comparing the number of villages and communities in need for information access, a formidable challenge of scaling up sustainable models in developing countries is imperative.

A different set of issues is to be confronted when scaling up information kiosks, say, from the creation of several pilots kiosks to thousands of kiosks: Firstly, relying on a limited amount of donors' grant is impossible. We need to identify models basically relying on the financially sustainable and commercially viable models with clearly defined scheme of government subsidy on public services. Secondly, the need to resource on local capacity for designing, creating and managing kiosks rather than relying upon foreign consultants. There is a need for a large cadre of domestic entrepreneurs and supporting staff capable of responding to community demands and managing innovative business models, maintaining high-tech equipment and providing services to the community in a socially and culturally sensitive manner. As described earlier the capacity to create information kiosks requires skills and knowledge on technical, managerial and social dimensions.

Financial Sustainability

Financial sustainability of kiosks is the prerequisite for scaling up of information kiosks. The definition of sustainability needs to be clarified in specific circumstances regarding developing countries. Some kind of public support may be warranted to preserve a kiosk, such as providing affordable access to the most vulnerable groups, providing e-government services, empowering the poor through basic computer literacy training, etc. According to experiences in the pilots, the key factor in achieving financial and operational sustainability is that the community gets involved in the making and running of kiosks.

The key to success is to identify the most crucial demand for services and provide "killer applications," like market price information for farmers, land registration services, or health information system. Computer literacy training is almost always in demand and provides a large income to kiosks. The most important success factor is that kiosk managers conduct a participatory demand survey and create their business plans according to the outcome of the survey. To conduct an effective participatory demand survey and to create a business plan, there is a need for sharing experiences among kiosk managers in and across other countries.

Building Local Capacity to Support Information Kiosks

In the creation of a local capacity to build information kiosks there are four key functions: Effective community organization to support the kiosks, efficient and innovative kiosk managers, telecom service providers, and Kiosk support institutions to provide technical, business and logistical support to kiosk managers. There are different models where different players supply these functions. In some models, the same players provide some of these functions (for example, community directly manages kiosks). In the typical commercial models, a kiosk manager is an independent entrepreneur who invests his capital in the kiosk and creates community organizations to guide his kiosk's activities, he is supported by a franchiser who provides technical, managerial support for the kiosk operations. Kiosk managers select one of the telecommunication service providers who provide communication access channels.

Role of the Community

For the sustainability of information kiosks, the role of the community is essential. There should be a mechanism for the community members, including the poor and vulnerable, participate in designing the services that the kiosk provides. A village community can create an information kiosk through contribution of capital and by forming a governing body. Alternatively, a village community may create an advisory body to support a kiosk manager on identifying community demands for services and providing mutual support and partnership arrangements. Capacity of kiosk managers and community leaders to conduct jointly a participatory demand survey and stakeholders meetings including the poor and vulnerable group in the design phase is essential for the success of the kiosks. In many cases, local NGOs could conduct the role of such capacity building most effectively.

Role of Local Entrepreneurs
For kiosks to be financially sustainable, the roles of entrepreneurs are crucial. According to the Canadian CEDA's pilot telecenter project in Thailand, private sector-managed centers have shown better performances in terms of achieving financial sustainability (e.g., producing current operational profit). There are also many examples where the kiosk manager's entrepreneurial dedication played a key success factor for kiosk operations. However, information kiosk managers require a combination of technical, managerial and social development skills that are sometimes difficult to learn spontaneously by local entrepreneurs. There is a need for a systematic capacity building program for local entrepreneurs to be able to become effective kiosk managers. This role will be generally provided by private and public entrepreneur support organizations, such as chamber of commerce, incubators and SME support centers. But various types of "Kiosk Support Institutions" can provide more information kiosk specific support.

Role of Kiosk Support Institutions
In scaling up kiosk networks, the role of Kiosk Support Institutions is crucial. They provide a kiosk manager with the necessary managerial support, such as manuals for operation, establishing a legal framework for kiosk, and technical manual and support for installation and maintenance of computers and other equipment, and necessary operational software. Kiosk Support Institutions may come in a variety of forms: NGOs, private sector franchises, public agencies, and academic institutions.

In the case of NGOs, they often have a long history of community capacity building and empowerment. They understand the importance of information in empowering the poor, women and other vulnerable groups. They sometimes have excellent capabilities for participatory community development skills. Some NGOs have already been working in using ICT to assist such vulnerable groups in urban and remote rural areas. With some more systematic capacity building on information kiosk specific knowledge, they can become an effective Kiosk Support Institution. In Sri Lanka, Sarbodaya, the largest NGO has already created several information centers as an integral part of its village empowerment program. In the e-Sri Lanka program, Sarbodaya will become one of the major kiosk support institutions.

Role of Global/Regional Support Networks
Information kiosks are still in a developmental phase, and there are no fixed viable models. This requires close international exchange of lessons learned and

the best practices of the kiosks across the border. There are numerous pilots of information kiosks, but there are relatively fewer evaluation reports, case studies and benchmark data available for kiosk managers to take stock. Global/regional network to collect and analyze these information and data and assist the local kiosk managers and support institutions are vitally necessary.

Creating Relevant Contents

When developing countries overcome the current communication infrastructure problem, the greater challenge they face would be the creation of locally relevant knowledge contents, software and educational materials.

Acute Shortage of Local Contents

There are countless web-based developmental knowledge contents written in English and other languages. However, there are surprisingly few knowledge contents written in languages spoken and written in developing countries. As for the empowerment of the poor or to create economic opportunities for the local people, the availability of locally relevant content, created by the local people are essential. The lack of such locally relevant contents is a serious challenge for the kiosk initiatives. The reasons for such shortage are complex: technical issues such as the lack of local language codes and software, lack of affordable web hosting services, restrictive policies on disclosure, etc.

Creating Local Contents by Local People

Creation of locally relevant contents in local languages requires a broad participation from the local community. Uganda's Health Net is creating health care information based on traditional medicine and on local knowledge, where Western medicine is not available or effective. India's Self-Employed Women's Association is creating training tools for women to acquire income-generating skills based on their local embroidery and crafts. Compared to the text information prevalent in industrial countries, the use of radio, video, voice-based communication and multimedia tools are much more effective for illiterate people in rural communities. Cost-effective and easy-to-use tools to author knowledge contents locally should be developed and to train the local community to participate in knowledge creation is essential. There is a need for aggregators of such local knowledge contents, so that local people could access to these materials systematically and easily.

Sharing of Global Knowledge Resources

At the same time, access to global knowledge is another important demand from grassroots organizations. Global knowledge contents, concerning development strategy, educational materials, and business information, created in developed and developing countries should be shared through a global knowledge sharing mechanism. Global knowledge contents should be translated and adapted to the local context and delivered to the local communities.

Need for Open-Source Knowledge System

The cost of creating such knowledge contents is more expensive than the cost to access Internet. Solving these issues will need global knowledge sharing system based on open-source, peer-to-peer principles.

Broader ICT Capacity Building

So far the capacity building needs are directly related to the creation of information kiosks. But the ICT in developing countries will not prosper unless the country addresses the more holistic package of ICT development strategy: regulatory framework to allow new types of communication industries to compete with traditional telecom careers; investment climate conducive to innovation and entrepreneurship; financial, legal and accounting infrastructure to support the creation of technology-oriented business; development of software, hardware and system integration industries; application of ICT at home, companies, government, schools and healthcare; flexible tertiary education system to support the innovative knowledge creation and utilization, and so on.

Information kiosks and rural connectivity are neccesary components to support the country's ICT development. Without the balanced development of these components, information kiosks will not survive or become self-sustainable. Capacity building and knowledge management for information kiosks should be planned in such broader contexts.

Recommendation for Open-Source Knowledge Sharing

Creation of such broad capacity building to support ICT development in developing world requires the creation of a global knowledge sharing system which can be accessed easily and freely by developing country students and professionals. There have been many important attempts at materializing such systems through "Open-Source Knowledge Management System". This utilized the Internet peer-to-peer file sharing and collaboration functions and creating a common and open-source platform for e-learning management system and voluntary contribution of knowledge contents and e-learning materials to be shared by all the partners.

The action-oriented group learning courses to promote interaction among the various stakeholders across the countries can complement this online self-paced learning. Application of such open-source knowledge system is being discussed under the initiative of Global ICT Education Program led by leading universities both from developed and developing countries.[1] A network of participating Universities and NGOs will be created to connect and pool the knowledge resources, to create a flexible combination of curriculums to match the needs of dynamic change in the educational demands. Under this system, developing country students can fully benefit from the access to the most comprehensive and updated knowledge available globally. This will help significantly to mitigate the Digital Divide between developing and developed countries. Information kiosk capacity building could be one of the pilots of such open-source knowledge sharing system.

Notes

1. See http://www.ecomlink.org/ictworkshop/agenda.asp

Satisfying the Demand for ICT Connectivity of Low-Income Groups

Ana María Fernández-Maldonado
Delft University of Technology

Abstract
In the milieu of telecommunications deregulation and privatization, poor people's demand for ICT connectivity has been highly overlooked by the private sector because they are not considered a valuable market for profitable business. The author challenges this assumption and discusses the importance of public access points as a way to satisfy this demand in the context of the Peruvian experience with cabinas públicas.

The level of ICT diffusion in countries, cities and regions is significantly related with their level of economic development. In affluent countries, where most citizens enjoy telephone connections and can pay for computer equipment and Internet connection, the level of ICT penetration is obviously high. In other words, the richer the country, the higher the connectivity. Further, ICT is not only widely used at home but also at work and school. In fact, one of the driving forces of the expansion of ICTs in affluent countries has been the transformation of work practices into ICT supported activities. Such transition can be defined as the transition for an industrial society into a knowledge society.

The case with developing countries is however different, as many countries are still in their transition phase towards an industrial society. For most people in developing countries the ICT revolution has meant or will mean the first exposure to computers and technical equipment. Because of this, developing countries have a double burden for the connection of their population to the global networks. While most people simply cannot afford the means for home connection, only a segment of their economies are supported by ICTs.

An additional burden for developing countries comes from the new rules of the game in the telecommunications sector, in which deregulation, privatization and free competition are the key words. In this new context, ICT services are being offered in places of high demand, where companies can get the most benefits. This fact punishes poor countries, cities and regions even further. The irony is that poor areas do have a high demand. Children and young people from all over the world are equally enthusiastic about computers and the Internet, and they constitute the largest portion of the population in developing countries. The reality is that poor peoples' demands are not taken into account because these people are not affluent enough to pay the high prices of the telecommunications services. They simply do not constitute a valuable market for profit-driven private companies.

In this highly difficult panorama the only realistic way to answer the demand for ICT connectivity in developing countries is by means of the implementation of places for collective access. This has been already widely recognized by institutions involved with development. The advantages are manifold. To name only two: people can develop their familiarity with computers and improve their technical skills gradually, investing time and money according to their own needs, pace and budgets. Further, the exposure of children and young people with computers and Internet at an early age ensures the improvement of the educational level of the future working force.

Governments, NGOs and the private sector have engaged in actions and programs to establish these types of places in disadvantaged regions of both the developed and developing world. However, the experience shows that to implement public access centers extensively is a big challenge. Even if developing countries' governments might be willing to implement them, which is not always the case, the endeavor requires a massive investments of funds that developing economies generally cannot afford. In some cases, governments have invested relatively large amounts of money but the implementation of public access places has not been successful enough to show an effective improvement in the overall penetration of ICTs at local or national level, with few exceptions.

On the other hand, NGOs involved with development have also become interested in establishing telecenters, and many projects have been implemented in all corners of the planet. The telecenters movement is highly dynamic but their main goal is not to provide access or improve ICT connectivity but to empower isolated or disadvantaged communities or target groups. For this reason the model becomes too expensive to be replicated extensively.

On the other hand, the private sector is increasingly successful in providing ICT connectivity to low-income communities. Indicators of Internet penetration in developing countries show a trend towards stagnation of home connectivity and the sustained growth of users connecting from public places. This is because the so-called cybercafés are gradually proliferating in crowded areas and neighborhoods of cities in developing countries, providing connectivity at affordable prices. Local people have properly identified the demand for ICT connectivity coming from the poor and are establishing small businesses to satisfy this demand, although without social pretensions.

The cybercafé model is highly different from the government or NGOs centralized and top-down initiatives. They are rather unpretentious commercial initiatives of local entrepreneurs to earn a living in the cities. The for-profit character of this type of businesses means that they are not addressing the very poor segments of the population. However, their increasing numbers are effectively providing an answer to the demands of connectivity of those groups which otherwise cannot afford home connectivity.

An interesting example shows the possibilities of collective access to ICT connectivity. In Peru, thousand of cabinas públicas de Internet have emerged since 1998 in the cities of the country, without any support from the State, NGOs or private firms. Thanks to their presence, many from the lower-income sectors of society are benefiting from cheap and widespread access to ICT connectivity. More than 85 per cent of the Peruvian users connect to the Internet in *cabinas*. Despite its poverty restrictions and low levels of telephone penetration, Peru has become the second country in Latin America regarding the percentage of Internet users, after Chile.

The effect of the existence of cabinas is visible in the Peruvian society. Cabinas have become a familiar urban facility at neighborhood level. Users express that Internet use is effectively improving their daily lives, especially the youth and the popular sectors. The use of computers and Internet by school and university students has become common. Teachers express that the use of computers by students is improving the quality of education. Peruvians have changed their recreation habits and since 2002 the visit to the cabina has become the main recreation activity. Besides, Peruvians are much better communicated with their relatives abroad than before, which has increased the level of remittances to the country. At the city level, cabinas are offering different urban services, which have been systematically denied to poor neighborhoods. The libraries, post offices, recreation facilities, study places, youth centers, training centers, etc., that have always been lacking in the poor neighborhoods are now present and combined in the multiple services offered in the cabinas.

Recently, public and private institutions have understood the fundamental importance of the cabinas as providers of ICT connectivity and are beginning to implement different programs to use them as a bridge between citizens and government or institutions. Different networks of cabinas are currently promoting e-government activities, payment of taxes and fines, and facilitating the use of Internet by SMEs. The presence of cabinas is an opportunity to rapidly reach groups that were previously difficult to access.

More important, cabinas have become a topic of high interest for the general population. Peruvians are proud of the cabinas, which they consider a national product. There is a high affinity of the general population towards these new technologies, which seems to have been promoted by the widespread aspirations regarding education as a tool for upward mobility. The popular sectors have been among the firsts to acknowledge the potentials of ICTs for improving their living conditions. Increasingly, popular groups are taking the initiative and demanding better services, facilities and a stronger leading role in the telecommunications sector from the side of the government.

On the other hand, the main limitation linked to this commercial model is its focus on technical access. If access is important, it does not constitute an end in itself but only a first step towards universal access to information. But this first step means much more for the poor than for the affluent groups. If for the affluent the Internet is a new invention that is complementing or slowly replacing other telecommunication media, such as telegraph, traditional mail, fax, and local or long-distance telephone, in the developing world access to the Internet makes a big difference. This is because it provides possibilities for communication among people who previously could not contact others who were distant from them, because of the absence, scarcity, inefficiency, or unaffordability of traditional communication services. In this way it opens a new world that was previously out of reach.

Cabinas are now considered as the "Peruvian model of access to ICTs", which the World Bank officials have celebrated as "the most viable model" for (universal access in) developing countries. The Peruvian model is evidence of the high demand for ICT connectivity coming from low-income groups particularly in cities. It shows that bottom-up alternatives can be effective to achieve ICT connectivity. It confirms that the path towards the "information society" has no blueprints and will develop differently according to local circumstances. Finally it means that satisfying the demands for ICT connectivity of low-income groups is an investment in the future that will pay back.

Basic Principles of Community Public Internet Access Point's Sustainability

Klaus Stoll*

Fundacion Chasquinet

Abstract

The author offers a more holistic approach to achieve information kiosk sustainability. This sustainability, he argues, can not been seen on the basis of Financial Sustainability alone. In order to reach the goals of Community development and financial sustainability, information kiosks have to integrate Social, Political, Cultural and Technical sustainability as vital elements into their planning and operation.

It is a fact that the vast majority of Public Internet Access Points, or PIAP's of all kinds and denomination, (these can be Cybercafé, Cabina Publica Internet, Telecentre, Infocentro, Multi-purpose Community Telecentre, Community Technology Centre, Locutorio, e-government centres, etc.), can in fact hardly sustain themselves independently in the long term and thus require outside funding.

The global telecentre movement can now look back on a more or less proud history of more then 20 years. Many initiatives and models have been tried and tested and some real success stories have emerged. But still one of the holy grails of the global telecentre movement seems to be out of its grasp: The real sustainability of Community PIAP's. But there are some remarkable examples emerging that show that real sustainability of PIAP's is indeed possible if some basic principles and rules are followed in their implementation and running.

It is very useful to distinguish at the start within the broad group of PIAP's three main subsets, on the basis of the fundamental vision and purpose of their creators and operators. Some PIAP's represent a mixture of two or even all three of the below mentioned subsets.

*I would like to express my profound thanks for the valuable input and comments of Prof. Michel Menou and Mr. Don Cameron. Guys, you are great!.

1) PIAP's of the first group are primarily meant as a small business providing connectivity to people who cannot have individual access (either because they cannot afford it, or are travelling). As any other business, the goal of these PIAP's is to be profitable for their owners, even though this fact and the induced socio-economic effects may have indirect consequences upon the condition of the community where they are based. A typical example for PIAP's of this group are privately owned Cybercafes.

2) PIAP's of the second group are primarily meant to aid the interaction between the public administration and the public through ICT's. These PIAP's are known as Government or Public administration or Public services PIAP's.

3) PIAP's in the third group are intended as facilities to overcome some socio-economic imbalances and/or support communities struggle for development. Connectivity is for them one more tool but not and end in itself, neither is sustainability. These are the so called Community based PIAP's or Community Development PIAP's. A typical example for PIAP's of this group are Telecenters created and maintained by a community for the community. This article in particular concentrates on Community PIAP's.

When one talks about PIAP's sustainability, financial sustainability of PIAP's is the first, and in too many cases only, thing that comes to mind. Obviously business PIAP's need to be sustainable. And yes, community development PIAP's should aim to be financially sustainable if possible after a reasonable time of operation, even if this sounds like a rather utopian goal in the light of many experiences. One good reason for it is that this would secure their autonomy. Another is that outside funding often dries up. One may however stress that to the extent the provision of universal service of information and communication is recognized as a fundamental requirement for societal effectiveness, if not even a right, the need for public, or community development, PIAP's to be self-sustainable is no more obvious than for schools, health care services, roads, museums, libraries, courts, chambers of commerce, or any other basic facility.

Because financial sustainability is seen as crucial, many PIAP's base their "business model" on the provision of ICT and related services to their respective communities or customer base. Many have found out that this on its own is often not a sufficient basis for achieving financial sustainability. This even more likely to be the case if the aim is the development of a community whose members have initially limited requirements for telecommunications and a very low purchasing power, if at all.

Some "Basic Principles" for PIAP's Sustainability

These principles are related specifically to Community development PIAP's. Those PIAP's that have integrated Social, Political, Cultural and Technical sustainability as vital elements in their planning and operation have made the experience that financial sustainability can indeed be achieved on this basis. Even fully commercial or governmental PIAP initiatives are making the experience that sustainability can not be achieved without taking these elements into account.

PIAP's Sustainability can not been seen on the basis of Financial Sustainability alone. In order to reach the goals of Community development and financial sustainability. PIAP's have to integrate Social, Political, Cultural and Technical sustainability as vital elements into their planning and operation.

Social and Cultural Sustainability

If the activities of a PIAP's are to be lasting and viable, they must take account of the social and cultural context in which it operates, and must respond appropriately to that context. If people in the community feel themselves empowered by the PIAP, they will be more active in seeking ways to keep it running.

Men and women have different needs and expectations that are reflected in their perception of telecentres, and different possibilities and interests with regard to its use. Similarly, young's, adults and elders have different needs and expectations. Significant differences can also be identified between urban and rural settings, between professions and income groups, among indigenous communities and minorities. If the telecentre cannot come to terms with these differences in its management, it will be neither socially nor culturally sustainable.[1] "The matter of Telecentre sustainability (and there is certainly a distinction between a Telecentre and a PIAP) can be overcome when the Telecentre itself is a "common" and thereby deemed to be worthy of community support."[2]

We can differentiate between two kinds of "commons": 1) The Social Commons and 2) the Physical Commons.

1) The Social Commons are expressed as shared community values. These can be analysed and documented using the following criteria:

- Participation in Networks: interlocking relationships between many groups.
- Reciprocity: taking care of each other's interests and the interests of the all.
- Altruism rather than egotism. This is a very important issue as egotists will decrease social trust and so people will tend not to float ideas within a group dominated by an egotist.
- Trust: ability to take risks within a social sphere.
- Proactivity: a community that designs a future for itself rather than is a victim of fate or worse still a victim of a poor self fulfilling prophecy. People are actively participating in a range of community activities.
- Social Norms: unwritten, inarticulated but with the ability to make you feel bad intrinsically when you have broken one, therefore it is even more binding and does not require enforcement.[3]

2) The Physical Commons as "public facilities as being of value and worthy of on-going community support". These can be   green spaces, recreational grounds, wells, means of production, public halls, libraries, schools, Telecentres and other places of identified community worth. The physical commons are the physical manifestation of the social commons. All social commons present in a community and put together represent a significant part of the Social Capital of a community. The stronger the social commons present in a community, the bigger are the chances for sustainability of the physical commons, such as a Telecentre.

Sustainable PIAP's have to fully integrate all the stakeholders in the community its serves and the specific needs of this community in the planning and the operation of the telecentre. There are no "one for all" models for PIAP's because the circumstances in which they are operating are different from case to case and as a result we can only talk about different "dynamics".

Communities that feel themselves empowered by their PIAP and feel the real benefits for their community and the individuals of this community will ensure the sustainability (including the financial sustainability) of a PIAP because it is in their own vital self interest.

Political Sustainability

Political sustainability refers to the importance of securing a stable regulatory framework in order to protect, promote, and support community telecentres and their activities, with special attention to the specific needs of the poorest sectors.[4]

Short term fiscal or political considerations often result in changes in the legal or tax status of telecenters that may jeopardize long standing efforts in a fortnight. The relative novelty of ICT result in high inconsistency in their definition by legislators and judges.

Sustainable PIAP's follow a "down-up" and not a "up-down" dynamic. As PIAP's and their sustainability is based on the community and its commons the role of government in a telecentre dynamic is not to "impose" a telecentre on a community, for what ever well intentioned reasons like to bridge a perceived "digital divide" but to create the conditions that allow community telecentres dynamics to develop. The same is true for international organizations active in the field of PIAP's development.

"In Australia 'Commons' are sustained by taxes and frequently supplemented through the contributions of volunteer administration groups. Our establishment (seed) funding processes for Telecentre's recognizes the value of 'commons' and works on similar principles that a community must want and make application for Telecentre funds. Telecentre's are not 'imposed' on our communities; and in fact communities must demonstrate very strong support for the Initiative before they will be considered for funding and on-going maintenance Support (access to State Help-Desks, additional equipment and low-cost broadband etc.)".[5]

Technological Sustainability

Although telecentres do not generally need to operate with the latest technologies, it is important that they have a clear plan for insuring their technological sustainability. This is especially the case since digital technologies are changing so swiftly, which means that equipment and programs rapidly become outdated. Connectivity and its related costs is still a vital issue in particular in rural areas.[6] PIAP sustainability can not be achieved without networking between telecentres. In order for PIAP's to make their work more effective and to reach their ams, they need to organize themselves in overlapping local, national, regional and international networks. This organization is important for four reasons: First, it allows users to interact with other communities at all relevant levels and for all relevant purposes thus expanding the range of their potential benefits; Secondly, to share technical know how, insight and experience, increasing their effectiveness and chances of success; Thirdly, it allows them to share resources, and to get access to resources more easily and cheaply; Finally, these networks need to engage actively in public policy debates and organization is a key step towards this.

Being part of local, national and international networks provides PIAP's with much needed scalability and the subsequent support to cope with these liabilities. One example for this is the ability to achive connectivity for a reduced cost through block deals between PIAP networks and the public sector.

Financial Sustainability

PIAP's sustainability can not be achieved on the basis of providing and selling ICT services alone. PIAP's sustainability can be achived if the provision of ICT Services is seen as the "tool" that complements the overall goal to achive positive community development. Community PIAP's are Community Commons with the element of ICT support. The community and its needs and assets stands in the centre of a Community PIAP not the ICT.

"Because the Telecentre is 'a common' the failure of any single Telecentre service (such as the provision of public Internet access or ISP services etc) must not result in the Telecentre itself becoming 'unsustainable'... It should simply mean that one particular service is no longer sustainable, which is then quite easily managed - I see this point as being the most fundamental difference between a PIAP and a Telecentre... a Telecentre is 'a common'; a PIAP is a service that may or may not be provided by a Telecentre or by any other suitable provider (libraries, commercial providers such as Cyber Cafe's, schools etc. etc.).

'Commons' are facilities identified as components of social capital that have worth extending beyond commercial viability or promise. As such these are community assets sustained for the benefit of current and future generations. Yet the activities and some of the business ventures of these commons will come and go (PIAP or ISP services etc.) we must be sure to carefully delineate between the service and the asset. The asset has long-term value; the value of the service is usually of shorter term (meaning new services can be added as community needs are continually identified) and can be discarded as needs wain or are met."[7]

Notes

1. Quoted from: Community Telecentres for Development, by Karin Delgadillo, Ricardo Gomez, Klaus Stoll, www.tele-centros.org/tcparaque

2. Quoted from an email of Don Cameron to the Telecentres-I list, 8th of December 2002

3. Susie Brown quoted by Don Cameron in his article: A Community-Rebuilding: The Coolah Story, www.regional.org.au/articles/development/coolah_revitalisation.htm

4. Quoted from: Community Telecentres for Development, by Karin Delgadillo, Ricardo Gomez, Klaus Stoll, www.tele-centros.org/tcparaque

5. Quoted from an email of Don Cameron to the Telecentres-I list, 8th of December 2002

6. Quoted from: Community Telecentres for Development, by Karin Delgadillo, Ricardo Gomez, Klaus Stoll, www.tele-centros.org/tcparaque

7. Quoted from an email of Don Cameron to the Telecentres-I list, 8th of December 2002

Digital Innovation in Communities: The Diffusion Effect

Richard Fuchs
International Development Research Center (IDRC)

Abstract
The author argues that the sooner broad cross-sections of people in a society learn about and decide how digital tools make sense in their world, the more likely it is that sustainable progress will begin to be made. He offers three basic, mission-critical lessons for consideration: First, find and support the social innovators; Second, start small with anchor "markets" and plan big on an inter-generational basis; and Finally, engage women in the process of ICT diffusion.

Why are so few lessons learned from "lessons-learned" asked the veteran ICT development professional[1] from the Caribbean? He was wondering why it was that wave after wave of community based digital innovation repeated the same mistakes and failed to learn from the experiences of digital innovators that had gone before them.

Over the last two decades people, communities and societies have begun to recognize that there is a direct relationship between income, employment, "development", access, and fluency with the tools of the digital world. Some have come to this realization quickly while others have taken longer to accept this post-industrial economic reality. The World Summit on the Information Society will crystallize global attention on many of the issues associated with developing world participation in the Information Economy. Many new leaders, community activists, government policy officers and private sector entrepreneurs will pass through the experience of WSIS in Geneva and Tunisia. Surely this is a propitious time to try to help distil the most important lessons of how to get started in the digital age.

Communities in the Information Society

Diffusing ICTs into community life is an essential element of successful participation in the digital world. At some point, the use of digital tools clearly has to go beyond the thin layer of elites that initially use these technologies in a society.

In very real terms, broad interest, access, awareness and fluency with digital tools helps to "make the market" for a domestic, rather than a solely export oriented, Information Economy. The building of community sophistication with digital tools is the principal mechanism through which the "politics" of legislative and regulatory reform become grounded and sustainable. Large groups of people learn to understand why connectivity and bandwidth are important in their schools, businesses, health clinics and local governments. Sooner or later their governments then come to reflect their interests in the policy decisions they support.

So, lesson number one, is that community participation is not an elective: it's a required course. The sooner broad cross-sections of people in a society learn about and decide how digital tools make sense in their world, the more likely it is that sustainable progress will begin to be made. Community participation builds awareness, skills, entrepreneurship and demand. Eventually access will increase and prices will reduce.

Where to Start? - Find the Social Innovators!

It's pretty clear that the rules of social entrepreneurship and engagement resemble those of private markets. In order for an innovation to be adopted, some particular group or segment of society needs to champion and lead the adoption process. They lead this process until broader cross-sections become convinced that the change is worth pursuing and paying for in greater numbers.

So the first place to start is to find these social entrepreneurs and innovators. Every society has them. They are often initially found in NGOs[2] but they can turn up in the most unlikely of places; schools, private firms, universities, even occasionally within a government agency.

Many government-led initiatives for community engagement are based upon the "spray n' pray"[3] approach to community involvement. Rather than taking the time to locate and support community innovators, this approach favours a "one-size-fits-all" programmed strategy. And, it almost never works.

Anchor Markets

As much as we'd like our well-intentioned approaches for community engagement to benefit everyone at about the same time, this is almost a sure-fired recipe for failure. The common experience is that, if everyone is supposed to benefit, then no one actually owns the innovation. While the long-term strategy can be a very inclusive one, some principal social segment has to be targeted for the adoption of the community based digital innovation. This need not be an exclusive arrangement but it almost certainly needs to be a paramount fixture of the start-up strategy.

In Indonesia, the Liberation Technologist, Dr. Onno Purbo targets university and secondary school students for his "quick course" in how to deploy WiFi in urban settlements. He gives public lectures with 300-500 participants, each paying $3 to enroll. What follows is instruction in "how to" inexpensively deploy the technologies along with access to his website[4] that includes 30 books he's written and had published in Bahasa Indonesian. While his aim is for the entire Indonesian society to become "knowledge-based", his hope is that the young students will sustain and spread their digital innovation over the course of one generation.

In Benin, West Africa, Fr. Godfrey Nzamujo has focused on an entirely different "anchor market". The sustainable agriculture NGO he started in 1985 now has six rural plantations with corresponding urban telecentres in three of the locations. Upwards of 700 adult learners come to these school-plantations every year to learn the novel Songhai[5] approach to environmentally renewable agriculture. The principal initial focus of this digital innovation is on these students and the 150+ faculty and staff that work there.

Having engaged this "anchor" market in the use of digital tools, the telecentres have opened their doors to the community at large. Yes, Songhai has had social investment from several agencies that has assisted with the acquisition of technology and systems. Importantly, however, they have always amortized the replacement cost of these investments as a part of their normal budgeting processes. Songhai has recently installed VSAT capability in its telecentre locations in Porto Novo, Savalou and Parakou, considerably increasing its bandwidth and the reliability of its connectivity. After five years of trial, some error, and perseverance, the revenue from the operations of its telecentres is a major element of the NGOs financial sustainability. They now help other NGOs install and operate VSAT as a new element of the services their NGO provides.

Fr. Nzamujo's longer term strategy is for African agriculturists to increasing use digital tools, including the Internet, to engage in continuous learning and the recruitment of new innovators. Like other social innovators, he's selected an initial anchor market with a longer-term intergenerational transformation in mind. Start small and plan BIG!

The Right Man for this Job is a Woman[6]

An entire literature and professional practice has, thankfully, emerged to help us understand and benefit from the ways in which gender roles are affected by development processes. The reasons for incorporating this into the business of ICT diffusion within communities go beyond the customary reference to an understanding of gender within a perspective of human rights. Simply put, if women are not recruited, engaged and involved within the social transformations associated with the Information Society, the economic transition to a knowledge-based economy will not succeed!

The evidence from the post-industrial economies[7] of the North is clear and straightforward. Within the two decades since the Information Economy has become ascendant, women's roles and contributions to science, technology, the labour force and business have risen very considerably matching and, in some cases, surpassing that of men.

I recently participated in an ICT Policy Workshop at the MS Swaminathan Research Foundation in Chennai, India. One of the presentations included the testimonials by nine (9) community animators in an engaging ICT program in Pondicherry. Six (6) of these presenters were women, very different from the gender mix of the people in the audience where women were in very small numbers.

At the end of this particular session, I asked the audience to close their eyes and imagine the presentation we had just seen and to then "erase" the six (6) women from the picture. Could we possibly imagine that what we had learned from the group would have been nearly as successful if these women had not been represented, and even over-represented, among those doing the ICT diffusion?

It is impossible to imagine how the participation of women scientists, researchers, entrepreneurs, knowledge workers, teachers and assorted other roles could possibly be "erased" from the Information Economy in the North. So too is it impossible to imagine how developing world societies and economies can engage the Knowledge Economy without the full participation of women.

This same case needs to be made, understood and acted upon in how we diffuse ICTs within communities if developing societies hope to succeed in the Information Society and Economy. If human rights is an insufficient motivation to include women in this information economy transformation, then it is important to know and to understand that success is impossible without their full participation and contributions in this sector.[8]

Conclusion

The first generation of developing world digital pioneers are now in sufficient numbers that we can benefit from the sacrifices they have made and the lessons they have to teach. I have offered three basic, mission-critical lessons for consideration. First, find and support the social innovators. Second, start small with anchor "markets" and plan big on an inter-generational basis. And finally, engage women in the process of ICT diffusion.

As the World Summit on the Information Society approaches, let's hope that it is a fertile arena for sharing, exchanging and generating new knowledge for how the developing world can benefit from and contribute to the next Information Revolution.

Notes

1. Personal conversation with Yacine Kheladi in October 2001.

2. For a whole host of reasons NGOs are the most likely places to find these innovators and they are also often the best places to begin the diffusion effect within communities. NGOs tend to be

"flatter" and unstratified. They also have a compelling need to "do more with less", just the type of environment in which ICTs thrive. Faced with a choice among an NGO, a school, a library or a local government agency, I would almost always start with the NGO for these reasons. But eventually, the innovation that is led by the NGO has to become adopted by more dominant institutions. The "staying power" of an NGO to remain engaged in this process is often a difficulty.

3. I first heard the "spray n' pray" reference used by a South African ICT consultant., Niki Roberts, at an IDRC Sub-Saharan Africa SchoolNets debriefing session in Johannesburg in February 2001.

4. http://sandbox.bellanet.org/~onno/

5. See www.songhai.org or refer to the Songhai Case Study included in this publication.

6. I used this reference in an earlier publication "If you have a lemon, make lemonade: A Guide to the Start-up of African Multi-purpose Community Telecentres", International Development Research Centre, 1997. I use it again to emphasize how mission-critical it is to long-term success.

7. Education at a Glance: OECD Indicators 2003.Paris, OECD, c2003. 451 p.

8. See The First Sex: The Natural Talents of Women and How They Are Changing the World. Ballantine Books, 2000 by Helen Fisher for an interesting analysis of why the information economy may be most well suited, of all economic eras, to women's successful participation.

Private Sector Kiosks and Government Incentives:
What Works and What is Sustainable

Robert Schware*
The World Bank

Abstract
Governments in many developing countries are making market-oriented reforms, in which they privatize and deregulate the telecommunications sector and fashion transparent regulatory frameworks. As a result, private sector kiosks are spreading at a fast pace in many urban areas of the developing world. The author suggests that private sector kiosks, with the correct government incentives, can become viable channels of distribution of ICT services and support development goals.

In the ten years since the information kiosk (or "telecenter") movement began, governments and international not-for-profit organizations have experimented with the kiosks to help poor communities in the developing world gain access to information and communication technologies (ICTs), but participation of the private sector has been limited until recently. The private sector was not greatly interested in investing in kiosks because of the opaque telecom systems in such countries, and doubt about the profitability of doing business in low-income communities.

This state of affairs is changing. Governments in many developing countries are making market-oriented reforms, in which they privatize and deregulate the telecommunications sector and fashion transparent regulatory frameworks. As a result, private sector kiosks are spreading at a fast pace in many urban areas of the developing world. Experiences from cabinas públicas in Peru, locutorios in Argentina and cibercafes in Mexico (Proenza et al. 2001) to Sonatel phone shops in Senegal and Wartels in Indonesia (Norton et al. 2000) show that there are sizeable markets in which private sector investment in kiosks can be highly productive. These kiosks are also fulfilling an enormous demand, particularly in urban low-income areas, for ICT services and they are doing it at a reasonable

*Lead Informatics Specialist, the Global ICT Department, World Bank, Washington, D.C. USA. The views herein are those of the author and should not be attributed to the World Bank or any other affiliated organizations

cost. Can they be expanded to rural and low-income areas in a financially sustainable manner? Can they create new jobs in rural areas? Are they an effective way of enhancing Government and international organization development programs? This paper seeks to show that if private sector kiosks can be given the correct economic conditions under which to flourish, they can become viable channels of distribution of ICT services and support development goals.

Elements That Make Private Sector Kiosks Financially Sustainable

Kiosks that do not achieve commercial sustainability in the medium and long run are constantly at risk of failure, for they drain resources through their endless dependency on external funding - either donations by not-for-profit organizations or subsidies from governments - after the start-up phase. This cycle limits the kiosks' usefulness in contributing in any way to economic and social development. A variety of approaches have been tried and the results so far are mixed. Although some stories of success have been documented using a variety of remedies, certain challenges threaten the viability of the kiosks as a tool for development, among them problems with equipment malfunction and the unreliability of telecommunications and electricity particularly in rural areas.

For a kiosk's success to be long term, it must behave more like a private enterprise in its administration and setting of goals, and since the objective of the kiosks is to provide sustainable services to a community, there must be incentive for sustainable growth. Government involvement can represent the common interest of social good, but lessons learned show that the public sector will not likely offer the promise of growth and new opportunities that private entities could bring to the table. Furthermore, the resources necessary to expand telecommunications infrastructure to underserved areas can only be achieved by spurring private sector investment and entrepreneurship (Norton 2000, Proenza 2001, Cannock, 2001, and Wellenius 2003).[1]

The vast majority of private sector kiosks rely on demand-driven approaches[2] for their sustainability, starting with basic services, and increasing their service' offerings in response to the demand of the local market. These approaches have proven to be responsive to community needs (Norton et al 2000) fulfilling first the immediate needs for basic services like telephone, photocopy and fax and steadily integrating more sophisticated ones, such as printing and typing/reporting services, training on how to use the computer, and Internet once the basics have been widely adopted by the community. In Indonesia, for example, franchised phone shops (Wartels)[3] , typically located in markets, bus stations, hotels, and airports, provide access to two to four telephone lines in the start-up phase with an initial investment of USD2,000-4,000. Where there is local demand, Internet kiosks (Warnets) offer more sophisticated ICT services (International Telecommunications Union (ITU), Indonesia Case Study: 2003).

Clearly an advantage of the demand-driven approach is that it fosters the entrepreneurship and management skills of local kiosk owners, since these ow-ners must become knowledgeable of the market they are serving in order to provide the services that better fulfill the demand of their customers, and they stand to make a profit or risk loss. Drishtee Ltd[4], a private company, is implementing a tiered-franchise approach to bring information and communication technologies into rural areas in northern India. Through Drishtee's franchise, kiosk owners offer a basic set of e-government services, but they may choose from an array of other services, such as insurance and microcredit, in order to increase their revenue streams and become more responsive to local needs. Although they offer different services this same advantage also applies to cabinas públicas[5] in Peru and Sonatel phone shops in Senegal (Fuchs 2000).

However, no matter how responsive a kiosk may be at the local level, it must be guided by a sound business plan and a medium to long-term strategy to ensure survival (Sabien 2001). Kiosks sponsored by the public sector often lack a strategic business plan and a performance evaluation process, running the risk of becoming tools of political propaganda or simply disappearing once the resources from the government are withdrawn. We can learn many lessons by observing the fate of the telecenter rollout program sponsored by the South African government.

This 1997 program, created under the auspices of the Universal Service Agency (USA) with the objective of establishing over four years 100 telecenters in poor areas that lack telecom infrastructure, had a beginning budget allocation of USD 4 million. The program ran into many difficulties, such as 1) the USA was politically pressured to establish as many telecenters as possible even though none did a systematic needs analysis of the telecenter sites; 2) there was a "one-size fits all" model that became known as "being killed by over-capitalization"; and 3) the bureaucracy within USA generated a centralized management that increased telecenters' dependency on the agency for equipment maintenance, "having a profound effect on the ability of the managers to maintain working equipment," stifling local adaptation and ownership (Benjamin: 30).

Early indications from the Thailand Canada Telecentre Project (proof of concept pilots) are that although there was a general inclination by communities to have their telecenters owned and run by government, after 4-6 months the local government administrations ("Tambons") realized that they were not the best organization to operate a telecenter. The major factor affecting financial performance is the lack of a market oriented revenue sharing arrangement that provides a financial incentive to the telecenters (CIDA 2002).

All this having been said, in and of itself the involvement of the private sector in kiosks cannot alone achieve the goal of universal telecommunications access[6] in developing countries. However, as the next section will show, the next step is to encourage partnership between private industry and government, so these privately sponsored kiosks can become viable means to deliver telecom access to rural and low-income areas.

Government Incentives to Private Sector Kiosks

It has been seen that kiosks that are self-sustaining have greater positive effects in developing communities, and we have examined the key elements that make private kiosks financially sustainable. Now we must explore how government incentives to privately-sponsored kiosks can help kiosks become viable distributors of ICT services for the purposes of development. These incentives generally fall into two categories:

1) those aimed at expanding telecommunications infrastructure into underserved areas (rural and remote),

2) those designed to enhance kiosk performance for development purposes.

Many countries are crafting market-oriented reforms intended to privatize and deregulate their telecommunications sectors and to improve access and investment in rural, underserved and unserved areas. Among the mechanisms they are implementing to spur private sector investment in the early stages of kiosks establishment are:

- license obligations to serve rural communities,

- minimum subsidies schemes,

- telecommunications development funds,

- variations of build-transfer-operate arrangements.

In such countries as Chile, Peru and Colombia universal access funds were established to provide one-time subsidies to extend fixed networks to underserved rural and remote areas, which in turn attracted considerable private sector investment.

In Chile, for example, a subsidy of USD 21 million became, in the hands of five firms that won the bidding process, USD 30 million in additional investment for the provision of public-access phones and more than USD 109 million in other services -residential and commercial individual access lines and value added services; this means that USD 1 of public subsidy leveraged over USD 6 of private investment in the country. In a similar manner, Peru created FITEL (Fondo de Inversión para las Telecomunicaciones) to subsidize services in rural areas; the initial subsidy of USD 1.66 million resulted in an additional investment of USD 3.3 million. This means that USD 1 of public subsidy leveraged over USD 2 of private investment (Cannock 2001, Sepulveda 2002).

In Colombia, COMPARTEL granted a minimum subsidy to a number of firms in order to build a total of 270 telecenters with three, six, or twelve computers each. "The competition for the subsidy is open to any type of business model, but the enterprises that won this particular subsidy follow the commercial franchising model" (Proenza 2001:8). Nepal, Sri Lanka, and Nigeria, are undertaking similar output-based contracts for rural services in which telecommunications operators bid for the minimum government subsidy to provide ICT services to the poor in targeted areas.

The World Bank Telecom Sector Reform Project in Nepal will finance one rural telecom operator in the eastern part of the country covering approx 4 thousand wards (villages), impacting 3 million people who have been excluded from commercial operations. Using the same formulae, Sri Lanka will improve rural access to telecommunications services by promoting private participation to some 500 kiosks in the south and northeast of the country (Singh 2003).

These and other experiences have shown that additional successful incentive mechanisms at the start up phase include publicity of the programs, establishment of solid monitoring and evaluation strategies, and training and support services for kiosks operators (Wellenius 2003).

Finally there are two ways to enhance kiosk performance for development purposes:

- grant tax breaks for those kiosks that provide e-government services on their premises;

- negotiate with telecommunications companies so kiosks in rural areas can obtain flat phone rates.

Conclusion

Successful kiosk development has always depended on a synergetic relationship among community members, not-for-profit organizations, private enterprise, and governments. The involvement of the public sector is of fundamental importance in the setting the scope and expectations for social development. Simultaneously, the participation of private organizations is also crucial to provide business acumen and discipline. In this context, the key issue becomes how to mobilize private sector investment and participation in kiosks that are not only driven by commercial interests, but are able to integrate development goals with appropriate government incentives.

The involvement of private organizations in social projects has two main benefits: private organizations bring a treasure-trove of expertise and much-needed capital, and private groups are driven by measurable results, which can be applied to efficient planning and lean execution. The relationship between the public and private sectors requires the adaptation of two seemingly inconsistent ideologies: government will be driven by the need to improve the quality of life of its communities, and private organizations will be motivated by the prospect of future growth and profits. Consequently, this relationship cannot be built by short-term goals, but rather on long-term relationships in which there is significant accountability on both ends. The government must reduce bureaucracy and smooth market conditions, and private organizations must be prepared to commit themselves to long-duration projects with some risk in exchange for equally long-term growth and profits.

Notes

1. This paper does not explore management issues related to kiosks/telecenters, or major internal factors affecting financial performance. Initial evidence from six telecenters in rural Thailand

suggests that women are better telecenter managers and operators. Women tend to be better retailers/small business operators, better at financial management and reporting than their male counterparts and more sensitive to privacy concerns of women customers. See CIDA, December 2002, World Bank, 2003, and Thailand Canada Telecentre Project case study in this book.

2. Norton et al. (2000) distinguish between two types of financing approaches: 1) driven by demand-side forces; 2) driven by supply-side forces. The latter receives its funding, especially in the initial phase, from international donors and NGOs, and although in theory these kiosks are designed to become sustainable, in practice there is no solid business plan created in the start-up phase. This model departs from the premise that providing a wide array of training and services will eventually generate demand, which in turn will provide sufficient revenue to achieve sustainability (p.15). Supply-driven kiosks face the risk of the high operational costs of underused equipment endangering the efficient use of financial resources.

3. Wartels were introduced in Indonesia in 1999 as a way to provide public access to telephone services in urban and rural areas in a country with a teledensity of 2.9 phones per hundred people (ITU 2000). As of today, there are close to 200,000 Wartels that together contribute US$700 million or 60% of the state-owned telecommunications enterprise revenue. For further information on this model please refer to the Indonesia case study in this book.

4. For further information please refer to the Drishtee case study in this book or visit the website at: http://www.drishtee.com

5. For further information please refer to the Cabinas Públicas de Internet case study in this book.

6. Universal access has been defined in many different ways, depending on the socio-economic context and availability of telecommunications infrastructure in the country. For example, in Ghana the goal for universal access is to provide one phone per 500 people; and in Mexico the goal is to install one telephone line into all villages and localities. Universal access is a more viable strategy in developing countries with deficient telecom infrastructure. See Benjamin and Dahms article in the bibliography for further reference.

References

Benjamin, P. and Dahms, M. (1999). "Background paper on Universal Service and Universal Access Issues," Prepared for the Telia Telecommunications in Society Seminar. Sweden, June 1999.

Benjamin, Peter. (2001). "Reviewing Universal Access in South Africa," The Southern African Journal of Information and Communication, Vol. 2, No. 1.

Benjamin, Peter. (2001). Telecentre Experience in South Africa 1997 - 2000.

Cannock, Geoffrey (2001). "Telecom Subsidies: Output-Based Contracts for Rural Services in Peru." The World Bank Group Private Sector and Infrastructure Network," Viewpoint Note Number 234, June.

Canadian International Development Agency (CIDA), 2002. Monitoring the Community Telecenters, Hickling Corporation and Syntel Consultancy, December.

International Telecommunications Union (ITU) Indonesia Case Study. www.itu.int/ITU-D/ict/cs/indonesia/material/IDN%20CS%20-%202nd%20part.pdf

Norton, Marlee, Michael S. Tetelman, Christiane Brosnan, Maria A. Kendro, Brian S. Bacon, Patrick Lohmeyer, Richard Fuchs and Kristi McBride (2000). "Initial Lessons Learned About Private Sector Participation in Telecentre Development: A Guide for Policy Makers in Developing Appropriate Regulatory Frameworks," Report Commissioned by NTCA, July 7, 2000 (www.ntca.org).

Proenza, Francisco (2001). "Telecenter Sustainability: Myths and Opportunities." Journal of Development Communication, Vol. 12, No. 2, December.

Proenza, F., Bastidas-Buch R., and Montero, G. (2001). "Telecenters for Socioeconomic and Rural Development in Latin America," Rural Unit, Sustainable Development Department, Washington, D.C www.iadb.org/regions/itdev/telecenters/index.htm

Sabien, Brett (2001). "Some Principles of Financial Sustainability Based on Telecenters and a Telecentre Network in Australia," Journal of Development Communication Vol. 12, No. 2, December.

Sepulveda, Edgardo (2002). "Minimum Subsidy Competitive Auction Mechanisms for Funding Public Telecommunications Access in Rural Areas," ITU Global Symposium for Regulators, Hong Kong, No.8, December.

Singh, Ritin (2003). Interview on Output-Based Contracts for Rural Services in World Bank Projects, World Bank, Global ICT Department, CITPO, Washington, DC, October.

Wellenius, Bjorn (2003). "Sustainable Telecenters: A Guide for Government Policy." The World Bank Group Private Sector and Infrastructure Network," Viewpoint Note Number 251, January.

World Bank, (2003). "Ensuring Gender Equality in ICT for Development." Gender and Development Group in PREM, and the Global ICT Department, consultant report by KM International Co., Ltd.

Expanding State Purchases from Micro and Small Enterprises:
A Promising Approach from Peru

Francisco J. Proenza*
Food and Agricultural Organization

Abstract
The author describes the Peruvian government strategy that is taking advantage of the country's extensive network of cabinas publicas to helps support SMEs development through online services. He argues that the Peruvian approach is making effective use of the Internet to help overcome the information barriers that have traditionally prevented SMEs from taking advantage of the purchasing power of the State.

The availability of services online enhances the value of connectivity. The generally low levels of access to infrastructure typical of developing countries hold back governmental offers of content and services online. Since there is no effective demand, there is little value in supplying these services. Where telecenters are ubiquitous, however, the potential for serving the poor through online services can be realized. Telecenter sustainability is also enhanced, as the value of connectivity increases and low income users become more willing and able to connect to the Internet through telecenters.

Peru has a dense network of about 2,000 cabinas públicas, mostly located in Lima and in other urban centers of the country.[1] Competitive forces have enabled increasingly lower service costs. By mid 2002 telecenter users in Lima were paying about USD 0.60 for an hour of use of computers and the Internet. In June 2001, 33 per cent of Lima's population was using the Internet at least once a month [Apoyo 2001].

Commercial telecenters (cabinas) are the most common form through which Peruvian citizens connect to the Internet (see Figure 1). Only 5 per cent of the lowest income category (E) used the Internet at least once a month; and only 21 per cent of the second lowest strata (category D). Within this small group of low

*The view presented in this paper are those of the author and do not necessarily represent the official position of the FAO.

income users (D and E), 91 per cent connected to the Internet using telecenters. Amongst women Internet users, 90 per cent connected from cabinas. Use of cabinas is not limited to low income groups; as many as 60 per cent of high income users (category A) connect to the Net through cabinas [Apoyo 2]. In 2001 the average number of users per Internet host was 2.3 in the US and 80.0 in Peru [Gallo 2003].

Figure 1. Place Where Lima Residents Connect to the Internet

Location	Income Status (A highest; E lowest)				Gender	
	A	B	C	D/E	Male	Female
Cabina Publica	**59**	**77**	**88**	**91**	**77**	**90**
Workplace	22	29	14	6	24	11
School	21	17	16	16	15	19
Home	15	17	2	2	14	8
House of friend or relative	10	4	4	9	9	2

Fuente: [Apoyo 2001]. Note: User's may connect to the Internet from more than one location.

Micro and small enterprises generate about three quarters of Peru's GDP and account for over 40 per cent of employment in the country. Peru's extensive telecenter network is making it possible for the Government to support them through online services. Especially noteworthy are ongoing efforts to increase the amount of State purchases that are supplied by micro and small enterprises.

Figure 2. Relative Significance of Peruvian Enterprises by Size, in Terms of Number and Contribution to GDP and Employment

Classification	Annual Sales in USD	Number of Enterprises		Percent Contribution to	
		Number	Percent	GDP	Employment
Micro	< 80,000	467,001	91.7	75.9	42.1
Small	80,000- 750,000	35,075	6.9		
Medium/Large	>750,000	7,348	1.4	24.1	57.0

Note: These figures exclude rural micro and small (mostly farming) enterprises. Source: Infante [2003]

A State purchase policy may seek neutrality and focus on transparency by increasing the amounts that are advertised and processed online, without introducing explicit measures that would favor small enterprises. This is, for example, the approach adopted in Chile. Alternatively, specific measures may be introduced to try to enhance the competitive edge of micro, small and medium enterprises in the bidding process. The latter approach is followed by the US Small Business Administration [Chellew 2002].

Peru has taken a proactive approach, through a set of low cost set of interventions that do not introduce distortions in market signals nor compromise the quality of products purchased. Instead they make effective use of the the Internet, to help overcome the information barriers that have traditionally prevented small enterprises from taking advantage of the enormous purchasing power of the State.

The Ley de Contrataciones y Adquisiciones (Ley 26850) which became effective early in 2001 has significantly increased commercial opportunities for Peruvian micro and small enterprises employing fewer than 40 workers. The law provides that these small enterprises be favored in the event of a tie in a public tender process. More important than this "positive discrimination", are

Figure 3. Consultation Periods of Low Value Purchases and Select Direct Tenders

		Low Value Purchases		Select Direct Tenders***	
		Minimum*	Maximum	Minimum**	Maximum
Civil Works		8,900	26,000	26,000	129,000
Goods		3,580	10,100	10,100	50,500
Services		3,580	4,300	4,300	21,600
Notification Requirements	**Civil Works**	7 days between the call for proposals and the deadline for their presentation.		10 working days between calls for proposals have been issued and the deadline for the presentation or proposals.	
	Goods & Services	Deadlines for the presentation of proposals may be set shortly after the call for proposals has been issued (even within the same day). Notification to PROMPyme must be simultaneous with issuance of invitations to tender.			
Period of Consultation and formulation of tender documents		Does not apply.		4-5 days of consultation and refinement of tender documents.	

parallel measures introduced by the law, requiring every State agency to notify PROMPyme of those tender processes involving small amounts. Low value purchases matter the most, because those are the kinds of purchases that small enterprises are in a better position to supply competitively.

The new law requires every State institution to inform PROMPyme of every tender process it launches involving Low Value Purchases (Adjudicaciones de Menor Cuantía) as well as of Select Direct Tenders (Adjudicaciones Directas Selectivas). These small tenders need to be awarded expeditiously and, accordingly, do not require written public calls for proposals. Select Direct Tenders are awarded after inviting no fewer than three suppliers, in addition to the requirement of a ten day advance notification to PROMPyme. Low Value Purchases involve smaller quantities. They are more numerous and more frequent and are generally filled by awarding the purchase to the best bid from suppliers. Traditionally Low Value Purchases are filled by predetermined suppliers that are invited to submit their bid; now they also need to consider proposals submitted by enterprises that learn of the tender from PROMPyme. In this case, notification to PROMPyme must be concurrent with issuance of invitations to prospective suppliers.

Once PROMPyme receives the calls for proposal, it immediately notifies enterprises through various means, including a one minute daily radio announcement, posting in its own premises and PROMPyme's website (www.prompyme.gob.pe/compras_estatales/).

In principle, failure to inform PROMPyme in a timely fashion may lead to the challenge and eventually the cancellation of the tender award. In practice,

Figure 4. Visitors and Visits to PROMPyme's Website

		Distinct Visitors	Visits	Average Visits per Visitor
	June	4,306	6,804	1.6
	July	8,564	15,969	1.9
2	August	15,332	35,334	2.3
0	September	18,213	43,027	2.4
0	October	19,452	46,393	2.4
2	November	17,845	39,821	2.2
	December	16,344	36,677	2.2
	January	18,989	46,292	2.4
2	February	19,868	49,308	2.5
0	March	21,522	55,990	2.6
0	April	22,215	56,705	2.6
3	May	24,468	62,514	2.6
	June	24,548	n.a.	
	July	24,690	n.a.	

PROMPyme has been able to persuade agencies to conform with the law and the number of properly informed tenders has increased from 77 per cent in September 2002 to 96.1 per cent by the end of 2003. The average number of business opportunities notified per month to PROMPyme has increased from 1,273 in 2000, to 2,883 in 2003. The process is also gaining in effectiveness, as government agencies are making increasing use of the Internet to notify PROMPyme. The proportion of calls for tender received via e-mail increased from 40 per cent in January-April 2002 to 55 per cent a year later; while at the same time calls for tender notified through other means fell in importance (32 per cent to 23 per cent by fax and 29 per cent to 22 per cent by courier).

Initial results are encouraging. PROMPyme's website is by far the principal means through which entrepreneurs learn of existing smallscale opportunities to sell to the State, and the number of visitors to this site has been rapidly increasing. A total of 3,285 users have subscribed to the PROMPyme portal and 2,787 have asked to receive notices of State purchases from PROMPyme by e-mail. More suggestive, the proportion of central government purchases that were supplied by small enterprises rose from 23 per cent in 2001 to 33 per cent in 2002.[2] In 2002, USD 400 million of goods and services purchased by State agencies were supplied by 67,635 small enterprises.

Conclusion

We do not know how many of these visitors use telecenters to connect to PROMPyme's website, but given the frequency of use of cabinas amongst Peruvian Internet users it is safe to say that a significant number do so. Most likely, it is not the informal microentrepreneur but the somewhat larger and more technically sophisticated small enterprises that are benefiting from the new policy. The increasing importance of smaller firms as State suppliers may also reflect an ongoing transformation in Perús industrial structure whereby smaller firms become more competitive than larger vertically integrated operations, as has happened elsewhere as a result of increased reliance on information techno-logy.[3] The Internet gives an edge to technically sophisticated small entrepreneurs with otherwise limited physical capital resources. Widespread connectivity opens up a window of opportunity for developing countries. It also brings to the fore the importance of parallel policies that raise a country's digital literacy and the general educational level of its population.

Notes

1. Perús cabinas públicas are small commercial microenterprises that in other parts of the world are commonly known as cybercafes. Although no one really knows, it is commonly believed there may be 1,200 cabinas in Lima and another 800 elsewhere in the country.

2. Purchases by central government agencies and regional governments, for which data is available, represent about half of all State purchases.

3. "In many industries, mass production by large, vertically-integrated, hierarchically-organized firms is giving way to more flexible forms of both internal organization and industrial structure. Work is increasingly accomplished through networks of smaller, more focused enterprises. The resulting structure of loosely coupled suborganizations blurs the boundaries of both firms and industries." [Brynjolfsson 1993, pages 2-3].

References

Apoyo - Opinión y Mercado, "Uso y Actitudes hacia Internet", October 2001.

Brynjolfsson, Erik, "Information Systems and the Organization of Modern Enterprise", Journal of Organizational Computing, December 1993. (http://ccs.mit.edu/papers/CCSWP200/)

Caroy, Miguel, "Introducción a las Compras Estatales" Presentation 2002a. (www.prompyme.gob.pe/pymeperu/evento/archivo/1)

Caroy, Miguel, "Los usuarios del portal de información de compras del Estado - ¿Están preparados los microempresarios de Cabinas de Internet para atenderlos?", Presentation to "Foro Virtual: Cabinas Internet, oportunidades para Todos" del 2 al 16 de diciembre del 2002b. (http://socinfo.concytec.gob.pe/foro_cabinas/)

Chellew, Patricio, "Compras del Estado: oportunidades para las pequeñas empresas", presentación en el V Foro Interamericano sobre Microempresas, September 2002. (www.iadb.org/foromic/Vforo/downloads/Chellew.doc)

Gallo Quintana, Máximo, "Masificación del Uso de Internet: El caso peruano", Presentación ante el Seminario Iberoamericano sobre: Estrategias de Mercadeo y Negocios en Internet para PYMES", realizado en Quito 21- 22 de agosto 2003 2003. (http://plananual.prompyme.gob.pe/micip.php)

Infante Alosilla, Juan, "Potencial de la Pequeña Empresa como Proveedora del Estado en la Macro Región Sur, Presentación, Puno, 21 de junio de 2003. (www2.prompyme.gob.pe/downloads/uploads/archivos/Presentacion_Prompyme_Puno_2003.pdf

SECTION III

Measuring Impact - Methodological Challenges and Evaluation Tools

Notes on Research for Telecenter Development
Raul Roman and Royal Colle

Beyond Profitability: A Framework for Measuring the Impact of ICT Kiosks
Priscilla Wisner

Prioritizing the Criteria for Success A Funders Perspective:
Jonathan Peizer

Notes on Research for Telecenter Development

Raul Roman and Royal Colle
Cornell University

Abstract
The authors provide an overview of the areas where research on telecenters is needed the most and explain the main challenges of doing field research on telecenters in the developing world. They argue that a comprehensive study of telecenters demands cross-linked levels of analysis and multidisciplinary inquiry. Furthermore, they suggest, there is a need to generate a "practical theory of access to public information systems" that can guide public policy and program planning.

This chapter is a brief review of two essential aspects in research on rural community telecenters: a) what are the areas of interest that need most pressing attention from researchers at this moment; and b) what are the main challenges to doing field research on telecenters in developing countries.

In other words, this chapter suggests what questions researchers need to focus on, and what methodological and theoretical problems researchers might confront in trying to tackle those questions. These two aspects are particularly pertinent today for several reasons. First, many of the telecenters established around the developing world as pilot (or 'research and development') projects are reaching a certain stage of maturity, and they start showing potential for valuable in-depth evaluation. Second, that in-depth evaluation of telecenter programs is sorely needed. Stakeholders inside the 'ICT for development' movement (policy makers, grassroots activists, and academic researchers, among others) need to know what is really happening in the field. It is clear that rigorous evaluative evidence of the performance of rural telecenters can help inform more effective public policy and program planning.

Rural telecenters have been attracting the attention of both academic and non-academic researchers for the past ten years. As a result of this interest, there is an increasing amount of publications on telecenters. Most of them are case studies and policy-oriented reviews of relevant telecenter issues (see the collection of articles in Colle & Roman, 2001; Gomez & Hunt, 1999; Latchem & Walker, 2001), but others also present original field research and data-driven analysis[1] (i.e., Blattman et al., in press; Proenza et al., 2001; Torero et al., in press). There are also a number of publications specifically devoted to the issue of telecenter research (Hudson, 2001; Roman & Blattman, 2001; Whyte, 2000). Additionally, the mounting literature on information systems in developing countries appears as an important reference for telecenter researchers (i.e., Heeks, 2002).

Nonetheless, it is clear that still a lot remains to be learned from the field, and there is much to be done in terms of development of research tools and interdisciplinary collaboration. The goal of this chapter is to continue the discussion among social scientists about some key aspects of research in telecenter development. Doing so in the framework of this book provides an opportunity for activists, policy-makers, and communities to understand how research can contribute to the telecenter movement.

A Research Focus: Impact, Access, and Sustainability
The core of a research program on rural telecenters in developing countries can be summarized in three broad interconnected areas:

- the impact of telecenters on social and economic change;
- the factors that hinder or facilitate access to telecenters;
- the conditions for the workability and long-term sustainability of such centers.

Put differently, telecenter research should attempt to provide a comprehensive picture of how information and communication work for community development, the factors that make that connection between communication and development possible, and the conditions necessary to maintain a communication system functioning effectively for development purposes. The remainder of this section provides some details on these three areas of research.

Socio-Economic Impact of Community Telecenters
The communication dynamics stimulated by telecenters can open the possibility for more participatory and self-directed forms of community development. This is a highly relevant subject of research today, although it remains largely unexplored. New information and communication tools give disadvantaged communities the opportunity to communicate their own ideas, to seek and request information, to produce and diffuse their own knowledge. In a very specific sense, this process is visibly translated into a change in communication behavior: a new movement by which deprived and isolated communities become knowledge producers and diffusers, and active information-seekers (Roman, forthcoming).

Observing the patterns of social and individual behavior change generated by information systems availability is a worthwhile topic of research in itself and the field of social psychology provides us with very useful tools to explore this path in the near future. Nonetheless, beyond the issues of individual and social co-mmunication-related behavior change, other very important questions remain to be explored: how is this change in communication behavior connected to aspects of community development such as education and health? How does the use of new communication and information tools affect local economic development? How do new communication technologies stimulate new forms of social and politi-cal organization at the community level? What are the policy mechanisms (at the international, national, and local levels) necessary to make this change possible? Providing answers to these questions is probably the most fascinating challenge in telecenter research today.

Factors Explaining Equal Access to Telecenters
The realization of the potential of telecenters to contribute to rural development partly depends on the capacity of such centers to offer equal access to informa-tion, independent of the socioeconomic status of the users. The study of access is critical in terms of the enormous concern shown about increasing information inequities, a concern explicitly articulated in the discussions about the so-called "digital divide". Our current research examines ways in which structural variables (such as level of education) and motivational variables (such as perceived impor-tance of specific information services) help explain access to telecenters among different social strata in rural and poor communities of South India.[2] The objective of our research is to identify the factors that facilitate egalitarian access to practi-cal and demand-driven information and communication resources provided by telecenters in order to define and mitigate (or help prevent) conditions of social exclusion and knowledge gaps.

This is a very important issue: extensive research in developing countries has consistently shown that the diffusion of innovations (such as new information and communication technology or any information perceived as new by community members) tends to widen the socioeconomic gap between the higher and lower status segments of a social system (Rogers, 1995). The basic questions are: what are the factors that explain and help predict the likelihood that community members will access information that is relevant to them? When developing an information system such as a rural telecenter, what are the barriers to access that can be identified in order to better meet the needs of the users? Recent research in rural India shows that, unless some strategies are proposed to reach the lower socioeconomic segments of society, telecenter availability may exacerbate already existing knowledge and information gaps (Blattman et al., in press).

Conditions for Financial and Social Sustainability of Telecenters
The issue of self-sustainability and long-term prosperity of development projects based on some kind of technology transfer (or innovation from outside the target

communities) has been on the agenda of development planners for a long time. It is clear that effective access to and impact of any telecenter project depends on the viability of such a project.

Telecenter researchers need to examine ways in which a mechanism that manages locally relevant information and communication resources becomes a financially and socially sustainable tool of community development (that is, economically solvent, affordable, useful and usable, and trusted by the users). Studying these aspects implies focusing on two levels of research: the micro and macro. First, at the micro level, it is important to identify the infrastructural, social, economic, and cultural factors that account for the sustainability of local institutions and, in our case, localized information systems in a rural developing context. Second, at the macro level, it is essential to outline the national and international institutional environment that frames information systems implementation, from public policy to contextually appropriate technological innovation, such as the introduction of simple computers and low cost telecommunications distribution mechanisms.

Telecenters remain largely an atheoretical area of research. However, to rigorously tackle the problems described above, research requires a strong theoretical base. Elsewhere we have suggested how 'diffusion of innovations' can serve as a general theoretical framework for the study of telecenters (Roman, forthcoming). Leaving aside any detailed theoretical discussion, one thing is clear: the study of telecenters demands cross-linked levels of analysis and multidisciplinary inquiry. A comprehensive research approach needs to establish a link between socio-psychological levels of study and more macro levels, such as institutional factors, to describe the different processes of social change associated with telecenter adoption.

Social psychology and the field of information systems offer many useful theories on individual perception and behavior change that can be applied to telecenters (i.e., Ajzen, 1985; Davis, 1989; Taylor & Todd, 1995), while institutional theory (King et al., 1994; Montealegre, 1999) can provide a macro framework to understand telecenter diffusion and adoption. Besides this, another important task ahead is to build a practical theory of access to public information systems in developing countries to guide public policy and program planning.

The Challenges of Fieldwork

Conducting research on telecenters in developing countries is not an easy task. As a general premise, data collection in developing countries presents situational, methodological, and ethical challenges that make it significantly different from conventional social science conducted in a Western context (Casley & Lurie, 1987; Devereux & Hoddinott, 1993). Nonetheless, beyond these usual fieldwork challenges, research on telecenters has specific characteristics that deserve to be discussed. This section presents a very brief account of some of these special characteristics common in telecenter research. Fieldwork challenges in telecenter research can be roughly divided in two groups:

- on one side, telecenter researchers confront methodological challenges (technical problems that condition how research is designed);

- on the other side, researchers need to resolve contextual problems (environmental obstacles that influence how research is conducted) to successfully complete their task.

Of course, both methodological and contextual problems are closely interrelated: "technical issues cannot be separated from the social environment in which research is practiced" (Roman & Blattman, 2001: 112). The remainder of this section expands on these two issues with examples from our own field research experience.[3]

Regarding methodological challenges, a couple of examples will suffice. First, at this early stage of telecenter development, it is difficult to find reliable measures of telecenter-related indicators. If we decide to carry out quantitative research, a strong theoretical base (and clear research objectives) can help in this direction, as indicated in the previous section.

In our work in India, we used the diffusion of innovations theory (Rogers, 1995) and the communication effects gap hypothesis (Rogers, 1976) to examine the socio-psychological and structural determinants of access to telecenter services. However, having a clear set of indicators operationalized in a survey instrument (as difficult as that might become) does not solve all the measurement problems, as any field researcher knows well. The issue is that, besides the common errors and mistakes by surveyors and respondents (errors that usually can be solved with training and supervision), there are measurement challenges that have to do with our topic of research itself.

This takes us to the second example of methodological challenges that we are presenting here. We conducted a pre-project survey in rural South India to assess the information and communication needs of the villagers (Roman & Colle, forthcoming). During the research process, it was difficult to measure demand of potential telecenter services among a population that had never had access to such services. Many villagers did not have the ability to judge the costs and benefits of access to technology and information (Roman & Blattman, 2001). This meant that they were not ready to answer the questions prepared for them.

The context of telecenter research is likely to affect the data collection process as well. Overall, each stakeholder in a telecenter project (including researchers, project managers, and villagers) has different priorities. In the telecenter project in India, for example, the managerial urgency to make-things-happen conflicted with the researcher's request to first understand the needs of the telecenter-hosting communities. In other words, the researchers wanted to base the design of telecenters on their research findings, while other stakeholders needed to push the project forward as soon as possible (Roman & Blattman, 2001).

As a conclusion, misconceptions about the role of research in telecenter development may frustrate the desire of a researcher to make research useful for other stakeholders in the project. At the same time, those misconceptions, and the ideological and cultural asymmetries between the different stakeholders of a telecenter project, can seriously affect the conditions under which research is conducted. For example, if research is perceived by villagers as a simple bureaucratic step towards getting a development project started in their village, the results may be far from optimal.

Beyond Formal Social Science: Research as a Managerial Routine

From the discussion above, it may seem that research for telecenter development might only be conducted by social science professionals and consumed by a limited portion of a specialized public. It may appear that this research is only for academics, international consultants, and program planners. That is certainly not the case. It is argued that research (in the shape of evaluation and needs assessment) should become an important element of any community telecenter project, and not used exclusively by external consultants for objectives that do not necessarily deal directly with the communities researched (Roman & Blattman, 2001).

For what has been presented in this chapter, it is necessary (as a principle) that telecenter-hosting communities participate actively in research - sometimes aided by external agents. In a telecenter project in India (See University-based Village Telecenter in Section V of this book), the research approach was instrumental in designing telecenter services, raising awareness about the potential of telecenters for community development, and recruiting volunteers for telecenter steering committees (Roman & Colle, forthcoming).

However, beyond participation in externally designed research, it is more important that communities include social research (in a formal or informal way) as part of their ongoing planning agenda. For example, local telecenter governing bodies should assess the needs and desires of current and potential users on a regular basis (through community discussions, focus groups, or other appropriate means), and monitor the quality of their services in a systematic way. In other words, research should find its place in the management routine of a telecenter.

In some cases, as implied above, help may be needed from outside: training materials on research methods to build capacity of telecenter communities might be pivotal in stimulating this kind of self-determined assessment (Colle & Roman, 2003). In any case, locally initiated research can contribute to the social and financial self-sustainability of telecenter projects by:

- fostering local participation in telecenter design and decision-making;
- stimulating a sense of community ownership; and
- establishing a solid mechanism to monitor the quality of telecenter services and the balance between community demand and telecenter supply.

A Look at the Future

Based on what has been discussed in this chapter, we conclude with the following recommendations for future action:

- There is a need to share research tools and experiences among the members of the telecenter movement in a public and open forum. In other words, a common place is required (open to all the research-interested community, not only those who can afford the cost of specialized journals) where survey instruments, indicators, reliable measures, focus groups guidelines, and theoretical applications can be shared.

- Training materials on basic research methods need to be developed for use at the grassroots level by members of telecenter-hosting communities. At the same time, there is a need to raise awareness about the potential of self-assessment research to contribute to telecenter sustainability.

- Finally, there is a need to determine the role of universities in 'ICT for development' initiatives. As noted elsewhere (Colle & Roman, 2003), universities represent a largely underused resource for telecenters, despite their traditional roles related to knowledge generation and diffusion, and to carrying out research. Not only might universities contribute human resources (for example, student interns) to the kinds of telecenter research needs noted in this chapter, but telecenters can provide an extraordinary social science research opportunity for university staff. A first step is to discover and overcome the obstacles confronting such a potentially valuable partnership.

Notes

1. In this sense, the International Development Research Center in Canada presents one of the most prominent examples of a commitment to telecenter research (see Etta & Parvyn-Wamahiu, 2003).

2. For more information about this research, contact the authors of this chapter.

3. A more detailed exposition of challenges in telecenter field research can be found in Roman & Blattman (2001).

References

Ajzen, I. (1985). From intentions to actions: A theory of planned behavior. In J. Kuhl and J. Beckmann, Action control: From cognition to behavior, (pp. 11-39). Berlin: Springer-Verlag.

Blattman, C., Jensen, R., & Roman, R. Assessing the need and potential of community networking for developing countries: A case study from India. The Information Society [in press].

Casley, D. J., & Lurie, D. A. (1987). Data collection in developing countries. Oxford, UK: Claredon Press.

Colle, R., & Roman, R. (Eds.). (2001). Telecenters for rural development: Critical perspectives and visions for the future, a especial issue of the Journal of Development Communication, 12 (2).

Colle, R. & Roman, R. (2003) Challenges in the telecenter movement. In X. Yu, S. Marshall, & W. John (Eds.), Transforming regional economies and communities with information technology, (pp. 75-92). Westport, CT: Praeger Publishers.

Colle, R., & Roman, R. A Handbook for Telecenter Staffs. Rome, Italy: FAO and ITU. [forthcoming]

Davis, F. D. (1989). Perceived usefulness, perceived ease of use, and user acceptance of information technology. MIS Quarterly 13 (3), 319-340.

Devereux, S., & Hoddinott (Eds.). (1993). Fieldwork in developing countries. Boulder, CO: Lynne Rienner Pub.

Etta, F. E., & Parvyn-Wamahiu, S. (Eds.) (2003). The experience with community telecenters. Ottawa, Canada: International Development Research Centre. [available online at: http://www.idrc.ca/acacia]

Gomez, R., & Hunt, P. (Eds.) (1999). A report of an international meeting on telecentre evaluation. International Development Research Centre, Canada. [available online: http://www.idrc.ca/pan/telecentres.html]

Heeks, R. (2002). Information systems and developing countries: Failure, success, and local improvisations. The Information Society 18, 101-112.

Hudson, H. (2001). Telecentre evaluation: Issues and strategies. In C. Latchem & D. Walker (Eds.), Telecentres: Case studies and key issues. Vancouver: Commonwealth of Learning. [available online: http://www.col.org/telecentres]

King, J. L., Gurbaxani, V., Kraemer, K. L., McFarlan, F. W., Raman, K. S., & Yap, C. S. (1994). Institutional factors in information technology innovation. Information Systems Research 5 (2), 139-169.

Latchem, C., & Walker, D. (Eds.) (2001). Telecentres: Case studies and key issues. Vancouver: Commonwealth of Learning [available online: http://www.col.org/telecentres]

Montealegre, R. (1999). A temporal model of institutional interventions for information technology adoption in less-developed countries. Journal of Management Information Systems 16 (1), 207-232.

Proenza, F., Bastidas-Buch, R., & Montero, G. (2001). Telecenters for socioeconomic and rural development in Latin America and the Caribbean. Washington, DC: Interamerican Development Bank [available online: http://www.iadb.org/region/itdev/telecenters/index.htm]

Rogers, E, M. (1976). Communication and development: The passing of the dominant paradigm. Communication Research, 3 (2), 213-241.

Rogers, E. M. (1995). Diffusion of innovations (4th Edition). New York: The Free Press.

Roman, R. Diffusion of innovations as a theoretical framework for telecenters. Information Technology and International Development. [forthcoming]

Roman, R., and Blattman, C. (2001). Research for telecenter development: Obstacles and opportunities. Journal of Development Communication, 12 (2), 110-123.

Roman, R., and Colle, R. D. Content creation for ICT development projects: Integrating normative needs and community demand. Journal of Information Technology for Development. [forthcoming]

Taylor, S., and Todd, P. A. (1995). Understanding information technology usage: A test of competing models. Information Systems Research 6 (2), 144-176.

Torero, M., Chowdhury, S. K., & Galdo,V. Willingness to pay for the rural telephone service in Bangladesh and Peru. Information Economics and Policy. [in press]

Whyte, A. (2000). Assessing community telecenters: Guidelines for researchers. Ottawa: International Development Research Center.

Beyond Profitability: A Framework for Measuring the Impact of ICT Kiosks

Priscilla S. Wisner
Thunderbird, The American Graduate School of International Management

Abstract

The author proposes a measurement framework that can be used to develop a set of performance measures useful for evaluating both the capabilities and the impacts of ICT kiosks. By describing performance from a variety of dimensions, she argues, the proposed framework allows the researcher to determine the type of value that is created by different stakeholders and the aggregate value generated by ICT kiosk projects at large.

Measuring the impact of Information and Communication Technology (ICT) kiosks is challenging from a number of perspectives. The kiosks represent a non-traditional business model - some are for-profit ventures while others are non-profit or partially funded by governments or by donors. The concept of the "customer" of the kiosk has to be expanded to include various stakeholders other than the direct users of the kiosks. Also, the measures of value created by the kiosks, such as educational, social and economic development, are much broader than the traditional business calculations of profitability and related measures of financial value. To accurately measure value of ICT kiosks, what is needed is a multi-dimensional set of performance measures that represent the value propositions of numerous stakeholder groups.

In a traditional for-profit organization, measuring value created for the customer and the organization is fairly straightforward. As shown in the organizational-profit chain presented in Figure 1, the organization delivers a product and/or a service to customers. The customer is the person or firm that is willing to pay for products or services. The customer's measure of value is a function of the utility over time of the product or service to the customer minus the sum of the acquisition costs and the price paid. Where the value of the outcome of this equation is positive, we can say that the customer is receiving value for the transaction. This results in an increased likelihood that the customer will buy more, buy more often, and will favorably recommend the product or service to others - all of which result in increased revenues and profitability for the organization. The profitability of the organization is then used to sustain or add to the organizational capabilities to develop and deliver more and better products and services to its customers. However, applying this organizational profit chain to a non-profit or a non-traditional organizational model such as ICT kiosks is problematic.

Figure 1. Organization-Profit Framework

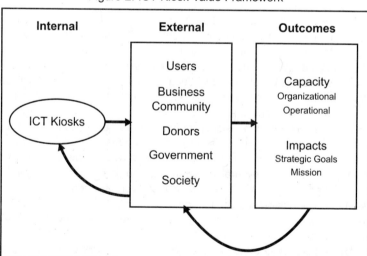

Stakeholders and Value Propositions

ICT kiosks are designed to offer technology-based services to communities and users that typically would not have access to computer technology. As shown in Figure 2, the value chain of the ICT kiosks is expanded to include a set of external stakeholders.

Figure 2. ICT Kiosk Value Framework

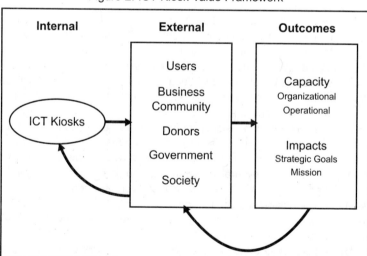

The direct users of the kiosk and the business community are both analogous to - profit customer; in that they are directly accessing the services of the ICT kiosks to achieve personal or business goals. However, one key difference is that the direct users and possibly the business community groups may not pay a fee for accessing or using the ICT kiosk services. Other external stakeholders of the kiosks - the donors of funding, materials or expertise, government, and society - are also customers in the sense that they are seeking the services of the ICT kiosks, but not directly for themselves. These stakeholders are enabling the kiosks to operate by contributing to the capacity of the program, which enables the kiosks to serve more clientele with potentially more and better services. The ICT kiosk could not exist without either type of stakeholders - the "upstream" stakeholders (e.g., donors, government, society) that provide the resources and the license to operate and the "downstream" stakeholders who need and use the services provided (e.g., users and business community).

These two types of stakeholders differ dramatically in how they judge the value of the kiosk services. Upstream stakeholders may be motivated by the ability to align their values with the values of the ICT kiosk project, or an enthusiasm for the mission of the kiosk project.

Figure 3. ICT Kiosks Stakeholder Matrix

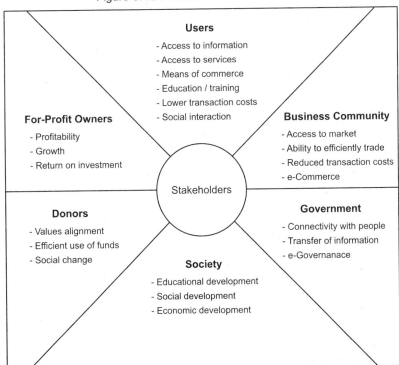

Upstream stakeholders may also be motivated by the opportunity to help others in difficult social conditions or to effect longer-term social change in a more effective and efficient manner than any individual donor could accomplish. Upstream stakeholders are therefore more motivated by the social mission of the organization, and the link to social value. Downstream stakeholders have a very different set of needs and expectations. As the users of the kiosk services, their goals and objectives are more activity-oriented, and they judge the kiosk value by how their individual goals are met, rather than the achievement of broader social goals.

As detailed in Figure 3, each of these external stakeholder groups has distinct value propositions. If the ICT kiosk is a for-profit operation, the owner has specific financial goals. The users of the service and the business community have specific transactional outcomes that they wish to achieve, such as access to information, access to markets, reduction in transaction costs, e-commerce transactions, etc. The government stakeholder may also desire specific transactional outcomes from the ICT kiosk projects, for example birth registrations, legal documentation, or community services information. But the government, donor and society stakeholders are more broadly looking to the ICT kiosks to make a difference in the lives of people and facilitate educational, social, and economic development.

Measuring Value

Assessing the value of the ICT kiosks therefore must take into account multiple dimensions of performance measurement. As shown in the ICT Kiosk Performance Pyramid (Figure 4), value of the ICT kiosks can be segregated into four dimensions of performance measurement:
- Organizational capacity: What are the resources?
- Operational capacity: How are the resources used?
- Strategic impacts: What are the programmatic goals?
- Mission impacts: What difference does it make?

Figure 4. ICT Kiosk Performance Pyramid

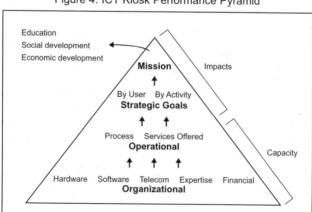

Each dimension of the performance pyramid is dependent upon the level preceding it - the operational processes and services are dependent upon having adequate resources. Meeting strategic goals requires an operational framework that enables users to achieve outcomes that they desire; and the longer-term mission-based impacts are driven by the achievement of the strategic goals.

To further describe the contents of each of these dimensions, the ICT Kiosk Performance Matrix (see Table 1) is a description of the performance measures that are relevant to each dimension of the pyramid. While this list is not intended to be exhaustive or a "one size fits all" listing of relevant performance measures, the performance measures given are relevant to assessing the value created by an ICT kiosk project.

The first two dimensions of performance reflect the infrastructure or the capacity of the kiosk:

- Organizational capacity is a measure of the resources of the ICT kiosk project, in terms of hardware, software, telecom, expertise, and financial capabilities. Organizational capacity is typically the easiest performance dimension to measure, because the resources are easily identifiable and tangible.

- Operational capacity reflects how the organizational capacity is used or positioned to create a service environment for the potential community of users. Measurement of operational capabilities should take into account both how effectively the technical resources are used to create a reliable and accessible process for the users of the system, as well as the actual service offe-rings of the ICT kiosks.

The top two dimensions of the performance pyramid reflect the outcomes or the impacts of the ICT kiosks:

- Strategic goals impacts measures the accomplishment of the ICT kiosk project's goals in reaching the targeted communities (user information) and having them take advantage of the kiosk services (activity information). The determination of the strategic goals of an ICT kiosk project is dependent upon the specific strategic objectives of the ICT kiosk project, as demonstrated in the example discussed below.

- Mission impacts reflects the ability of the ICT kiosks to impact broader educational, social, and economic development goals. Measurement at the mission level is the most difficult, given that these impacts are longer-term in nature and are less tangible than other outcomes. Also, impacts at the mission level are affected by a myriad of factors, and it is very difficult to accurately measure the actual ICT kiosk impact on these societal changes. However, by using the framework described by the performance pyramid, it is possible to show the linkages between the ICT kiosks and mission impacts.

Performance Framework Example

The performance pyramid framework can be applied to ICT kiosk projects that have broad technology-access goals or to kiosk projects that have more specific application goals, such as specific e-commerce, e-health, e-education, or e-governance applications.

Table 1. ICT Performance Matrix

Capacity Measures		Impact Measures	
Organizational	**Operational**	**Strategic Goals**	**Mission**
Hardware	**Process**	**User information**	**Educational development**
·# Computers	·Up-time (avail hrs/	·Size of user com-	·IT literacy
·Processor speed	total hrs)	munity	·General literacy
·# Terminals	·Response time	·# Users (by relevant	·Increase school
·# Printers	·Local language cov-	demographics)	capacity
·# Copiers	erage	·% of target popula-	·Access to informa-
·Other equipment	·% of local population	tion using	tion
·# Kiosks	with access (cover-	·% of local population	
·Age of equipment	age)	using	**Social development**
	·Access to informa-	·# New users	·Healthier population
Software	tion providers	·# Repeat users	·Community safety
·# Programs	·# Available hours		·Community building
·Types of programs	·Capacity utilization·	**Activity information**	·Reduced mortality
·Age of programs	System reliability	·Average time on-line	Economic develop-
	·Power reliability	use	ment
Telecomm	·Telecom reliability	·Average time off-line	·Farm productivity
·Bandwidth capacity		use	·Employment
·# Links	**Services Offered**	·# People taking	·Reduced transaction
·Types of links	·Services scope (e.g.,	classes	costs
	e-mail, fax, printing,	·# Sites visited per	·Reduced poverty
Expertise	databases, transla-	user	·Wealth creation
·Technical help avail-	tion, training, word	·# Look-ups per site	
ability	processing, video)	·# On-line transac-	
·Application help	·# Different classes	tions	
(software, data, etc.)	offered	·% Time system used	
	·# Class hours	·# Health consulta-	
Financial	offered	tions	
·Revenues from	·# On-line classes	·# Government cor-	
grants	·# Off-line classes	respondence	
·Revenues from fees	·# Community links	·Software package	
·Revenues from ads	·# Intranets	usage	
·Operating self-suffi-		·Other equipment	
ciency (fees ÷ costs)		usage	
·Internal rate of			
return			

Consider, for example, an ICT kiosk project that is designed to give technology access to the agricultural community. The organizational capacity measures would be similar to those described in the performance matrix, such as hardware, software and telecom capabilities. Expertise capabilities would reflect the availability of technical help to keep the system functioning, since having good technical resources but a system that constantly "crashes" will impact the ability to offer services and the likelihood that people will use the services. Expertise might also be needed to help farmers with the applications- to fill out forms for illiterate farmers or to translate between the farmers' language and the language recognized by the various applications. The operational capacity measures, in addition to those suggested on Table 1, would include measures such as:

- average distance between the farmers and the terminals;
- the local language coverage of the system;
- the accessibility (in a local language) of sites that provide weather, market price, and farm practice information;
- the accessibility of vendor information.

Strategic goals related specifically to agriculture would include building intranets of farm cooperatives so that farmers could communicate with each other more easily, increasing farmers' use of the kiosk system, vaccination of farm animals to reduce diseases, increasing farm productivity, and moving goods to markets more efficiently. Achieving these strategic goals can logically be linked with broader societal or mission impacts such as access to information; healthier populations (through healthier animal populations and better farming practices); and wealth creation for the farmers through reduced transaction costs, improved farm productivity and better market information.

Conclusion
As described above, the performance measurement framework can be used to develop a set of performance measures that are useful in measuring both the capabilities and the impacts of the ICT kiosks. It is robust enough to use for ICT kiosk projects that have broad application goals or for projects with more specific application goals. By describing performance from a variety of dimensions, the framework helps to determine if value is being created for the many different types of stakeholders that have an explicit interest in the success or failure of these initiatives. It only by having a multi-dimensional set of performance measures that reflect the impact of the kiosks from the viewpoints of multiple stakeholders that a determination can be made about the value created by the ICT kiosk projects.

Prioritizing the Criteria for Success: A Funders Perspective

Jonathan Peizer
Open Society Institute

Abstract

The author explores different strategies to evaluate, approve and expedite technology grants for ICT projects. It these grants cannot be evaluated, he argues, then an alternative process should be put in place where an unallocated, or venture, fund is managed by a small group capable of making decisions regarding the grant process fairly quickly.

Where should resources be primarily focused to insure successful development of Information Kiosk projects? Should they be focused on design, on implementation or on evaluation? There is a growing call for adequate metrics to measure social return on investment (SROI). Unlike profit making enterprises that have clear and measurable indicators of success, projects that generate social value are much more difficult to assess. Clear metrics do not exist, and if they did, it would be easier to quantify, duplicate and scale successes. It is easy to point to billions of dollars poured into a variety of public sector initiatives with little discernable impact and to blame this on inappropriate assessment tools and techniques.

There is value in developing social metrics that adequately assess the breadth and depth of a project's efficacy. However, too many evaluations are left to the end of a project and are used to answer the question, "has a social value mission been achieved or not?" To ensure a project's success, it's best to intervene in the design and implementation phase when changes can still be made to modify outcomes. Metrics are best focused upon the scale of success rather than whether total success has been achieved or not. The best evaluations provide a continuous feedback loop of objective and subjective data.

I started the Soros Foundation Network's Open Society Institute Internet program (OSI-IP) as a novice grant maker. Instead I relied heavily on a decade and a half of operational ICT experience to assess the elements of a successful project. This served me well in an extremely time sensitive sector. Grantees are looking to the Internet to improve efficacy in meeting their missions. They are also looking to public funders to resume the leadership role they held in the past by tackling these new social endeavors with funding and other support. Below are the implementation strategies that could be far more significant guarantors of a project's success, rather than focusing solely on after-program metrics of evaluation.

Grant Evaluation: Because the traditional grant making process has spawned professional proposal writing, it is incumbent on the funder to go beyond the proposal to thoroughly vet the people behind the vision. Is the project simply a brilliant plan or are there people behind it who can actually carry it out and make it work? What is their experience and commitment to the project? The questions above need to be answered by people with expertise in the proposal area.

Flexibility of Project Criteria is a Must: Technology and opportunity evolve at a rapid pace in the Internet space, and a funder must be able to react to this by being flexible and, sometimes, rewriting the rules of project evaluation and implementation. Rather than pre-defining programs through stringent prerequisites for grantees, what should be used are highly flexible criteria, especially as one funds Information Kiosks projects.

Venture Capital: Treat Information Kiosks as social ventures and have funding available throughout the year for innovative efforts. This is an imperative for all technology related funding. A year is a long time in the technology space and pre-allocating all funding means missing important opportunities.

Soliciting Partnerships: Every good venture capitalist knows that it is better to go into a project with partners than to go in alone. The Soros Internet Program made an extra effort, on many of the projects it was funding, to find funding partners. Consequently, it raised its total budget by two-thirds through partner funding over seven years.

Follow-up: Once an investment or grant is made it is important to follow-up and check progress with the grantee on an ongoing basis. Funders and investors should help to resolve bottlenecks, if possible, and to determine what further assistance the grantee needs, whether resources or expertise. Internet grants lend themselves to follow-up. One can go on-line to determine progress and even call up objective statistics.

Trust the Project Implementers: Both the vision and implementation skills of the grant seeker should be evaluated before making a grant. However, once that has been accomplished it is equally important to trust the grantee's instincts regarding the best implementation on the ground. A big mistake made in public sector funding is the funder's assumption that they know better than the person on the ground does. While the funder can provide a lot of value-added consulting support and facilitation, the project should not become an invention of the funder, based on what it "thinks" is required on the ground. What a funder should be doing is building on the vision of the grantee and supplying implementation advice, based on the grantee's conception of the project, without redefining it. If a funder is doing this then a reconsideration of funding should be made.

Approach the Training Component of a Project with the Priority and Seriousness it Deserves: The most critical part of an Information Kiosk initiative is not the technology deployed, but the people deploying and maintaining it and the training they, and the users, receive. Most funding agencies have come to realize that training is a necessary component of a successful Information Kiosk project and that you can't just plunk technology down and expect it to work by itself. Yet, many projects still pay lip service to the training component in their proposals while actually allocating little time or resources to it. Training is a core component of any ICT project. It is a key determinant of project success or failure. It decides if a technology implementation and its benefits remain with the agencies deploying it or are transferred to the local constituencies to own, manage and disseminate it long after the original funder departs.

Approach Supply-Side Projects with a Healthy Degree of Skepticism: Technical projects that have the attitude "if you build it they will come" should be carefully scrutinized to determine if there is really a demand and a constituency ready to make use of what is delivered. While supply-side projects work well when the objective is building bridges and dams, they tend to be less appropriate when trying to affect human behavioral change. This is particularly true in the technology field because it is not intuitive to most people. Technology tends to be expensive and changes fast. If thousands of dollars are spent up-front on technology and it takes a year to entice people to use it, then, using a three-year depreciation standard, roughly a third of the investment is wasted in the first twelve months.

The most effective technology projects are demand based, with a supportive and willing constituency of users who are eager to make immediate use of what is supplied. They will become stakeholders and ask for the next level of technological assistance once they are ready to use it. For example, E-mail may very well be adequate before full Internet access is provided. For the most part the focus should always be on meeting demand and then taking it to the next level rather than creating supply.

Use Formative Evaluation Methodologies: From a bewildering range of evaluation methodologies the formative evaluation process is the one that best lends itself to these projects. Formative evaluation is an iterative process that can be used throughout the design and implementation of a project to analyze results against objectives rather than waiting until after the fact to determine whether a project has failed or succeeded.

Internal Project Leverage: Project funding should be a strategic consideration, with resources provided to help foster expected results. Funding and resources should not be withheld to the extent that they restrict a project from accomplishing its goals. However, funding in phases based on meeting predefined milestones is an effective leveraging tool. Consider first loaning equipment and later granting it, rather than granting equipment outright before a project has achieved any of its objectives.

Cross-Project Leverage: Look upon each project as much on its own merit as on how it might leverage another project. In the case of the Soros Internet Program, if an education or healthcare project was thriving in Romania, the Internet Project would make sure that a project in, say, Slovakia that was proposing something similar was talking to the Romanian team. It encouraged different projects in one country to connect with each other and with successful projects in other countries as well.

Vendor Leverage: As the Soros Network Program funded new initiatives, it became clear that different projects required similar products from the same vendors. Therefore, the Internet Project aggressively sought regional discounts from these vendors, and got them. Successful new technology solutions were also shared between projects so that people would consider them in the project planning and implementation phases of their own initiatives. This created a pool of vendors who we trusted and who understood our needs and could satisfy them across sectors and geographic borders.

Scrutinizing the Grant Making Process: If the process of grant making has become so time consuming and bureaucratic that it eclipses proper grant over-sight, then it is time to look at how it can be streamlined. This is particularly true for decision-making around technology grants, where the approval processes must be compressed, expedited quickly, but still be adequate.

Conclusion
The Internet has created a new potential for social sustainability with its low entry costs for reaching a much larger constituency. NGOs have started thinking about for-profit ventures as adjuncts to their not-for-profit activities. The irony is that often they do not fit neatly into standard foundation evaluation criteria and are therefore hard to evaluate. Yet, these ventures may well offer the long-term sustainability that most foundations currently expect from their grantees.

If technology grants cannot be evaluated, approved and expedited using the standard grant making process, then they are best made using an alternative process. I would suggest an unallocated, or venture, fund pool managed by a small group who can make decisions and make grants quickly. The makeup of this group should consist of staff with programmatic and ICT expertise. If the projects being evaluated have a sustainable, revenue-generating component as well, then adding someone with financial expertise to the group is advisable.

SECTION IV

New Approaches to Information Communication Technology for Development

Innovations to close the Digital Divide
Allen Hammond and William Kramer

Village Information Kiosks: A Commercial View
Deepak Amin

Innovations to Close the Digital Divide

Allen Hammond and William Kramer
World Resource Institute

Abstract
The authors present some of the most innovative projects in different areas that are using information and communication technology for development. Based on a research effort directed by the World Resource Institute's Digital Dividend project, the authors suggest that a significant number of innovative models across different development sectors are emerging at the enterprise level and they provide specific examples by sector.

This article presents preliminary findings of the World Resource Institute's Digital Dividend (DD) project; a research effort intended to generate knowledge about innovative approaches to the use of information and communication technology in international development (ITID). In particular, Digital Dividend seeks to identify appropriate models that could be widely implemented. The research has been focused at the enterprise level.

The Digital Dividend Clearinghouse, as is widely known, now contains about 800 enterprises serving Asia, Africa, and Latin America. The Clearinghouse is available online at www.digitaldividend.org and is intended to track activity, capture broad trends, provide baselines against which to identify novel approaches, and serve as a tool for communication with and among enterprises. Some emerging patterns in the data are highly suggestive. For example, some 60 per cent of the enterprises are NGO activities, 20 per cent private sector, 12 per cent government, and 8 per cent donor agencies. Clearly, NGO and private sector enterprises dominate the chart.

From the database, it has been identified that potentially significant innovations are modeled with pragmatic approach, and have very strong capabilities of scaling up. If such models are scaled up and replicated, they could have significant development impact. As a matter of fact, exceptionally promising enterprises, which are documented in case studies of Clearinghouse, involve field assessments by MBA students from leading business schools, including interviews, research into operations and enterprise records.

Case studies are collected in "What Works" series online. Untraditional "project evaluations" of completed projects, are instead forward-oriented assessments of projects or enterprises in progress, seeking to understand and evaluate their innovative approach. DD believes it is the enterprise's plan or strategy for achieving its objectives - its business model - that is the key to developmental and business success. The research suggests that a number of innovative models, spanning most core development sectors, are emerging at the enterprise level. Following are some examples, by sector.

Agriculture

In India, ITC Ltd. is developing an internationally competitive agricultural business by empowering, not eliminating, the independent small farmer. The company has set up a network of Internet-connected kiosks, known as e-Choupals, to serve the soy, coffee, wheat, and shrimp farmers in its procurement network. An e-Choupal is a high-tech version of the traditional Choupal, or village gathering place in Hindi, where farmers can get current weather reports, local and international produce prices, and information on the best farming practices. The kiosks also serve as procurement and purchase points, allowing farmers not only to sell their produce directly to ITC, but also to buy agricultural inputs and consumer goods for daily household use.

A significant element of e-Choupal's success is its reliance on local expertise. The kiosks are typically managed by respected farmers and located in or around their houses. ITC saves money by eliminating middlemen and buying its produce directly from farmers; the farmers, knowing the current market prices, can negotiate better deals when attempting to sell their crops. In addition to increasing their incomes at the point of sale, farmers are also able to increase the quality and quantity of their harvests thanks to the information the kiosks provide. This "win-win" business model helps ensure the e-Choupal network's sustainability, while also making it highly scalable.

Health

Voxiva, a start-up company, has developed a technology solution that links rural and urban clinics, other healthcare providers, and public health authorities in Peru. Healthcare workers can log on to a Voxiva server via Internet or toll-free telephone call, and then use voicemail menus to submit case histories, retrieve data or trends, or communicate with peers throughout the network. Data submitted is automatically transferred to the Peruvian Health Ministry, and reports of specific diseases generate emergency notifications by e-mail, voicemail, or text messaging. More than 26,000 cases were reported in the first eight months of operation.

The Voxiva system combines interactive voice response with voicemail, unified messaging, and Web-based transaction and management tools, and can be customized to meet the needs of different customers. While accessible by Internet, it is equally accessible by cellular or landline phones, which are far more widely available in Peru. By providing both routine and emergency alert systems and making real-time epidemiological surveillance possible, this private-sector solution has given Peru's Health Ministry a powerful but relatively low-cost tool to advance public health and give frontline providers the information they need to provide high-quality care.

Civil society, however, has also originated some interesting models for using ICT to improve the quality of care available to the poor. One such initiative is Community Access to Sustainable Health (Cash) in India, which equips providers with handheld computers. Nurse/midwife practitioners, who are often the primary health providers in rural Indian villages, use the handhelds and custom software to collect patient information and make on-the-spot diagnoses, based on medical histories and diagnostic scripts or checklists stored in the devices. Each device also holds a simple geographic information system that captures patient location on a digital map. When the nurse/midwives synchronize their handhelds with computers in their home clinics, the records are uploaded to a central database, and the result is real-time epidemiological data enabling authorities to track the spread of diseases more effectively and take corrective actions sooner. Similar systems are likely to be replicated rapidly as the device costs drop.

Education and Training

Aptech Ltd. is an Indian multinational offering affordable computer training in India and 52 other countries. In India, there are 2,200 centers - some 800 of them in rural areas - that vary in size and range of services offered. All operate on a franchise model, with Aptech's revenues coming from royalty fees paid by the local entrepreneurs that run its training centers. Aptech's Vidya program is an introductory computer literacy course that has been translated into local Indian languages. It uses a variety of methodologies, from teacher-in-the-classroom to CD-ROMs, to deliver content. Aptech's business model allows it to offer the course at a subsidized price of about $20 in rural areas (the actual cost is more than double that amount). To date, approximately 500,000 students have been trained in India alone.

Microfinance

FFP Prodem, a microfinance organization that has been offering credit and other financial services to poor communities in Bolivia for 14 years, is setting up a network of multilingual, smart card-enabled ATMs (SATMs). The machines make use of smart cards that store all the customers' personal details, account numbers, transaction records, and fingerprint - allowing cash dispensers to operate without permanent network connections and facilitating service delivery even in rural areas where connectivity can be problematic. The machines have touch screens and help overcome language barriers and illiteracy by offering voice commands in Spanish and several local dialects. Its SATMs have enabled FFP Prodem to expand its client base significantly and to increase its profits. The SATMs reduce the company's cost of funds capture, and have paid for themselves in less than two years compared to what originally projected. This business model enables FFP Prodem to make the SATMs available to users free of charge. A total of 30 SATMs have been deployed to date, with more to follow, both in Bolivia and elsewhere.

Connectivity and Information Services

Vodacom, a South African cellular operator, has had success using a shared access model - phone shops owned by local entrepreneurs - to provide affordable phone services in townships and other poor urban areas in that country. They serve millions of customers via 4400-phone shops that provide more than 24,000 phones - each of which averages 100 hours of use per month. Despite mandated prices less than one-third the commercial rate, phone shop entrepreneurs are mostly profitable, typically generating $1000 in revenue per month.

An entrepreneurial Indian company, n-Logue, has expanded the shared access model to offer voice, Internet, and other information services in rural India. n-Logue uses one kiosk per village, owned by a local entrepreneur. About 500 villages are linked to a central node at a distance of as much as 30 kilometers. Each node, also run by a (larger) local entrepreneur, connects to the phone system and the Internet via leased line or optical fiber, and also typically generates some local content or services of interest to its customers. n-Logue offers a broad range of information services through comparatively high-bandwidth service. The tiered franchise model also contributes to lower costs, allowing n-Logue to buy connectivity at bulk rates and share it among as many as 100,000 users per node. The company also uses low-cost kiosks and multilingual software of its own design. It now offers services in nearly 10,000 rural Indian villages and is growing rapidly, finding demand for voicemail; video mail and video conferencing; photography services; tele-medicine, tele-veterinary, crop consultancy services, and financial services.

Conclusion

What these approaches have in common are close attention to real needs at a community level in designing information services; innovative use of technology to provide services that are easier to use or accessible to more people; and new business models that suggest sustainability, scalability and replicability.

Village Information Kiosks: A Commercial Overview

Deepak Amin
Digital Partners (USA)

Abstract

The author suggests that truly self-sustaining information kiosks are possible only if they are setup as a commercial business. Furthermore, the author adds, the help from governments, international agencies and NGO's is critical, especially at the early stage of experimentation. Financial help as well as business and domain expertise are key to proving that it is possible to setup self-sustaining Information Kiosks that serve the underserved people in rural parts of the world.

Introduction

In the past few years, Village Information Kiosks have unequivocally proven their benefits to the local population where they have been deployed. The benefits have been not only operational efficiencies delivered through effective and timely availability of information but also services that are, so to say, "information" based, like purchasing land records, price of crops in remote wholesale markets, procurement of goods by governments agencies, bill payments, etc. In addition, the social benefits of these kiosks to the least privileged are clearly visible in most cases, though not in an easily measurable way. Examples of these include reduction in corruption, social recognition of women, exposure to computers and technology leading to an increased desire to get an education, realization of hitherto unknown opportunities, reduction in class and caste barriers, reduction in terrorism, etc.

However, there is a high amount of variance in the approach of these projects towards financial sustainability. On one end are projects that from the very beginning are structured to depend on grants on an ongoing basis. This may entail funding from various government agencies and non-governmental agencies. Examples of such projects include COMPRASNET (government eProcurement,

Brasil), E-Seva (Andhra Pradesh, India) and Poupatempo Centers for Attending to Citizens (Brasil). On the other end are projects that are driven as pure businesses with an initial investment for kick-starting the business and eventually attempting to achieve financial sustainability through profitable service offerings. Social returns in these businesses are an important goal but an operational side-benefit. Examples of such projects include E-Chaupal, Drishtee, Tarahaat, etc. In between these two ends of the spectrum are a wide range of projects that are a hybrid of these two models. Some are started by politicians to get credit for introducing apocryphal visionary schemes in their constituencies. Others are started by well-meaning NGOs who are working in the field to provide specific services to the villagers. Still others are initiated purely as experiments to gain a better understanding of how technology can benefit the underserved segments of society.

Grant Versus Investment

Village Information Kiosk (VIK) projects that are modeled to survive on grants are doomed for failure. If there isn't a self-sustaining business model behind the project, then it is continuously running on a fund-raising treadmill. Initial funding typically comes relatively easily and sometimes even continues past the initial state, albeit intermittently. Eventually the grants move on to other projects and other priorities, politicians follow other vote-grabbing schemes of the day, government agencies get new mandates, international organizations experiment with something else and NGOs eventually run out of money to fund these projects. Additionally, setting up these projects without the rigor and discipline of a self-sustaining business model will automatically attract entirely different kind of persons to run these kiosks. These are people who will not have incentive to make the kiosk more profitable or to expand its service offerings. Most of them have a false sense of assurance that these projects are going to be funded forever by external agencies. The "brand" of supporting government bodies typically makes it worse because the citizenry in these segments typically thinks of the government as its "provider", at least in its mind, if not in practice.

On the other hand, if VIKs are modeled from the very beginning as businesses to be operated locally by entrepreneurs who look upon these as investments that they can grow and reap benefits from based on their own efforts, then there is a strong incentive for them to work hard. Similarly, knowing that the kiosk will not be funded externally after a certain stage makes them work harder to ensure survival of their livelihood. They can see that working harder and smarter can lead to increased rewards. That can lead to higher interest and commitment from the local operators. Fear and greed. Carrot and stick. Both working in conjunction.

Governments, international agencies and NGOs still have an extremely critical role to play in such VIKs. From showing political support and providing seed capital, to offering business help to entrepreneurs, these groups are necessary for overcoming initial friction. They play the role of experimenting with new opportunities and ensuring an equal "starting line". However, a self-sustaining commercial focus must be the driving factor.

The strong role of external agencies with an interest in the success of the VIKs improves their chances of success while the experimental stage of these ventures simultaneously reduces the chances to some extent. The net effect of setting up the VIKs in this way is having as good a chance of succeeding as any other business. That's the best one can hope for. After all, one cannot offer services to people that they don't see value in. That value has to be a combination of two things: (1) the consumer willing to pay for the service and (2) a collective benefit, measurable or at least perceivable, for which the collective unit is willing to pay (e.g.,governments and self-help-groups). The former is the basis for setting up the business and keeping it self-sustaining. The latter is the social benefit that governments and international agencies are chartered to do. The former is the business ROI, the latter the social ROI. VIK projects cannot bring about SROI without first focusing on the business ROI.

The VIK Business Model
As with any business, one needs to look at the VIK business in a structured manner. What is the market opportunity? Where is the market opportunity? What products and services can you offer to this market? What will it take to "make" and "deliver" these products? What is the competition? What are the challenges? What are the financial needs? What are the sources of funds? What are the revenue projections? What does the "management team" look like? For the SROI part, one can ask other pertinent questions like what are the social benefits of the venture? What specific segment of the village does the business serve? What kind of opportunities does it create for the underprivileged sections of society? What kind of productivity gains does the villager see? Let us look into the key components of this VIK business model:

Market opportunity: While each region needs to have its own local market analysis done in detail, there are several broad trends that stand out when we look at the various VIK projects all over the world. The biggest opportunity is in the offering of government related services. In some cases, these services are missing altogether in the village or are being currently offered in a highly inefficient manner (For example getting land records, caste certificates, government incentive schemes, government procurement, etc). Interaction with government is one of the biggest areas of opportunity in this segment of the population. Moreover, offering government services initially also lends a high level of credibility to the VIK.

A second broad category of opportunity is in financial services. This includes services such as insurance, micro-credit and banking. A third category includes agriculture related products, including information about market prices for various products, weather forecast, crop information, seed information, fertilizer information, etc. A fourth category is health services. This includes health related services for people as well as animals. This category is so critical and so obvious that there are projects that address only health needs of the villages. A fifth category is education. This includes things like computer education, language learning, multi-media courses on specific topics like desktop publishing, distance learning, etc. This even includes education programs that are subsidized or funded by the government. Examples include AIDS awareness, water conservation, etc.

After these five broad categories, opportunities get more specialized. These include government-reporting, census, information dissemination, supply-chain management, Dairy Information Service Kiosk (an excellent and very successful example of a vertical approach to deploying VIKs, done in the state of Gujarat in India), government procurement kiosks (Chile, Peru), etc. Note that we are only looking at market opportunities in rural parts of the world.

If one looks at VIKs as the proverbial "sockets" into villages, one can then think of them as information and service enablers through which corporations, government and other entities can offer their services. The VIK can act as an intermediary and collect a fee for providing access to the end market for corporations. It can also provide the services themselves to the villagers, something that would not be possible without the kiosk infrastructure. The more services one can carry through the VIK "socket", the more benefits that can be brought to the villagers. It has the potential for being a win-win-win situation for the villagers, the VIK operators as well as corporations and governments who provide the services.

Products and Services: There is a dazzling list of products and services that are being offered today through VIKs in the various projects all over the world. The opportunities abound in a wide range of areas, with a bulk of them obviously being in the five broad categories listed above. It is in fact very interesting to look at services that are being offered outside these five broad categories. Most of them are not financially self-sustaining stand-alone. However, if one builds the right "bouquet" of service offerings, the marginal increment in revenues with each additional service offering is substantial. One has to be very careful while putting together such a bouquet so as to avoid operational and deployment problems that each of these services comes with. Overloading the kiosk operator with too many services with not enough revenue increment can lead to degradation of service quality arising out of lack of attention, lack of training, etc. In addition, a one-size-fits all approach has been shown from many existing projects to have failed, E-Seva in India being one of them. The point is that there is a wide range of services that have been identified for many markets. The key is to pick the right products and services first, generate sustainable revenues from them for a given segment and then expand from there, both with more services as well as into more regions.

Partnerships: Where does a Village Information Kiosk operator source this bouquet of products and services? The key is partnerships. First and foremost, government related services need to be provided through strong support and partnership with the local government agencies, and most preferably with one central agency that takes interest in and responsibility for the success of these services.

Other services can be offered through partnerships with corporations and other entities that look upon the rural regions as a target market. Partnerships with financial institutions, healthcare providers (private as well as public), content providers, etc are critical. Partners don't need to build their own networks and the VIK don't need to build their own products and services from ground zero. For example, financial institutions in India are interested in providing loans and insurance to rural parts, partly as a market opportunity and partly in compliance with legal requirements.

Clearly, forming such partnerships with each corporation and government entity for every locality by the various kiosk operators individually is not possible nor is it desirable. The right structure is for an umbrella organization to form relationships with the various entities, set up best practices for the kiosk operators to use in setting up, operating and growing their kiosk based businesses. In other words, some form of a franchise model that takes into account local market sensitivities within a broader well established operating framework for all VIKs. We will not delve deeper into partnerships here because they are discussed in more detail in other chapters of this book.[1]

Technology: Formulating and executing such a plan that covers a wide range of products and services that are widely distributed across disparate regions with multiple different languages and in some countries differing cultures is impossible without the effective use of technology. This is where ICT plays the crucial role of enabling such a model to be deployed in a decentralized manner, yet allows for efficient centralized management. Implementing the right technology that enables corporations to deploy their services easily, to manage them on an ongoing basis, to improvise and do course-correction in mid-stride and to do detailed market analyses with near-real time data is critical. Technology has only now matured enough to a point where such solutions are not only possible but also are cost-effective.

The various hardware components of the technology infrastructure include a PC, power supply with backup (wireline, solar panel, generator sets, etc), Internet connectivity (telephone line, some regions even have fiber optic high speed connectivity, cable, satellite), video camera/speaker/microphone, printer, camera, scanner and fax. Some are now beginning to experiment with 802.11 WiFi for local wireless access to the Internet. Typically, a basic kiosk consisting of a PC and a modem with backup batteries can be setup fairly inexpensively ranging from USD 500 to USD 1500 depending on the kind of services that the kiosk wants to offer. These costs are dropping every year as new technologies that are better and cheaper replace old ones.

The key however, is the software that enables the delivery of the services, including housekeeping functions like accounting, tracking, reporting, transaction handling, notifications, etc. Typically, such software ends up in the form of a browser-based application on this client side and some proprietary database driven application on the server side. For example, ordering copies of land records, loan applications, complaints, email, data entry, etc. In addition, other custom client software may also be required that enables services on the client alone. For example, training, scanning, photograph printing, desktop publishing, custom applications, etc. Again, other sections in this book discuss technology issues in more detail.[2]

Costs: There are basically two cost components involved in running a kiosk. First is the fixed cost that includes hardware, initial setup, a telephone connection, and training and in some cases a license fee to ensure seriousness and to cover some basic setup costs on the part of the umbrella franchisor. The second component is the monthly running cost that includes telephone charges, electricity, maintenance, service fees, etc. Typically, the fixed upfront part of the cost is covered by some sort of a loan, either through discounted government schemes or even through commercial banks. The running costs are expected to be covered by transactional revenues from service and product fees.

Revenues: For the VIK business model to be worthwhile for the local kiosk operator as well as the franchisor, the revenues have to not only cover the fixed investment and the recurring operational costs, but have to reap enough profits so that the kiosk operator does not look at other options, including going back to doing what he or she was doing before. In other words, cost of opportunity lost. In the case of VIKs in India, this can be 7000 rupees (approx USD 150) per month and higher. While many project promoters come up with seductive revenue opportunities, few have consistently reached such levels. Worldwide, there are very few truly self-sustaining business driven kiosk projects, and none that have actually achieved financial sustainability. There are several that are government schemes but their longevity is questionable as discussed earlier. There are a few kiosk models that are in fact financially self-sustaining but they are part of a large corporation's initiative to reach out to the rural parts of the region that they already serve. E-Chaupal from ITC in India and Dairy Information Service Kiosk (DISK) from the National Dairy Development Board of India are two examples of kiosks that serve as a distribution and collection infrastructure, for soybeans and milk respectively.

Business Structure: One way to structure a business driven kiosk model is as a franchise. The franchisor would setup the overall business model, setup best practice guidelines for the technology and services, sign business relationships with service providers, build the software for delivering the services, collect revenues, track activity, do market research and ensure efficient operations of the business. They would recruit qualified franchisees in the villages, train them, help them setup the kiosks, get the loans and provide them the overall operating platform to run the kiosk profitably. The franchisee would run his or her kiosk like a business. The franchisor would typically charge a setup fee and an ongoing monthly fee, either flat or a percentage of the service fee that the customer pays. The fee splits would need to ensure that there is enough incentive for the villager to consume the services, for the kiosk operator to make a comfortable profit while leaving enough money on the table for the franchisor and the original service provider. Note that all the parties do not have to necessarily be involved in every transaction. For example, the kiosk operator can offer desktop publishing as a service without having to pay the franchisor a percentage of the fees he charges his customers.

There are examples of commercially viable projects that have been setup in ways that are not franchises. E-Chaupal has been setup as a distribution and collection center as part of an existing profitable large corporation in India. Amul Dairy in the state of Gujarat in India is setup as a co-operative where each producer of milk becomes a member of the co-operative and hence a part owner.

Management Team: Success of a business depends first and foremost on the core team that is setting up and driving the business. In the VIK model, there are two teams that are key. The first is the management team of the franchisor organization. These are people who must set up effective operations for running a distributed service model, be technically savvy, have the ability to strike beneficial business relationships with service providers, have the ability to drive kiosk growth in a franchise model and have a strong focus on driving transactional revenues from the kiosks. Understanding the local market needs and translating them into the right mix of services that villagers are ready to pay for is critical. The second "team" is the kiosk operator. This could be either a self-help-group (SHG) or an individual entrepreneur. In either case, the team needs to have an entrepreneurial streak, have the discipline to run a business, must be local, have high school level education at least and must have a good understanding of how the business operates. To find the right person with the right incentives who is willing to do this business is difficult. The right person, especially if motivated and knowledgeable about the local market, can make all the difference to the success of the kiosk.

Funding: In a franchise model, funding is required at two levels. The franchisor needs to be funded to setup the business as described earlier and the franchisee in the village needs funding to franchise and start his kiosk business. The former is typically in the form of an investment or a loan structured for a business with all its intricacies. The latter is typically setup with the help of the franchisor who has established a partnership with a bank to provide a loan for setting up the kiosk with favorable bulk terms and a pre-qualification process that is part of the recruitment of the kiosk operator by the franchisor.

Challenges

Setting up such VIK projects is not an easy task by any means. Broadly speaking there are two big categories of challenges. First is the business challenge and second is the social challenge. From a business perspective, it takes a very high level of commitment by one or two key people who are passionate about making it happen. In addition, these people need to have experience in running a highly distributed service business, preferably in some sort of a franchise model. Putting together such a team is not easy. Once this team is in place, a core technology platform needs to be developed, more so on the software service delivery side because the hardware is relatively straightforward. Knowing that one-size-fits-all will not work and doing solid market research to understand the needs of the various market segments in the rural areas is very important. Business partnerships with service providers like financial institutions, government bodies, health providers, etc. need to be put into place. Revenue collection and tracking mechanisms in a distributed model can get tricky, including revenue splits between the service provider, the franchisor and the kiosk operator. Putting together such an initiative takes a good amount of investment that needs to be raised either from private investors or from government and international institutions.

Simultaneously, many social challenges need to be overcome to make such a project succeed. The most disruptive effect of a VIK is the introduction of efficiency. Where there is a lack of information or availability of services, there are entrenched middlemen who are exploiting the situation to make large sums of money. Typically, these middlemen are or have become very powerful because of their position in this inefficient "supply-chain" ecosystem. They see kiosks and kiosk operators as a threat, and justifiably so. Dealing with them, their aggressive moves to disrupt and discredit the kiosks can mean one of two things. Either the VIK can take it in stride and try to fight it or alternatively try to include the middlemen in the process in some clever way so they have an incentive in the success of the kiosk. Other social issues include the exclusion of lower caste or poor classes of people from the benefits of such projects, the kiosk operator himself becoming the exploiter of opportunity (e.g., how do you handle a complaint against the kiosk operator who is offering a service of filing complaints against the local government officials?), education leading to empowerment of certain sections like women or lower caste people that in turn leads to the privileged people feeling threatened, etc. The experience of Grameen Bank while offering micro-credit to women self-help-groups illustrates many of these social problems in detail. Such projects need strong support at the political level to overcome these barriers. A catch-22 situation, to say the least!

Conclusion

The case being made in this article is that truly self-sustaining VIKs are possible only if they are setup as commercial businesses. Help from governments, international agencies and NGO's is critical, especially at the early stage of experimentation. Financial help as well as business and domain expertise are key in proving that it is possible to setup self-sustaining VIKs that serve the underserved people in rural parts of the world. A lot of experimentation with such commercial models is happening all over the world today with an overwhelming majority in India.

Some of these projects are on the brink of breaking through. Supporting them and learning from their successes and failures can help the projects in the rest of the world in reaching out to the underserved people. People who need an opportunity to run with, not opportunistic handouts.

Examples of Business Driven VIK Projects

Drishtee (Rajasthan, India): is a franchise model of VIKs that offers services in e-governance, education, financial services and health services.[3]

E-Chaupal, Hoshangabad (Madhya Pradesh, India): is ITC's Business Division that provides information, products and services required in Soya farming.

NDDB (Gujarat, India): has more than 1,000 milk collection centers setup, as cooperatives in rural India were women sell cow and buffalo milk. Middlemen have been effectively sidelined.

Warna Wired Village Project, Kolhapur (Maharashtra, India): has 70 villages that provide benefits to members of sugar cooperative as well as other villagers through a network of kiosks.

Tarahaat.com, Jhansi (Uttar Pradesh, India): has setup kiosks in a franchise model to offer services like market prices, information, news, mail, procurement, payment services, etc.

N-Logue Tele-centers Project, Madurai (Tamil Nadu, India): has helped setup 30 kiosks that provide telemedicine and several other web based services.[4]

Notes

1. For further information please refer to Proenza, Sherry & Ilahiane, and Stoll in Section 1 of this book.

2. For further information please refer to Jhunjhunwala and Jensen in this book.

3. For further information please refer to the Drishtee case study in this book or visit the website at: http://www.drishtee.com

4. For further information please refer to Jhunjhunwala's article in this book.

SECTION V
Analysis of Selected Case Studies: Lessons from the Field

AFRICA

NIGERIA - Owerri Digital Village
Njideka Ugwuegbu

BENIN - The Songhai Network of Telecenters
Morenike Ladikpo

ASIA

CHINA - Poverty Reduction through Access to ICTs in Rural Areas
Paul Ulrich

INDIA - Drishtee Village Information Kiosks
Digital Partners

INDIA - University-based Village Telecenter
Royal D. Colle & Raul Roman

INDIA - n-logue
Osama Manzar

INDONESIA - Internet Warnets
Rudy Rusdiah

THAILAND - Thailand Canada Telecentre Project
Warren Wong, David Barr, Jingjai Hanchanlash and Vasoontara Chatikavnij

EASTERN EUROPE

HUNGARY - Hungarian Telecottages
Tom Wormald and Mátyás Gáspár

LATIN AMERICA

CHILE - Red de Informacion Comunitaria
Pedro E. Hepp and Rodrigo Garrido

EL SALVADOR - Infocentros
World Resources Institute

PERU - Cabinas Públicas de Internet
Ana Maria Fernandez-Maldonado

BENIN

The Songhai Network of Telecenters

Morenike Ladikpo
International Development Research Center

Project Summary

The Songhai centre is a zero emissions research institute for training, production and development of sustainable agricultural techniques. The centre was founded in 1985 by a Dominican priest and trains about 700 students each year with a staff of 150 people on its seven sites. In early 1999, Songhai created a network of 3 community telecenters on three of its sites in the following towns in rural Benin: Porto-Novo (south-east of Benin); Savalou (centre of Benin); and Parakou (north of Benin). Plans are currently being made to expand this network to Lokossa (south west Benin) and Amukpè (Delta state in Nigeria) to answer the growing demands for the telecenter's services in these regions.

The Songhai telecenters are good examples of the "adoption model" in that the telecenters were integrated into the existing research, training and production centres and adopted by the local entrepreneurs, students and staff. This approach has been the strength of the Songhai telecenters since they were able to rely on the centre's administrative and budgetary systems and thus concentrate their efforts on the provision of quality service. The Songhai telecenters have been embedded in the realities of these research centres, forcing them to become more productive and competitive. The telecenters are therefore not stand-alone units.

Socio-Economic Impacts

The telecenters have had an impact on both the Songhai centre and the rural communities across Benin in which they have thus far been established. Here are a few:

- Provided the rural communities with the means of overcoming their geographical and infrastructural constraints. VSATs have been installed in each of these telecenters to overcoming the limited telecommunications infrastructures in these areas and provide access to the Internet;

- Increased the level of understanding of the information and communication tools among the staff, students and communities around these telecenters. This has been achieved through the various training and awareness raising programmes organised by the telecenters;

- Provided social, economic and professional opportunities to their communities. For example, farmers come to the telecenters to use the Internet to look for agricultural equipment for their farms, entrepreneurs use its resources to look for new partnerships for their projects;

- Increased Songhai's productivity and helped optimize its organizational system thus reducing administrative costs. eg. Reduced transportation and telephone cost since a lot can be solved over the Internet;

- Help disseminate Songhai research results and experience using the information and communication technology tools such as multimedia CDROMs of Songhai training modules, online training courses etc;

- Increased awareness of Songhai at the international level through the website they created;

- Developed and encouraged the culture of information both within the centre and in the rural communities around.

Sustainability Model
The telecenters have been integrated completely into the activities of the Songhai centre as a whole. They are now considered as one of the key sectors of the Songhai system feeding into and receiving inputs from the other sectors.

Figure 1. The Songhai Adoption Model (from Songhai website)

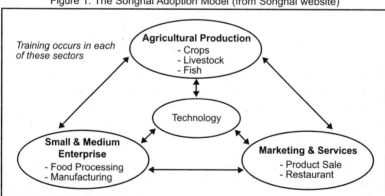

The Telecenters Organisation
The telecenters function in a decentralised manner. Each of the Telecenters has a manager and also an overall coordinator supervising all their activities. The

telecenters coordinator is given a certain amount of autonomy to enable him to carry out his function effectively, he however has to report to the management committee of the Songhai centre on a regularly basis. The telecenter coordinator although not necessarily a very technical person, has to love the technologies and have a good human relationship capacity.

The Role of the Telecenters in the Songhai Centre

- It is at the telecenter that all the new information and communication tools are tried out.

- The technical team of the telecenter ensures the networking, maintenance and repair of all the computers of the Songhai Centre as well as those of their clients.

- The Songhai website developed in the telecenter has increased the request for collaboration and training (from outside) in sustainable agriculture over the past few years.

- The marketing and entrepreneurship sections of the centre have also benefited from this website through which they now sell and market their products. An e-commerce module has even been added to the website. Most of the Songhai staff now access their e-mails through the telecenters.

- The telecenters have developed multimedia training modules on each of the key sectors of Songhai. They are also developing online versions of some of these training modules.

- Staff and students of the centre use the Internet access there to get updated information in their fields of interest.

The Role of the Songhai Centre in the Activities of the Telecenters

- The Songhai centre provides the telecenters with accounting, organisational and administrative services.

- The Songhai centre recruits, trains and manages the technical staff of the telecenters.

- The Songhai centre also provides the telecenters with a steady clientele (its staff, students and clients who come to the Songhai farm shops, restaurants, conference centres etc). The services currently provided by the telecenters can be divided into two groups:

  1) Internet and computer Services: Internet phone, Navigation, Internet fax, e-mail, Distance Education, E-Commerce, Computer training (Internet, graphic design, website creation), computer repairs.

  2) Office services: Telephone, Photocopy, Word processing, Lamination, Publishing (badges, business cards, greeting cards, logos), Digital pictures, Fax, Creation of multimedia products.

Technology
Connectivity
There is a VSAT installed in each telecenter linking the telecenters together and also to the outside world. The computers in each telecenter are connected to each other and also to the other departements of the Songhai Centre by a local area network.

Hardware
In the Porto-Novo telecenter there 45 computers of which 6 are servers. In the Savalou there are 18 computers while in the Parakou telecenter there are 15 computers. Most of these computers are Pentium IIIs and IVs.

Software
Linux is used for the mail server in each telecenter while the other computers use the Microsoft operating system. CyberCafePro is used for managing the Internet connection in each telecenter. Softwares such as Flash, Adobe Premiere, Photoshop, Dreamweaver are also available for editing and graphic design.

Partnerships
Non Governmental Organizations and Educational Institutions
The Songhai telecenters have established partnerships with the schools, non-governmental organizations and associations in their vicinities. They offer varied services ranging from badge making for the organization personnel to training in the use of computers and the Internet.

International Organizations
International Development Research Centre (IDRC): The Songhai VSAT and distance education programme are being put in place with the support of IDRC.

United States Agency for International Development (USAID): The telecenters were created with the financial and technical support of USAID.

Lessons from the Field
Songhai has put into place a system for monitoring the daily visits to the telecenters and the types of services sought out by their clients. Here are some findings obtained from the data gathered:

Financial Sustainability
On the whole there are about 1500 people visiting the telecenters each week with a majority of the clients coming for Internet related services (mainly Internet navigation, e-mails, Internet phone). Other services such as photocopying, word processing, telephone services however remain very popular because of the partnerships with the associations and NGOs working in those localities.

The demand for computer training is also on the increase because of the partnerships made with the schools in each locality to teach computer courses.

In some cases, Songhai provides the instructor and computer equipment, in other situations, they only provide the equipment. Songhai has already trained 350 people in the use of computers and the Internet during the first 8 months of the year. All the telecenters had to organize a very strong awareness raising campaign when they started. They went about this by first organizing training for the Songhai centre staff and students since they were to be the champions of the telecenters. Information sessions were also organized for the rest of the population. During such sessions, they were introduced to the uses of the computer and how the new technologies could benefit them.

To draw peoples' attention, services such as Services to which most people were already used to such as photocopying, telephone, Fax, word processing, lamination, creation of badges were offered at the beginning to draw people to the telecenters. People started coming in for the Internet services only after they had been made aware of its benefits. The telecenters started with 5 per cent of their clients demands being Internet related. Today, they have reached a 75 per cent demand for Internet related services.

Much effort had to be put in initially by the telecenter staff to assist their clients. They helped them type their e-mails, helped and taught them how to navigate and search for information over the Internet. Today, this has paid off since the majority of the clients are now autonomous and require very little assistance.

The telecenters charge a small fee for services rendered. The fees are generally lower than what is being charged in private telecenters. They have been established so that they cover the running cost of the telecenters while leaving some for equipment renewal. The Porto-Novo telecenter after its first two months of operations was already covering its operational costs. Today the Porto-Novo telecenter has a turnover of above USD 7500 each month. This covers its costs (operational, capital depreciation) and also leaves a profit margin. The other two telecenters, which are in more remote areas have not reached this level of sustainability but are moving towards that progressively. The telecenters are in a peculiar situation since they have to be both sustainable and also meet the Songhai development objectives. The telecenters are open for long hours, from 7:30am in the morning to 10pm everyday. The telecenters intend to extend the opening hours till midnight so as to satisfy the growing demands for their services.

Technology
All the telecenters have a VSAT connection with a 128kbps uplink for the Porto-Novo telecenter and 64kbps in the other two telecenters. Download speeds vary between 300-800kps. There are generators on each of the Songhai sites that take over when there are power outages. This is quite frequent during the raining season.

The Community
The Songhai telecenters (with their VSATs) have provided Internet access to remote areas which otherwise would not have had any. This is most especially true in the case of the Savalou telecenter with people coming in from towns as

far as Bantè (50km from the telecenter) Dassa (30km from the telecenter), and Glazoué (55km from the telecenter). The total population of these three towns put together is estimated to be over 170,000 people. The only other telecenter in the area (apart from Songhai) recently stopped operations because of connectivity problems.

The telecenters have been seen as having opened doors of professional and social opportunities for its users, having trained them and increased their awareness of the benefits from using these tools. The telecenters with their development of the Voice Over IP services have also helped reduce the costs of transactions for the farmers.

Scalability/Replicability
Here are some of the elements that ensured the success of the telecenters:
- Their embedding in a well-known development and research centre. This made it easy to attract the clients already used to coming to the Songhai centre for other services. It also provided a market for the telecenters made up of Songhai students and staff. The partnerships formed with NGOs, associations, and schools have also ensured a steady clientele and thus financial sustainability. The embedding of the telecenters in a centre with a strong accounting, administrative and organisational structure allowed the staff to focus more on offering quality services;

- The strong awareness raising campaign and trainings offered at the beginning helped launch the telecenters;

- The status of the Songhai centre (a non-governmental organisation) removed all the elements of bureaucracy or politics associated with government organisations;

- The Songhai culture of ownership has also had a very positive impact on the telecenters since all the telecenter staff feel that they are responsible for the telecenters and so do all in their capacities to ensure that they meet their objectives.

Limitations of the Model
- High cost of VSAT access: The Songhai telecenters can be sustainable even after deducting VSAT access costs primarily because of the great number of users. This might be a more difficult challenge for smaller telecenters with a lesser clientele;

- One other problem the Songhai telecenters face is the turnover of telecenter staff. Since the telecenters are located in rural regions, there has always been that problem of finding highly qualified staff who are willing to work in such remote areas.

Other Initiatives in the Country

CED-Bénin: Propose distance education courses on the ICTs (web development, networking, etc.). http://www.cedbenin.org

Fondation de l'entrepreneurship du Bénin (FEB): Uses the information and communication tools to promote entrepreneurship in Benin. Provides computer training and a VSAT Internet access. http://www.fondationbenin.org

ORIDEV: An NGO which promotes ICTs in the country through training, publications and provision of Internet access points. http://www.oridev.org

Website and Contact Information

Songhai Center
http://www.songhai.org

Father Nzamujo, Founder
nzamujo@songhai.org

Leonce Sessou, Telecenter Coordinator
lsessou@songhai.org

NIGERIA

Owerri Digital Village

Njideka Ugwuegbu*
Youth for Technology Foundation

Project Summary

The Owerri Digital Village (ODV) was launched in September 2001 in Imo State, Eastern Nigeria by Youth for Technology Foundation (YTF), an international not-for-profit organization based in Nigeria and the United States. The mission of YTF is to create enriched learning communities in Nigeria by providing youth with the technology tools and resources they need to achieve their potential and create self-sustaining communities. The vision of YTF is simple yet powerful. In this vision, rural Nigerian communities become enriched learning environments in which technology used well enhances and expands opportunities for the marginalized, the poorest of the poor.

An actualization of YTF's vision is the Owerri Digital Village, a community technology and learning center in eastern Nigeria. The mission of ODV is to promote rural community development by providing technical, educational and entrepreneurship skills training to disadvantaged individuals in an effort to create social and economic opportunities that can change peoples' lives and transform communities.

The Eastern region of Nigeria is evidently underserved as a result of the Biafran war, 1967-1970, where between 500,000 and 2 million Biafran civilians, especially children, lost their lives to malnutrition and died from starvation during the war. The ODV is a community technology and learning center (CTLC) that offers IT skills development and training to Nigerian youth in an effort to develop entrepreneurial spirit, skills and passion for technology. ODV is a one-stop center where young people have access to need-based information, acquire vocational skills and master the tools for fostering social awareness.[1]

YTF primarily targets youth, between the ages of 8 and 25 for participation in the programs, as they are typically quick learners with the longest productivity horizon. Many of these young people come from desperately poor subsistence

---

*This case study was prepared with the assistance of Digital Partners, a Seattle, Washington-based nonprofit organization dedicated to the economic empowerment of the poor through the appropriate use of technology.

farming communities, have low educational achievement, receive little or no parental support and, in the case of the female children, are vulnerable to teenage pregnancy and abuse.

The Owerri Digital Village currently offers four core programs:[2]

1) *Tech Kids: Introduction to Computers*. Designed for youth between the ages of 8 and 12 to learn to use computers as a tool for learning. Program goals include improving critical thinking, information synthesis and problem solving skills among students through inquiry-oriented learning modules.

2) *Tech Teens: Computer Fluency Education*. Designed to prepare students (ages 13-18) for a career in the field of information technology. Participants gain the skills to use technology as a tool for learning and gain the necessary entrepreneurial skills to be future job creators. After successfully completing the TechTeens program, graduates spend up to 8 weeks at a local community business as TechInterns.[3]

3) *Tech Enhancement: Workforce Development Program*. Designed to meet the needs of individuals who are currently in the workforce but need to develop or enhance their skill level. Participants in this program partake in bi-monthly workshops offered at the Owerri Digital Village on career development and writing business plans, with an emphasis on technology as a key enabler for business and professional success.

4) *Tech Communities: Community Enlightenment Program*. This program targeted towards women producers in the community. Participants in this program attend workshops and are mentored on how technology can provide greater access to markets for their products, such as traditional handicrafts, textiles and jewellery.

All ODV programs are experiential in nature and are designed to increase problem solving, critical thinking, and information absorption and communication skills.

Socio-Economic Impacts

- Reduce youth unemployment, rural poverty and illiteracy by helping youth to develop self-confidence, self-esteem, discipline and teamwork.

- Improve academic performance and foster a positive attitude towards technology developed among Nigerian youth.

- Increase exposure to employment opportunities by empowering youth to become not only users but also creators of local content and applications.

- Develop local capacity at the grassroots through the utilization of information and communication technologies.

- Serve as a scalable and replicable model for future Youth for Technology Foundation Nigeria Digital Villages.

- Empowering people on the bottom of the economic pyramid, often women, by providing them with management training and leadership skills and by opening for them new venues to market and sell their products.

Sustainability Model
The Owerri Digital Village is the first of Youth for Technology Foundation's community technology learning centers (CTLC) and the first of its kind in West Africa. The community and local government showed the greatest interest and commitment. Imo State has the lowest levels of illiteracy in Nigeria. The cost of infrastructure (electricity, rent, phone, etc.) is relatively low compared to the other locations selected during the research process.

The ODV model is founded on three main pillars:
1) *Social appropriation of technology* a community-based approach that allows the meaningful uses of ICTs that can address specific community needs. In addition, the involvement of community members and leaders fosters the social sustainability of the center, since people are able to integrate and adopt those ICT-solutions that are relevant to their indigenous lifestyles and solve concrete problems or realities;[4]

2) *Knowledge transfer and capacity building* through the provision of training programs at the Center that contribute to the alleviation of poverty, create a new generation of IT literates among the young population and help the marginalized achieve their potential;

3) *A network of partnerships among communities*, private sector, international not-for-profit organizations and the Nigerian government. This pillar enables the cooperation among different stakeholders and increases the chances to achieve economic sustainability of the Digital Village in the long run opening the possibility of replicating the model in other rural Nigerian communities.

The ODV was funded, in part, by a grant donated by Microsoft Corporation for the acquisition of computer equipment, software and servers and subsequently by small in-kind financial donations from different international and local Nigerian not-for-profit organizations. The local government provided the physical space and the generator for the CTLC and the Owerri community contributed with a parallel, in-kind, investment by becoming responsible for the Center's maintenance, security and basic operational functions.

Technology Infrastructure
The center is comprised of fifty multi-media connected PCs, printers, educational software and technology books available for program members at the center.

The Center also has four classrooms, three administrative offices, one technology resource center, a boardroom and a seminar room. During the initial period the Center used a dial up connection for accessing the Internet, however, the high cost of phone bills and the unreliability and slow speed of the telecommunications infrastructure made this form of connection unsustainable. Currently, the Owerri Digital Village is exploring the possibility of establishing a rural connectivity paradigm where initial investments can be made in VSAT and wireless technologies provided there is a shared bandwidth approach with other local schools or organizations.

Partnerships
State Government
YTF has taken a community-based approach of involving Owerri's community leaders, who understood that not having access to information and communication technologies was marginalizing their local citizens. Support received by the local government in Imo State has been significant in the overall success of the project. Some of the donations include the facility that houses the Owerri Digital Village as well as a generator that provides electricity to the center. This commitment highlights, not only good governance but most importantly, the relevance that the local government places on information and communication technology to the overall development of its people.

Non-Governmental Organizations
Youth for Technology Foundation has been working with the Ministries of Education and other not-for-profit organizations to make the case for the necessity of making the use of information technology mandatory at all levels of educational institutions through adequate financial provision for tools and resources. YTF has developed partnerships with international not-for-profit organizations like Digital Partners and the Global Education and Tele-Community Initiative (GEI). The mission of both of these partnership is focused on ending the education, gender, and culture divides by stabilizing a global economy through education revitalization and establishing global collaboration between diverse populations and cultures.

Lessons from the Field
Financial Sustainability
Sustaining a community technology and learning center is not cheap. Be creative without diverging from your organization's mission statement. There are services that the community needs and will be willing to pay for provided the center can supply these services, for example long distance phone calls. Organizations should create annual CTLC operating budgets as if there were no donations (grants, fundraising etc) expected. Services for fees and contracted services (e.g., provision of state and local government services) should account for the majority of the budgeted income.

Technology
- State-of-the-art technology may not be the most appropriate mechanism to address the needs of the local community. There must be an organic process through which customized technology is chosen depending on the specific needs of the people.

- Dial up connections to the Internet are costly and unreliable underscoring the need for alternative access strategies via VSAT or Wireless technologies.

The Community
- Critical to involve the community in every stage of the project. The synergy and active communication between the CTLC and the community ensures the social sustainability of the center by making it highly responsive to the particular needs of the people.

- YTF ensured that its community-based technology programs were designed by first gauging the needs of the community and developing an understanding of how technology can be used to enhance their lives, create jobs, reverse urban migration leading to self-sustaining communities.

Scalability/Replicability
The majority of Information Kiosks models start thinking on replication at very early stages and this might not be the best approach. Rather, the Youth for Technology Foundation is channeling all its efforts for the Owerri Digital Village to become not only the best model but also a paradigm for other communities who can leverage the best practices of the model, adjusting them to their specific needs.

Limitations of the Model
The biggest obstacle the ODV is confronting right now is finding qualified trainers, with strong background in technology, to work at the center. The lack of high-skilled employment opportunities in this Nigerian region is causing a brain drain towards bigger cities. Highly qualified individuals find it difficult to give up the salaries offered by the private sector to work for non-for-profit organizations. The unreliability and high costs of dial up connection has limited the ability of the ODV to provide Internet access. As previously mentioned, the center is sear-ching for alternative technology solutions, in the form of VSAT or Wireless, that are more affordable and reliable.

Website and Contact Information
Youth for Technology Foundation, Owerri Digital Village
http://www.youthfortechnology.org

Njideka Ugwuegbu, Director
njideka@youthfortechnology.org

Notes

1. Youth for Technology Foundation, Our Projects, Owerri: http://www.youthfortechnology.org/owerri.html

2. Ugwuegbu, Njideka (2002) ""The Owerri Digital Village: A Grassroots Approach to Bringing Technology to Nigerian Youth". TechKnowLogia, July - September 2002 © Knowledge Enterprise, Inc. retrieved from 09/03/03 from http://www.TechKnowLogia.org

3. Youth for Technology Foundation, Our Programs, Tech Teens: http://www.youthfortechnology.org/frames.html

4. Ugwuegbu, Njideka (2002) "Owerri Digital Village: A grassroots approach to empowering Nigerian youth and their communities". Digital Divide Network retrieved on 09/13/03 from URL: http://www.digitaldividenetwork.org/content/stories/index.cfm?key=240

CHINA

Poverty Reduction through Access to ICTs in Rural Areas

Paul Ulrich
Independent Consultant

Project Summary

As a three-year pilot program of the United Nations Development Programme (UNDP) and the Chinese Ministry of Science and Technology (MOST), the project aims to reduce poverty in China by providing useful information services to the rural poor. Scheduled for completion at the end of 2003, the project is largely a home-grown effort: although the UNDP provides one quarter of the funding, principally for training and consultancies, one third comes from the central government's Ministry of Science and Technology, with the rest - approximately 40 per cent of the total - contributed directly by the benefiting counties themselves. Within each county, funds come not only from the county-level government but from the participating towns and villages, as well. Based on the quality of their applications and ability to finance their share of the project, five counties, each in a different province, were selected for this pilot effort. The five chosen "winners" and current participants are as follows:

- Yuyang district of Shaanxi Province;
- Wu'an city of Hebei Province;
- Huoshan County of Anhui Province;
- Shangcheng County of Henan Province; and
- Tongnan County of Chongqing Municipality.

The project has a pyramid-shaped support structure. At the center is the MOST office in Beijing with several technical staff that make frequent visits to the project sites in each province. Field staff, down to the village level, has also gone to Beijing to receive training, while some county-level managers and government officials have gone on annual overseas training tours to visit centers in Europe and elsewhere. The Beijing office has a central website at www.cstap.org.cn, linked to those of each county center. Each county in turn has an Internet center, with high-speed access to the Internet and about ten computer terminals for providing training to village and town project staff. Reporting to each county are two township Internet centers, providing training and services to local townspeople and surrounding villages. Every project town then has two village centers under it for providing training and services to local villagers. At each village and town center are from two to five staff, assigned by the local government to work full or part-time at the centers. One person manages the operation while the others provide training and solicit suggestions from local users on types of information or services that would most benefit them.

Socio-Economic Impacts

The project is conducting a formal social-impact-assessment survey in the fall of 2003. Rapid appraisals in 2002 found that many of the village sites and households had impressive stories to tell about rapid advances in their incomes, attributable to new information accessed via the Internet. In some instances, such as the case of pig farmers in Yuyang, the rise in their annual incomes from higher sale prices due to better pricing information exceeded the project costs by a wide margin. Others-particularly doctors-cited the benefits of help found online for treating difficult cases or for broadening their understanding of specific ailments. The most frequently mentioned benefit related to better information on useful agricultural technology and market prices, with successively fewer mentions of successes from health, educational, or job searches online, respectively.

Sustainability Model

Given the project's objectives, charging for services to generate revenues and cover costs was not considered to be an appropriate objective. Since the world's richest country, the United States, has spent USD 2bn to subsidize its own library and school Internet connections via the E-Rate program, it seems odd to expect programs in poor countries, and in particular, poor rural areas, to use revenues to cover their operating expenses. The elusive quest for sustainability in such ICT projects dooms those that succeed to narrow their targeted users to the groups that can afford the services-typically urban dwellers and the better off. Instead, donors should encourage developing-country governments to follow the Western model of cross-subsidizing ICT development in poor areas from taxes on more basic telecommunication services.

For the current project, lobbying the Chinese government on national policy changes to cross-subsidize universal Internet access remains a long-term goal to ensure sustainability. In the medium term, however, counties with higher cost structures should look at ways to minimize their costs without charging for services. Cost cutting measures could include the following:

- Assign redundant staff to other projects or more pressing government work;
- Work out monthly contracts rather than hourly rates with Internet service providers;

- Reduce printing costs by saving more materials on the computer and inviting interested villagers to read them there;
- Transfer unused PCs to centers needing them rather than purchasing new equipment;
- Buy second-hand PCs rather than new ones, particularly as supplemental training PCs.

Technology Infrastructure

In terms of infrastructure, all centers use computers made by Legend, a local Chinese company and the leading manufacturer and vendor of PCs in China today. Each village center has a dial-up line for accessing the Internet from one, or sometimes - in the case of town centers - from two PCs. Visitors may use non-wired PCs for learning or practicing typing skills or to watch and listen to VCDs. Every center has a phone and fax machine for sending periodic reports to its respective county center. Due to intermittent and slow Internet connections at the village level, faxing may be more reliable and convenient than sending e-mail. Some town centers, like the county centers, have ISDN or faster connections to the Internet. Most village and town centers also have a separate room for viewing videos or VCDs where users can watch training programs on, for example, new agricultural technologies.

Partnerships

As an initiative funded largely by the local and central government to serve areas and a clientele not profitable to the private sector, the project has not formed strategic alliances with private firms. However, the project has shown exemplary cooperation with, among others, academic institutions who have often provided consulting and advice at little or no cost. Local government officials at every level of the project are actively involved in its implementation. At the county-level, county executives provide guidance and organize local government experts from different sectoral departments for regular advisory meetings on, for example, Internet-based information needed by the county. At the village and town levels, governments often second staff to work at the centers. In some counties, the government departments themselves are among the heaviest users of the services. The project centers are located in government-provided facilities, usually adjacent to the local government's central offices, while a few centers are in village school buildings.

Lessons from the Field

The project generally makes appropriate use of available technology and is adept at providing useful information at the macro-level to local governments running the projects, and to a lesser extent (due to constrained resources) at a micro-level for individual users. However, the project has fallen short in the "C" aspect of ICT-in communicating best practices internally, among the five project counties, but more importantly, in demonstrating that the Internet, unlike TV or radio, is a valuable channel for two-way communication. Few villagers have received training in e-mail, despite the fact that repeated national surveys of Chinese Internet users have shown e-mail to be, by far, the number one application for the nearly 70 million individuals who, as of mid-2003, were going online in China.

Sustainability/Replicability

At a project-wide level, the MOST-UNDP initiative has a clear, organizational structure, highly motivated staff, strong government support at all levels, and a commitment to training, as detailed in instructional manuals. Overall, a remarkable degree of uniformity characterizes the structure of the project in each of the five provinces and reflects a conscious decision of the project planners. Nevertheless, in implementing their mandates, and as determined by local conditions or priorities, each county differs to some degree and achieved best practices that the other counties should emulate.

Tongnan county had the following examples:

- A fifty-page instruction manual developed especially for training village and town staff;
- An excellent often-visited website offering not only free e-mail accounts but also a separate page of agricultural technology video clips for those with high speed access;
- A practice of paying staff according to results based on monthly in-person reviews, conducted in conjunction with half-day training sessions;
- A well-planned advertising campaign including weekly 3-5 minute television spots, dozens of wall posters, signboards, and bus banners describing the project;
- A well-thought out training program that includes final exams to test that staff have properly absorbed the lessons;
- A close working relationship with China Telecom, the county center's broadband provider, despite using the cheaper Internet access services of Unicom in the village and town centers.

In Yuyang, the district's close cooperation with the county broadcasting bureau has resulted in an important and popular innovation for the households lacking cable TV. The bureau copies useful site data from the Internet and develops its own programs for regular broadcasts, received by cable TV at the information centers, viewable by VCD, or viewed at homes-either through cable TV or via a low-cost (USD 13) receiver.

Sound and pictures are especially important for those with limited reading skills, and in remote areas relying on slow Internet connections, microwave broadcasts or delivered VCDs are the most appropriate delivery vehicles for key developmental programs.

Yuyang has also achieved a higher rate of usage for its centers by subsidizing the village's costs of Internet access and locating the centers in more accessible village schools rather than in local government offices.

In Wu'an, some centers have had special training sessions for women and weekly newsletters for distribution to villagers or visitors. In one of Wu'an's villages, primary-school teachers - on their own initiative - recently bought for about USD 7 a set of five computer-training CDs, developed by China's renowned Qinghua University. With sound and animation on PCs supplied by the project, the CDs have enabled elementary students to learn on their own how to use a computer and enter information. This is a singular example of a cost-effective tool for learning that has applications in even the remotest locations that currently have poor access to phone communications.

In Huoshan county, one site closely coordinated its activities with those of a large Dutch-funded poverty-alleviation project and another made special efforts to train farmers in the use of e-mail, thereby providing added incentives for them to come frequently to the center.

Shansheng country demonstrated one of the more active community outreach programs by designating ten model households per village. These households had benefited from information provided by the centers and in turn told others about their experience. The centers also designated staff to go into the community to find out what information was most needed. To encourage active participation from those lacking their own TVs or VCRs, the centers offered screenings of movies and music videos in addition to technical ones.

Limitations of the Model
A few of the information centers are located in nationally designated poor counties, where average incomes fall below the government's poverty line. Overall, the project currently serves relatively poor rural areas but has not made use of satellite infrastructure to reach the poorest and most remote towns and villages, which tend to be located in China's mountainous areas. Such localities, lacking in fixed line or mobile telecommunications infrastructure, are the most expensive to reach and also the least able to contribute to the funding of their own projects. At present, even in the project counties, the poorest villages are not necessarily being served, and it is unclear whether the very poorest in each village are using the information services. Like other development projects with limited budgets, this one has had to balance the extent of its reach with the depth of how far down among the poor it extends.

To date, the centers are largely acting as information sources - as a kind of online library - rather than as vehicles for communication via, for instance, e-mail. Hardly any users or staff has their own e-mail accounts even though those are freely available at websites like Sohu and Sina, the Chinese counterparts to Yahoo or Hotmail. Instead, each center will have a central e-mail address on behalf of those few users who need to have information sent to or from another web address.

Other Initiatives in the Country

MOST has a related initiative run by its Science and Technology Bureau in Sichuan province. There the agricultural information network has distributed thousands of training VCDs to a thousand villages in the province. A group of expert advisors also meets several times a week to respond to farmer questions via e-mail, often replying within a day or two.

China has thousands of privately funded, for-profit cyber-cafes primarily in urban areas. Their reach, however, does not generally extend below large townships serving as county seats. Much of their revenue comes from youngsters playing online or computer games. In addition, China's nearly one-quarter of a billion cell-phone users have become devotees of short messaging services (SMS), and are likely to account for over one half of the world's total short messages sent in 2003.

The Chinese Ministry of Education also recently announced a USD 1.2bn initiative to develop online learning facilities for every primary and secondary school in rural areas during the next five years. The money will be used to build satellite receiving centers and computer classrooms across the country, and to develop educational material on CD-Rom discs.

Moreover, since late 1999 China's State Administration of Radio, Film and Television, with support from UNESCO, has run an "Every Village" (Cun Cun Tong) program of ensuring that each village in China has at least one satellite receiver to receive TV broadcasts. In the remotest areas, these already existing broadcast systems might be able to form the basis for two-way Internet centers.

Website and Contact Information

MOST
http://www.cstap.org.cn (in Chinese)

Mr. Bai Qiyun, Project Director
cstap@263.net.cn

Mr. Chen Guoyong, Project Officer
cstap@263.net.cn

Beijing, China
Tel. 8610-6851-5810

Dr. Daniel Wang, UNDP Project Officer
Beijing, China
Tel. 8610-6532-3731 ext 318
daniel.wang@undp.org

Paul Ulrich, External Evaluator
Hong Kong and New York
Tel. 852-2877-6254 or 1-914-238-4890
paul_ulrich@aya.yale.edu

INDIA

Drishtee Village Information Kiosks

Digital Partners
Seattle, Washington (USA)

Project Summary
Drishtee is an organizational platform aimed at fostering rural networking and the provision of ICT-enabled services to rural and semi-urban populations in India. Since its creation in 1999, Drishtee has expanded its operations throughout the northern states of Rajasthan, Haryana, Bihar, Punjab and Madhya Pradesh and currently has licensed 146 Village Information Kiosks.

Drishtee is based on a tiered-franchise model that enables the establishment of Village Kiosks that are owned and managed by local villagers. This model ensures the scalability of the franchises throughout different districts, fosters rural entrepreneurship and facilitates the provision of ICT-enabled services to underserved areas in the country. Kiosk owners offer for a fee, a wide variety of customized e-government services - filing grievances, land records, drivers' licenses etc. - and some Village Kiosks also offer private services such as computer training, insurance and internet access for email and web browsing. Users access Drishtee services via customized software that requires minimum data entry and is localized in the Hindi language. Drishtee's franchise mechanism is designed to give Kiosk owners the flexibility to adopt those services that better suit the needs of the communities they are serving.

Kiosks are strategically located within the range of 20-30 villages (between 20,000-30,000 people) in order to have a large enough serviceable market for Kiosk owners to provide services at affordable prices. This strategy establishes a context where Kiosks have a better chance to achieve financial sustainability by selling services to a bigger market. The Village Kiosks are connected through an intranet to the District Offices (DOs) that are responsible for processing the requests for e-government services that come from the Kiosks and for administering the kiosks under their umbrella.

The DOs are then connected to Drishtee Headquarters, which oversees operations of the entire network and develops strategic alliances with government, private and non-governmental organizations to increase the basket of services available to Kiosk Owners.

Drishtee Village Information Kiosks are a marquee example of an ICT-led development initiative based on market principles and strategic partnerships with the government, private sector and non-governmental organizations. The continued success of this model will lay on the ability of Drishtee to further increase the basket of services available in Kiosks, the level of efficiency at which District Offices can process the requests from Kiosk users, and the extent to which Drishtee addresses the problem of unreliable electricity that is affecting the performance of Village Kiosks in some areas.

Socio-Economic Impacts

Drishtee Village Information Kiosks are expected to empower rural villagers by:

- Expanding networking infrastructure and access to services and information in underserved areas;
- Strengthening the rural economy by creating employment and income opportunities;
- Reducing bribery and corruption through the provision of e-government services, fostering transparency and good governance;
- Bypassing brokers and middlemen by offering alternative providers to different services;
- Promoting the use of IT as a tool for education;
- Increasing rural household savings by reducing travel expenses to government offices;
- Nourishing rural entrepreneurship and a new generation of IT-literates.

Sustainability Model

At the organizational level, Drishtee has a 3-tiered structure. At the top is the Drishtee Dot Com Ltd. as Corporate Office that manages the Drishtee Regional Offices (DOs) and oversees all the operations. Each District has one Drishtee Regional Office, usually located at District Headquarters. At the village level are the Kiosk Operators/Kiosk Owners (KOs) who actually operate the kiosk and sell services to the customers/villagers. The employees at Drishtee Corporate Office and Drishtee Regional Offices are employees of Drishtee Dot Com Ltd. The Kiosk Owners are independent franchisees/ entrepreneurs.

Drishtee is designed as a tiered-franchise model aimed at expanding networking capabilities to rural areas through the establishment of Village Kiosks that are owned and managed by local entrepreneurs at a license fee. Kiosk owners are identified locally and they are required to be educated at least to high school level and demonstrate entrepreneurial skills. This franchiser/ franchisee partnership establishes the following responsibilities for both parties:

1) The Role of the Franchisee
- A Village Kiosk requires and initial investment of approximately 1,526 USD (70,000 INR), which includes a one time Drishtee's license fee (200 USD), equipment, furniture and stationary. The owner is responsible for baring this investment and the subsequent operational monthly costs of the Kiosk (approximately 45 USD) including phone and electricity bills, equipment maintenance, and continuous advertising of Kiosk's services;
- From the monthly revenues generated by Drishtee services, the Kiosk owners keep eighty percent while Drishtee receives the twenty percent left. Kiosks are expected to become profitable after the 10th month of operation;
- Kiosk owners need to be knowledgeable of the market they are serving in order to provide those services that they deem locally relevant for the community and can contribute to the financial sustainability of the Kiosk.

2) The Role of Drishtee
- The license guarantees to the franchisee access to a wide selection of e-government services that are enabled through Drishtee's intranet and the efficient processing of the requests by the users at Drishtee's District Office;
- Governmental services available through Drishtee are: public grievances, certificates, land records, loan applications, pension applications, driving licenses, auction centers for agricultural products and matrimonials;
- Private services that are continuously being integrated into the basket are: computer training, career guidance, insurance policies, microfinance schemes, adult education, etc;
- Drishtee also provides a three-week computer and business management training and offers support to Kiosk owners for identifying different loan schemes provided by the government of India and State governments;
- In order to increase the chances for sustainability of the Kiosk, Drishtee is responsible for ensuring that the market it will serve comprises between 25-30 villages (between 20,000-30,000 people).

Technology Infrastructure
Three nodes form the hardware backbone that supports Drishtee's intranet:
- The Web server that acts as the network management and main administrator of the entire system coordinates communication between districts and kiosks and acts as a content provider at a national level;
- The District Server, which is responsible for providing the local content, relevant data and for processing the requests of local kiosks;
- The Village Kiosks that have a dialup connection through local exchanges, on optical fiber, or UHF links - depending on the area - and use a database

that is updated every time that the Kiosk is connected to the district or web server. The intranet allows Kiosks to connect to Drishtee servers but it does not allow access to the Internet. If Kiosk owners are interested in obtaining Internet access they have to contract an Internet Service Provider.

Drishtee uses customized software that facilitates access to e-government and private services. The software developed by Drishtee it's a very simple menu-driven application that uses LINUX as its operating system, MySQL and PHP as the programming language. The program requires minimal data entry and the user interface is in the Hindi language.

On average each Kiosk is equipped with 1 or more Windows-based PC computers with MS Office, one printer, 28 or 56 kbps modem, Intranet dial-up connection, photocopier, a back up battery for electrical outages, furniture and stationary. Depending on the village, some kiosks have more sophisticated equipment such as digital cameras, scanners, electric generators and Cable TV (the latter is available only in the district of Jaipur, Rajasthan).

Partnerships
Drishtee is building upon its platform by establishing relationships with partners to offer e-commerce, e-education, research and BPO products/services in their kiosks. In order to accomplish this task Drishtee has been taking active steps to increase kiosk revenues and establish new business relationships. This is important not only to foster long-term financial sustainability for individual kiosks, but also to provide Drishtee with the ability to expand operations into new areas and to recruit high quality kiosk operators.

Government
It is a focal point for Drishtee's strategy to bring government services to rural villages. Government officials receive computer training from Drishtee and they are responsible for understanding the proposed system and for making necessary modifications in government-based processes in order to respond efficiently to villagers' requests. There is no extra financial remuneration for local governments but the common understanding that by integrating ICT to government services will improve efficiency and good governance.

Non Governmental Organizations
- SRISTI: an NGO that promotes environmental information and eco-friendly solutions in local languages. Through this partnership SRISTI will provide content to the Village Kiosks on environmental and biodiversity issues that is relevant to the local communities.

- Digital Partners: an NGO based in Seattle, WA provides Drishtee with financial support, loan executive services and strategic planning to help it expand and diversify its operations and services.

- Grameen Technology Center (GTC): Drishtee is partnering with GTC and Asa (a Grameen Microcredit Organization) in Tamil Nadu State to set up similar kiosks there.

Private Sector
- Aksh Optic Fibers Ltd: Aksh has setup an optic fiber network in Jaipur district through which they provide cable TV and Internet connectivity to Kiosk owners who then sell it to villagers. So, Kiosks are able to connect over this optic fiber network to the Drishtee servers and services.

- Max New York Life: Drishtee has executed an agreement with Max New York Life to act as a corporate agent and offer life insurance policies through their kiosk operations, providing MNYL with rural penetration

- Mahindra & Mahindra: Drishtee is working on an agreement with Mahindra & Mahindra to canvass tractors and jeeps through kiosks. Kiosk owners will be paid for generating leads, and thus connecting potential customers with dealers for these items. Drishtee and Mahindra & Mahindra are in the midst of deciding which states the model should be established in, as well as negotiating commission rates to be paid to kiosk owners.

- ICICI Bank: Drishtee and ICICI are in the process of signing a MoU where ICICI credit card payment services, loans, micro-finance and other financial services will be offered through Drishtee kiosks. ICICI is also interested in providing loans to finance the opening of individual kiosks.

Lessons from the Field
Field research was conducted on 25 Village Information Kiosks during the period of 3 months (April - June 2003) and it entailed interviews to Drishtee managers and Kiosk owners, surveys to 30 Kiosks' users and site visits.[1] From the data gathered in this research the following are the key findings:

Financial Sustainability
- The top revenue streams for the Kiosks are government-related services. On average, the most popular services requested by clients are filling grievances, applying for certificates, driver's licenses and, in some Kiosks, gun licenses as well. Non-government related services that contribute, although to a lesser extent, to the monthly revenue of the Kiosks are rent of computers, photocopying, photos for passports and email.

- The majority of Kiosk owners did awareness campaigns to advertise the Kiosks in the surrounding villages and continuously publicize new Drishtee services that are made available. The investment in publicity campaigns ranged from 50-218 USD (350-10,000 INR).[2]

- To date all the Village Kiosks surveyed have not yet met projected revenues but owners have high expectations to achieve the target of 218 USD per month (10,000 INR) that would ensure the sustainability of the Kiosks, particularly so if new Drishtee services are provided.

- The revenue of the Kiosks is highly influenced by the quality of services and the support provided by Drishtee District Offices (DO). This includes response times to clients' requests, skills enhancement and staff training. Some Kiosk owners surveyed in the districts of Jaipur and Morena face inefficient service response and poor support from Drishtee DO and are concerned about loosing clients.

- Even though the majority of Drishtee Kiosks have not yet met the revenue target of 218 USD per month to become financially sustainable the model has the potential of achieving such target if Drishtee addresses some of the challenges being faced by Kiosk owners.

Technology
- Almost all Drishtee Kiosks have dial up connections (28kbps - 56kbps) that links them to the District Server. Kiosk owners reported not having major connectivity problems with the server with some rare exceptions where the dial out time was 10-15 minutes to get connected.

- Close to sixty per cent of Kiosks offer Internet access as in a cyber café, which provides additional revenues for Kiosks owners.

- The major technological challenges for the Village Kiosks are electrical outages. All Kiosk owners interviewed, without exception, expressed frustration regarding the unreliability of electricity. In the district of Madhubani State of Bihar, for example, electrical outages last on average 19-23 hours. This could have a direct impact on the future sustainability of Kiosks in that area. The majority of Kiosks have UPS batteries that last around 6 hours and very few own electrical generators. An additional investment of 207 USD (9,500 INR) would be necessary in order to acquire a generator, imposing a higher debt-burden on Kiosk owners.

- Drishtee must consider the need to develop a partnership with a company that could sell electrical generators at bulk price, relieving part of the debt bared by owners and ensuring that electrical outages would not have a major effect in the sustainability of the Kiosk.

The Community
- The major benefits perceived by the people using Drishtee services were savings in time, money and income, since people would not need to take a

day off from their jobs to travel to district offices. In addition timely processing of their requests to the government seemed to be a strong incentive for people to keep using Drishtee Kiosks.

For example, in a small village called Kalawali in Sirsa district of Haryana, a contract farmer by the name of Biker Singh was interviewed. He grows sugarcane for the government's sugar factory and had filed a grievance through the Kiosk as the crop was not being cut and taken by government even after crop was ready. He received a response within 3 days and the government paid him the agreed amount for his crop. If he had tried directly at the District Office, his complaint would not have been heard.

- The educational level for interviewees ranged from Std 10 to Bachelors degree with the exception of one illiterate woman who approached the Kiosk to obtain a land record.

Scalability/Replicability
The model used by Drishtee, albeit with some limitations, contains unique elements that under the appropriate circumstances could be replicated in different countries:

- Conceiving Drishtee Village Kiosks as a social for-profit enterprise with the possibility of achieving financial sustainability is an important element that should be considered for other similar initiatives. For-profit models can foster entrepreneurship and management skills in rural areas without the burden of relying on national or foreign donors to sustain the Kiosk.

- Another interesting aspect of Drishtee's model is that local market demand determines the number and quality of services that each Kiosk provides. Demand-driven Information Kiosks provide basic services at the start-up phase and increase services in response to the demand of the local market.

- Tiered-franchising is actually being used in some countries with certain degree of success and Infocentros in El Salvador and RCP (Red Cientifica Peruana) in Peru are marquee examples of initiatives of this sort. Franchises required, however, sophisticated management from the central hub in order to ensure the efficient provision of services to Kiosks. In addition, there needs to be continuous effort to increase and diversify the basket of services available for Kiosk Owners.

- Becoming the bridge between the government and citizens living in remote areas is probably one of the most appealing elements of Drishtee's model. We perceive this as a win-win situation where villagers benefit from faster responses and time savings and government officials are incentive to provide efficient services and foster good governance.

- Developing a network of partnerships with different actors is another key element for the financial sustainability of Kiosks. Drishtee has created a diverse set of strategic alliances with government, private and NGO sector in order to ensure the expansion of Kiosks to other regions in India and, most importantly, to offer a wide variety of services that Kiosks Owners can provide depending on their market demand.

Limitations of the Model

- High dependency on government-based services is one of the major constrains that Drishtee is facing. In fact, more than 80% of the network-based online revenue is coming from the services offered by block or district Government offices. Drishtee has been able to move faster in states and districts which are IT aware and which have dynamic decision makers.

- Connectivity has become a major constraint for the vertical spread of Drishtee within a district. There are kiosks in "Sirsa", for example, that have not received promised telephone connections even after 6 months of operation.

- Market segmentation[3] and the right service mix for each segment of village population still eludes Drishtee. Present services are largely focused on landed farmers and there is little to offer for other segments like women, children elderly people and the landless/artisans. If Drishtee has to reach anywhere close to its assigned revenue target of 218 USD (10,000 INR) per month it needs to expand and diversify its basket of services to include those in fields such as health, education, entertainment and employment to name a few.

Other Initiatives in the Country

e-Choupal: established by the Indian Tobacco Company (ITC) to facilitate trading and market information of agricultural products. (http://www.echoupal.com)

n-logue: established by TeNet Group of the Indian Institute of Technology (IIT) in Madras and uses wireless technology (corDECT) to bring connectivity and information access to rural India. (http://www.n-logue.co.in)

TaraHAAT: combines a mother portal supported by franchised networks of village cybercafes to provide a full range of services to its clients. (http://tarahaat.com)

Website and Contact Information

Drishtee: Connecting India village by village
http://www.drishtee.com

Mr. Satyan Mishra, CEO
satyan@drishtee.com

Mr. Rishabh Sinha, Sr Manager
rishabh@drishtee.com

Notes

1. Field Research and Data Analysis: Catalyst-Social Development Consultants Pvt. Ltd with support from Intel Research and Digital Partners.

2. US Dollar = 45.88 Indian rupees

3. Drishtee website: www.drishtee.com

INDIA

University-Based Village Telecenters

Royal D. Colle and Raul Roman
Cornell University

Project Summary

The Tamil Nadu University of Veterinary and Animal Sciences (TANUVAS) recognized the importance of broadening its range of tools for transferring technology to the rural areas of the State. It further recognized the importance of reaching low-income people - especially women for whom small-scale economic enterprises are important to the welfare of their families. TANUVAS used existing institutional resources - its off-campus University Training and Research Centers (UTRC) and community-based self-help groups (SHGs) to establish a Village Information System (VIS) that would have strong university-related information and communication resources to support its operations. The core of the scheme consists of village information centers created as extensions of the UTRC hub.

Socio-Economic Impacts

In one district of Tamil Nadu, the Dhan Foundation established information kiosks in 40 villages and these were interconnected through Internet and wireless technology. The kiosk operators of nearby villages send veterinary queries to one of the TANUVAS VICs, which is managed by two veterinarians. In October 2002 one of the kiosk managers sent an e-mail message to the VIC (the nearest phone to the kiosk was 2 kilometers distant) indicating that several sheep had died and hundreds were sick. With technical support from the UTRC hub, the immediate problem was solved, and the Animal Husbandry Department of the District was alerted, and it arranged for the vaccination of other healthy sheep. It was an example of partnerships, cooperation and timely communication that saved sheep valued at some Rs 623,000 (USD 1385).

The introduction of modern ICT resources such as the phone, audio and video recordings, computers and the Internet has had a variety of individual impacts that are revealed in anecdotes such as the one above concerning women's new micro-enterprises. Other signs of socio-economic impact include the increase in computer literacy - where previously information access was something beyond the reach of villagers, now it has become part of their daily life. More than 150 men, women and youth in the three villages have created their own e-mail ID and have started communicating.

Likewise, TANUVAS reports that women who accessed computers, the Internet, digital cameras, and other ICT resources are gaining new respect by their husbands, the local community, and local government authorities for their newly obtained ICT skills. In addition there is a "mind shift" among all women in the community who now incorporate communication as part of their thinking about economic empowerment.

Sustainability Model

The project has two principal dimensions. One is the establishment of a team of people within its UTRCs who serve as "hub" to support the Village Information Center (VIC); the other consists of SHGs who represent a further extension of the hub. The hub part of the project started with a grant from Canada's International Development Research Center (IDRC); UNESCO supported the SHG extension. Communities contributed by supplying volunteers and locations for the VIC. In addition, SHG women provided their households as locations where other women could come to access ICTs. TANUVAS and various state and local agencies contributed information resources and services to the system as part of their on-going responsibilities to the public.

Steering committees at each VIC site were vested with the responsibility of regulating the activities of the Center. One of these responsibilities is approving rates for the use of the information and communication facilities. For example, typical rates are Internet browsing - Rupees 20 (approximately USD .50, e-mail sending/receiving - Rs. 10, VIC membership fee - Rs. 50 for the first 6 months and Rs 20 for each 6 months renewal. In one community where poverty restricted people's ability to pay, the payment of fees for some services was relaxed (resulting in a considerable increase in the number of persons who came for browsing and mailing).

Technology Infrastructure

Each VIC has a collection of ICT hardware including a telephone, a computer, and software based on the local information needs (as determined through field research) and in the local language. In addition, each has a library with books, Tamil daily newspapers, and magazines.

Partnerships

The driving force of the VIC and SHG components of the TANUVAS project were the studies of the communities' information and communications needs. These involved a number of intersecting partnerships. Included among the participants were the TANUVAS administrative team, the UTRC field staff, representatives of the M.S. Swaminathan Research Foundation, the University of Madras, and

Cornell University (USA), and the VIC steering committees. In addition, a major agricultural enterprise in India, EID Parry, which "franchises" a group of telecenters, joined the project through sharing its Wireless in Local Loop Technology.

There continue to be other partnerships as the hub personnel support the VICs in obtaining quality information for the communities. For example, one group of women wanted training in several specialty skills. Through the VIC, training programs were arranged for them with the help of the community polytechnic scheme of the Thanthai Periyar Government Polytechnic. After completion of the courses the trained women started a beauty parlor, a screen printing operation and tailoring and have started to earn money through these small enterprises. Similarly information was collected from the local government's line staff and was made available through electronic and non-electronic media in the VIC.

Lessons from the Field
Several major lessons emerge from the Tamil Nadu experience:

- The central role played by the Tamil Nadu University of Veterinary and Animal Sciences demonstrates the vital and practical role a university can play as a catalyst and supporting partner in establishing and sustaining a community information system that focuses especially on the welfare and development of the community. The university motivated and worked with local people who mobilized the community human and physical resources. The University was instrumental in conducting initial needs analysis studies upon which a service agenda could be built. The University also advised on management issues, and provided relevant training to people in the community. The University helped the VICs make contacts and build partnerships with other organizations that could support services wanted and needed by the community. The TANUVAS involvement in this information and communication technology for development activity presents a model for universities in other regions of the world to study and adapt to their own circumstances.

- Awareness is a vital element in the start-up of a local communication enter-prise. Villagers in Tamil Nadu needed to be motivated and persuaded to try out the telecenter. In one case, a VIC organized two "animal camps" to popularize the VIC and build rapport with the community. The veterinarians from the UTRC and the local government veterinary dispensary treated 422 animals and 143 birds, and 48 additional cows for infertility. In the process the VIC became visible as a place where people could deal with pressing needs.

- The TANUVAS program confirmed the importance of involving women in the New Information Society. During its first year of operation, women were not using the VICs very much. The lesson is that, for some groups, special efforts need to be undertaken in order to have a telecenter be inclusive in its attempt to meet community information and communication needs. This realization led to the component in which ICT facilities were made available in SHG households, where women would feel safe and comfortable in learning about ICTs and their values, and where they became more self-confident women molded from illiterate women.

Financial Sustainability

The three centers established with the assistance of IDRC and TANUVAS became financially independent in July 2003. TANUVAS entered into a Memorandum of Understanding with each community in which the community agrees to maintain its center. However, the TANUVAS system (the UTRC and the university itself) continues to provide information and service support for the centers as part of its institutionalized rural development mission. TANUVAS learned that a vital element in a strategy to build sustainability is the strong commitment to systematic and participatory needs analysis matched by resourcefulness in meeting those needs. With credible knowledge of the communities' needs, partnerships can be orchestrated with organizations that already have missions related to those needs. This reduces the cost of a telecenter reinventing these existing services. A second vital element is building awareness. The TANUVAS plan included animal camps, various kinds of competitions for youth, and other activities that would bring people into contact with the VIC. This rapport building resulted in an atmosphere in which most people were willing to pay for information and communication services at the VIC - although early research in the communities (prior to the VIC) revealed a reluctance to do so.

Technology

The experience in Tamil Nadu reinforces the idea that telecenters are more than computers and electronic networks. While connectivity to the world beyond the village is very important, a significant service is provided to the community through the availability of information and training materials in a variety of media and formats. These include the phone, CDs, video cassettes, and audio cassettes. The project leaders also built into the information, "technology" printed materials such as daily newspapers, magazines, books and other publications - which, like the games that were made available, induced people to come regularly to the telecenter. The lesson is not about the importance of the Internet, but about the necessity of observing, studying, and analyzing the human environment to see what media most respond to the needs of the community.

The Community

Steering committees bring a sense of community ownership to the VIC. In the TANUVAS effort, steering committees formed with a variety of members. These included a local development worker, a retired military officer, unemployed youth, largescale farmers and smallscale farmers, public call office (telephone) owner, student, SHG representative, village school teacher, village panchayat (government) officers, veterinary assistant surgeon, and a bank manager. Having steering committees that represented a broad spectrum of the community helped give the VIC visibility across a similar spectrum of the local population. This helped the VICs' managers to gain guidance that would make the VIC relevant to the community. Involving a steering committee from the planning stage made the transfer of the VIC to the local community a relatively easy transition.

Scalability/Replicability
The TANUVAS project suggests that using already established institutions such as universities and natural units such as Self-Help Groups is a feasible strategy. Where such entities exist (e.g., most Chinese provinces have at least one major agricultural university), the experience in Tamil Nadu can potentially be replicated.

Limitations of The Model
The main issue is to involve university leadership to endorse the development-oriented initiative that has been described in this case study. Universities do not have a reward system that factors in this kind of outreach activity. Therefore, unless there is top leadership support, the lower levels of university administration may resist this type of innovation. The TANUVAS project was carried out because the Vice-Chancellor of the University, and other influential personnel, provided institutional support right from the beginning.

Other Initiatives in the Country
A wide range of organizations in India have become involved in the establishment of telecenters or the more narrowly focused information kiosks. EID Parry Ltd has created what it calls Parry's Corners, privately operated computer and Internet facilities in agricultural areas in Tamil Nadu. The efforts of the M.S. Swaminathan Research Foundation are widely known, especially in relation to its innovative efforts at Pondicherry. Also in South India is SARI, a joint project of the Harvard University, the Massachusetts Institute of Technology, the Indian Institute of Technology at Chennai and others, establishing many information kiosks throughout Tamil Nadu and nearby areas. The Dhan Foundation (mentioned earlier) is also a prominent actor. Other organizations in India active in this and related fields are mentioned in other documents in this collection of case studies.

Website and Contact Information
Tanuvas
http://www.tanuvas.com

Dr. F. R. Sheriff, Project Director
sheriff@md4.vsnl.net

Raul Roman, Project Research Coordinator
rr66@cornell.edu

Royal D. Colle, Project Consultant
rdc4@cornell.edu

INDIA

n-Logue:
The Entrepreneurial Information Kiosks

Osama Manzar*
Digital Empowerment Foundation

Project Summary

India has the world's second largest population and one of the highest numbers of English speakers, which is still only 5 per cent of the total population of the country. India has more than 18 languages spoken by more than 80 per cent of Indians as their language of preference. More than 75 per cent Indians are naturally oral and not written, meaning they would impart and gather all the information orally but would be largely illiterate if it comes to reading and writing. India also has the highest population of youth; about 30 per cent of the Indians are young by category. For more than a billion people, India has less than 40 million telephone connection and barely 3 million Internet connections.

In contrast, India exports more than USD 8 billion worth of software services. India has the highest number of ICT for Development deployments in the world among the developing and under-developed nations. Among the fraternity of NGO granters, and social investors, India is at the top of recipients.

As matter of assessment, India is considered to be potentially the most viable country for ICT deployment, and putting all kind of efforts to bring the 80 per cent Indians on the map of information society.

Incidentally, born out of the technology developed by Indian Institute of Technology Madras, n-Logue Communication Pvt. Ltd. is an answer to India's humongous problem of connecting more than 400 million people with sustainability and economic scalability having majority of daily need services through integrated information kiosks.

Socio-Economic Impacts

Imagine an illiterate farmer in rural India talking to his son in Mumbai over a video conferencing session from the local village Internet kiosk. Imagine him using the same facility to consult an agricultural expert at the local university on protecting his vegetable crop from pests or getting advice on crop rotation. Further still imagine

*The author is indebted by PG Ponnapa, the project director of n-Logue for his immense contribution in providing information as close to the format as was required.

him getting proof of ownership of his landholding from the government database through the same village Internet kiosk, which will enable him to secure a loan. Consider any stakeholder having a multi-party video conferencing with a large number of village kiosks for faster and better information dissemination. While this was a pipe dream just a couple of years ago, all these are happening today in various parts of rural India, on account of a unique and remarkable project being executed by n-Logue Communications (P) Ltd.

Villagers are already experiencing the powerful impact that n-Logue's village Internet kiosks is having on their lives. However current offerings are only a fraction of what the digital rural platform can really offer. They will soon be able to have their pressure, temperature, ECG readings and stethoscope readings taken, and relayed using a special device. This will enhance the value of remote medical consultation with experts. They will soon be able to withdraw money from their "virtual bank account" deposited by relatives through a low cost rural ATM at the kiosk. Village events can be recorded and uploaded at the village kiosk and relayed as local news. Many more ideas are being devised, leveraging this unique platform to reach a market of 150 m. This will make it a truly powerful digital platform in the future.

Partnerships

n-Logue is uniquely positioned to tap the large rural market for Internet and Telephony, which is not being addressed by any other service provider. Nearly 76 per cent of the Indian population lives in rural areas but only about 1.4 per cent has telephone connectivity. With over 650,000 villages in India, the untouched market for connectivity exceeds 350 m people. Rural markets represent a large untapped opportunity but are challenging and have high entry barriers.

There are multiple and complex tasks involved which include: selection of LSP (Local Service Provider) partners and handholding them, procuring project finance, creating and driving applications, educating villagers, marketing the concept at the village level, tying up alliance partnerships for software, applications and content (in local languages) and securing partnerships with government institutions and corporate for basic services that can be delivered remotely using the platform. N-Logue has managed to successfully put together this "rural jigsaw puzzle" to effectively deliver services. It has already demonstrated in its initial markets over the past 2 years that it can successfully build a business in these "low revenue" areas.

"The key reasons for n-Logue's success are a unique combination of its founders, the Telecom and Computer Networking (TeNET) group of IIT[1] Madras, the choice of suitable technology, the focus of the organization, a proven business model and the core team," claim the industry experts. n-Logue leverages the strength of the TeNET group, IIT Madras and offerings of different companies incubated by the TeNET group in delivering a very cost effective solution for rural communication, and developing new rural applications.

n-Logue has access to the R&D of TeNET as well as all other TeNET companies. One of the benefits was corDECT, the low cost telephony and Internet combo solution selected by n-Logue, which has now come to be regarded as the most cost effective rural communication solution. Thirdly, the organization stays focused exclusively on the rural markets (i.e., markets outside the top 150 cities and towns) abiding by its motto "To think and act rural". Fourthly, n-Logue has devised a "cost effective, rural market attuned" business model to fulfill its mission. The fact that it leverages local entrepreneurship not only allows n-Logue to share project risks but also increases the chance of success significantly.

Lastly, n-Logue has managed to build a committed core management team, which has been together for the past two years executing the project, and have tremendous professional experience in the corporate sector. This ensures that the efforts of n-Logue, though in the social sector, should be professional and sustainable. These advantages can't be replicated easily and n-Logue will continue to remain a unique service provider company.

Technological Innovation

n-Logue was born with the belief that the rural market for telephony and Internet provides a large opportunity with no service providers (telecom or Internet) focusing on this market, given the challenges. The Telecom and Computer networking group (TeNET) of IIT Madras founded n-Logue in 2000 to fulfill the needs of this market.

The TeNET group is focused on providing and enabling communication technologies and applications to help create and drive rural micro-enterprises. Micro enterprises need three key elements - finance, information, and the ability to transact. Village folk are today able to apply for micro-finance over local kiosks. They have access to prices of commodities in nearby markets to make optimal decisions. In a recent development, kiosk operators are using credit cards to allow village folk to purchase online. The TeNET group strongly believes that these factors will act as catalyst in doubling rural per capita GDP to about USD 400 from present levels, creating greater disposable incomes and improving quality of life.

Sustainability Model

n-Logue's business model has been inspired by the success of long distance Public Call Offices (PCO) model and the Cable TV Operator models in India. The 950,000 PCOs, which are roadside booths offering telephony services, account for about 25 per cent of the total fixed line telephony income in India. The success of these ventures proved that demand aggregation, a "basket of services" approach and local entrepreneurship could combine to make a rural Internet cum telephony kiosk operationally viable. These principles are the foundations of n-Logue's approach.

n-Logue leverages local entrepreneurship and resources at two levels - the Taluk level (county) and the village level. At the Taluk level, n-Logue partners a local service provider (LSP), who co-invests in an access center[2] that can provide about 500 - 1000 Internet/telephone connections. Each LSP provides Internet connections to subscribers over an area of 3000 sq. km (radius of 30 km). On an average, the coverage would include 2-5 small towns and about 400 villages. The LSP, typically a local entrepreneur, is a project partner to n-Logue and shares the risks (investment) and rewards of the project.

At the village level, the LSP enrolls kiosk operators, who provide telephone, Internet and a host of other services to the end customers - the village population. Each kiosk operator invests about Rs. 50,000 (USD 1,000) in kiosk infrastructure, which includes a corDECT subscriber terminal, Pentium/Celeron PC with a color monitor and multi-media, a webcam, power back up, local language software, relevant applications and a printer.

n-Logue's investment requirements are very modular in nature - i.e., the investment model comprises of a series of access centers that can exist independently and become viable. The total investment per access center is about Rs. 4.2 m (USD 87,500) which includes corDECT hardware, software, base station and repeater towers and also implementation and service launch related expenditure. The investment is phased out over 2 years and is shared by the LSP partner.

In this model, n-Logue breaks even once about 10,000 kiosk operators are fully functional, which could be easily achieved with about 50 to 75 LSP projects. Each LSP breaks even once it has about 150 kiosks or connections, each contributing revenues of Rs. 750 - 1000 per month (USD 15 - 20). The kiosk operator breaks even at about Rs. 2500 per month (USD 50). Salient achievements of the project, as of today, are as follows:

- n-Logue was well placed to complete 24 LSP projects by August 2003. As of May 2003, 13 projects were live.

- A total of 500 kiosk operators are functional and the monthly ramp up is exponentially increasing. n-Logue's immediate target is to reach 10,000 kiosks, within the next 12- 15 months.

- Presently over 30 per cent of kiosks already earning over Rs 2000/ (USD 40) per month. The highest monthly earnings recorded were Rs 10,000/ (USD 200) in a month in May 03 at a kiosk in Tamil Nadu.

- Over 70 per cent kiosks are heading towards break even in a 6-9 month period of going live.

Scalability and Replicability

The pilot project was initiated under the name SARI (Sustainable Access to Rural India) and had four partners - IIT Madras, MIT Media Lab USA / Media Lab Asia, Harvard University CED (Center for Entrepreneurship Development), and I-Gyan Foundation. The project initiated in Madurai District in Tamil Nadu and went live in November 2001. The project presently has over 80 villages with Internet kiosks within a small geography, which is the highest density of rural Internet kiosks anywhere in the world. The Tamil Nadu state government approved and committed to extend the project across the state.

The pilot demonstrated the powerful impact of the Internet and PC based services on the lives of villagers and more importantly, that villagers are willing to pay for these services. The success achieved by n-Logue in the last 2 years has brought significant recognition and support for the project. n-Logue has won key clients and struck a number of partnerships and alliances.

There has been significant support from the Central Government. The Rural Development Ministry plans to cover kiosk loans under specific schemes with small subsidies. The IT Ministry has plans to aid LSP infrastructure roll out and the Agricultural Ministry has committed buying time for agricultural extension.

Recently, the National Institute of Agricultural Extension Management (MANAGE), an autonomous agency under the Ministry of Agriculture, Government of India, provided a grant for a LSP project in Maharashtra. Based on the success of the same it has committed to expand the project scope to cover 28 other districts.

Many State governments are getting into the act having seen initial success stories. The Tamil Nadu government has announced a project "RASI" (Rural Access to Services through the Internet) in which it plans to cover every village in 10 notified Districts in 2 years. In May 2003, the Gujarat government sanctioned a grant of Rs. 22.5 m (USD 500,000) to part fund 15 LSP projects across 15 districts. Other states that have indicated interest in the project include Haryana, Rajasthan, Punjab, Madhya Pradesh, Karnataka, Andhra Pradesh and Jharkhand.

Acceptance by Financial Institutions

Convinced with the viability of the project, kiosk loans have been cleared by various financial institutions such as the State Bank of India - India's largest bank with a branch network that covers over 9000 branches. Other banks such as ICICI Bank, Indian Bank, UCO Bank and NABARD have also approved project loans. ICICI Bank has also finalized equity investment in n-Logue for Phase 1 of the project. The USAID is sponsoring 50 kiosks in Rajasthan and plans to extend the scope of support after evaluating success.

Investments and ROIs

The key advantage is that n-Logue's investment requirements are modular. Hence the total project has been divided into 3 phases:

Phase 1: This will cover a total of 50 new LSP projects. USD 1.9 m of 2 million project funding for the Phase 1 growth has already been tied up from different sources through a mix of equity, government grants and debt.

Phase 2: This will cover 500 new LSP projects in the states of Gujarat, Karnataka, Rajasthan, Punjab, Haryana and Andhra Pradesh. Phase 2 will span 2004 - 2006. The net investment requirement during phase 2 is estimated at USD 20 m, which will be financed through a combination of debt and equity.

Phase 3: This will cover implementing about 600 more LSP projects in the remaining states during 2006 - 2008. The net investment requirement in this phase will be financed through a mix of debt and internal accruals.

n-Logue is seeking to raise USD 5 m of equity to bridge Phase 1 deficit and part of Phase 2.

The uniqueness of n-Logue's business model is that after the project execution phase, or once this phase is stopped, significant costs taper off. Post this phase, operating margins and net margins are very attractive as the revenue stream is fairly steady and growing without any significant further investment in marketing.

Website and Contact Information

n-Logue
http://www.n-logue.co.in/

Prof. Ashok Jhunjhunwala
ashok@tenet.res.in

Related Website: http://www.tenet.res.in/nlogue.html

Notes

1. Indian Institute of Technology is among Asia's top 10 Engineering Institutes. The TeNET Group is India's leading telecom research hub. It consists of a group of 15 professors.

2. Access Center - The switch and base station infrastructure of the corDECT system, which can provide last mile wireless connectivity to 1000 independent subscribers over.

INDONESIA

Apwkomitel: Future Community Warnet - MCI Center

Rudi Rusdiah
APWKomitel (Indonesian Association of Community Internet Center or Warnet)

Project Summary

The Vision of APWKomitel is the successful running of MCI (Multipurpose Community Internet) in Indonesia. A cyber café in Indonesia is called a Warung Internet (Warnet). Warnets are mostly SME (Small and Medium Enterprises) owned and entirely financed by the private sectors.

In Indonesia, 4,000 Warnets are responsible for 42 per cent of Internet access. Warnets are scattered in cities across the giant archipelago. Statistics say that until 2002, Indonesian Internet users were around 4.4 million, while Internet subscribers were only 500,000 - about 8.8 users sharing 1 Internet subscriber line.

Most of the Internet users share public Internet access facilities such as Warnets. Majority of the society in Indonesia cannot afford to buy PCs at home thus sharing pubic facilities becomes the only way to have access to the global Internet society.

The mission of the MCI Centers is to provide value-added services beyond ordinary Internet services, such as e-mail, chat, browsing to serve the community. It is strongly assumed that by providing value-added services, the MCI Centers will have sustainable and long-term effects compared to traditional cyber cafés.

Unlike many such initiatives across the world, where the approach is always top down - financing and facilitation usually coming from donors, governments, incumbents or a combination of these, the approach in the case of Indonesia's MCIs is unique and simple. By empowering existing SME and Warnet, which were already in place and operating in the market and society, it is a not top-down but a grassroots approach, from community to community.

Socio Economic Impacts

APWKomitel MCI Center (Warnet) provides a range of services, which can be classified as social, economic and commercial services. Some of them are:

- Extending public Internet access to serve people with no computer or Internet access at home;

- Providing value-addition to small and medium businesses in the community, strengthening the economy by creating employment and business opportunities;

- With the support of the Ministry of Industry and Trade, setting up of Warsi (Warung Informasi or Information Center) near small traditional industry clusters;

- Providing Internet access and literacy to the small businesses in the community and cluster;

- Promoting the products and services beyond local and traditional markets, to global and national reach;

- With Open University and OSOL, programs to promote the use of IT as a tool for education;

- Providing tourists, travelers and commuters with Internet access.

Sustainability Model

Since the grassroots approach is using Warnets that are already in operation in the market, the need to enhance these Warnets using MCI Centers is very crucial.

Warnet Association (APWKomitel) internally will provide the platform for collaboration among members. Externally, it will facilitate communication with the Government and players in the telecommunication supply chain as per institutional framework.

The MCI Center is simply providing multipurpose value-added Internet services to the community. Previously, with any traditional cyber café or Warnet, the services were usually limited to traditional Internet services such as Internet access, e-mail, chatting, browsing.

Technology Infrastructure

Negotiations with the government are underway, where proposals are in the pipeline for special tariff rates for members who provide public Internet access to the community for educational purposes and other community services.

Issues of SLA (Service Level Agreement) are very important, because sometimes the bandwidth supplied to the members do not meet the level that was previously offered. With non-standard level of bandwidth, it is difficult to provide value-added services to the community, especially with application such as VoIP (Voice Over Internet Protocol), Video Conferencing (VC) for distant learning etc.

In rural areas where there is no telecommunications infrastructure, outdoor Wireless LAN (WLAN) is simple and affordable technology. To share bandwidth for public Internet access in urban and rural areas, this technology could prove to be very economical.

Satellite footprint covers the whole Indonesia, but most Warnets cannot afford to have their own VSAT. An interesting cooperative model is in Makassar, a remote capital city in the Sulawesi Island. Here, several Warnets cooperate together to share a VSAT bandwidth that is otherwise expensive for one Warnet to bear. The last mile from the VSAT to the individual Warnet is through cheap and affordable WLAN (2.4Ghz 802.11b) that cost less than USD 3,000 for one link.

Unfortunately, recently there have been discussions to impose tax on the use of this free industrial frequency. This may hamper public Internet access across school and government offices' to use the frequency freely and economically.

On the other front, there has been decent effort to use open source software and applications. The association of APWKomitel is working with Micronics Internusa PT (distributor of DELL and Redhat) to setup classes for Linux training for Warnet engineers. APWKomitel plans to develop billing system software on Linux platform and move from Microsoft Windows. The effort to migrate from proprietary software to open source software is because of strict and unaffordable licensing policy of proprietary software.

Business Model and Classification of Warnet
- Small Warnets
  Majority of the players is small Warnets equipped with 3 to 12 PCs. These Warnets usually do not have proper business licenses. Many Warnets are operated by young startup entrepreneurs as their family business and quite informally. Such Warnets use fixed line dial-up modems to access Internet.

  Investment in small Warnets is as small as USD 5,000 - 10,000, where family or friend owns the building. It is difficult to collect data from these small Warnets, but they may represent more than 40 per cent of the total member-ship strength of the association. They provide traditional and basic services like classic Internet applications (e-mail, chatting, browsing), PC rental for student and SME; and some venture into a small basic IT training class (MS Windows and recently Linux etc.).

- Medium Warnets
  A typical medium sized Warnet would have 12 to 24 PCs. These Warnets are usually equipped with business licenses since many of them are located in crowded and commercial areas such as near bus-terminal, malls, etc. Some of their value-added services also include edutainment such as LANGames.

  The Investment necessary to start a medium Warnet ranges between USD 10,000 and 25,000, and a majority of them uses broadband connections such as Cable, ADSL, or Leased-lines. This category also enjoys 40 per cent of the membership capacity of the association.

- Large Warnets
  Equipped with more than 24 PCs, large Warnets usually operate near strategic commercial areas in the city (malls) or near Universities or Colleges (Campus). Many of the large Warnets operate professionally and closely

resemble the business model of an MCI Center serving the community. It usually provides edutainment, classic Internet services, and café and some have other unique services. Investment required here would range between USD 25,000 and USD 100,000 or may be even more. Broadband connections with a combination of VSAT, Cable, ADSL and lease line are used in large Warnets.

Partnerships

APWKomitel's strategy to achieve its mission is through partnerships and co-llaborations. Partnerships with various stakeholders will facilitate the exchange of information and resources to foster the development of the MCI Center.

1) *OSOL - One School One Labs:* With the help of public and private initiatives Warnet derived "One-School-One-Lab". Under this initiative, school premises are used as MCI centers after school hours, and in lieu of the provision of space, school uses the MCI PCs for their computer labs.

2) *MOU - Open University Distant Learning:* Public - Private partnership initiates MOU between Indonesian government-owned Open University (Universitas Terbuka) and APWKomitel. The University has no physical campuses, so the MOU can facilitate Warnet as a virtual campus on a remote island, while the university can focus on providing educational contents. Previously students had to use traditional technologies like fax to send and communicate with the University, but now they can use Internet for communicating with other students.

3) *MCI Center - APEC E-marketplace collaboration model*: During the APEC Workshop on e-marketplace in Jakarta in 2002, cooperation between Warnet and community content providers such as: e-business content (textile, mining industry, e-travel, arts & crafts), community content (Indian community), news content (detik.com) was initiated. It is supposed to be win-win collaboration where the content provider needs Internet users to access through Warnet, while Warnet needs content so that its customer can use the Internet.

4) *Warsi* - Warung Informasi or Information Center: Collaboration between APWKomitel and Director of SME, Ministry of Industry and Trade (MoIT) is underway. The strategy is to use a Warnet for future Warsi, so that SMEs in industrial clusters on an island can use the Internet to empower their business. Another win-win collaboration where small and marginalized SMEs do not need to buy and maintain PCs and Internet connections, while Warnet gets an additional customer from the cluster.

5) *Indonesian Directory*: Warnet, Hotspot and MCI Center will be published in October 2003. This is a sole initiative to empower its member and publicize

member services through the publication of a directory (hardcopy). The idea is to promote the Warnet network throughout the country so that any foreign tourist, traveler and commuter who visit any city in Indonesia can always find a Warnet.

6) *Makassar Broadband City*: Warnets in Makassar in West Indonesia have cooperatives to share their bandwidth provided by VSAT. This is a success story, where several small Warnets initiate collaboration sharing VSAT connections to Internet via outdoor wireless LAN 2.4Ghz. After years of operation there are more than 30-50 Warnets sharing broadband Internet around the city.

Private Sector Partnerships
- *Micronics Internusa PT*- Implementation of ICT technology for SME and Warnet (www.indopc.com)
- *AsriCitra Pratama PT*- The owners of Millenia Net Café. Developed the School Warnet (OSOL) using WNET the facility at Wijaya High School
- *PSN (Pacific Satellite Nusantara) PT*- VSAT provider for Warnet in rural areas (www.psn.co.id)
- *IM2 (Indosat Mega Media) PT*- This is an Indonesian ISP with national coverage (www.indosatm2.com)

Lessons from the Field
A proper field report has not been prepared due to limited resources, but most of the information gathered is by talking to partners.

Financial Sustainability
- Although many new Warnets are being setup every month, many are also closing down, due to competition or poor business models. In the beginning of 2003, the total number of Warnets having positive growth was about 4,000. With this model of an MCI Center, APWKomitel can prevent SMEs from terminating their businesses and provide better financial sustainability.
- The top revenue streams are from Warnets located near shopping malls, universities and tourist areas.
- Government policy to provide a favourable pricing policy for Warnets to operate in urban and rural areas is much required for future expansions.
- Usually a Warnet operates for longer periods and should get bulk Internet access tariff.
- Public policy to foster cooperation between financial sectors and small business Warnets.
- Access to capital market is needed for future expansion.

Technology
- There are various enabling technologies such as Wireless for outdoor LAN, to distribute bandwidth from the Internet POP (point of present) to the Warnet (see Makassar broadband city).
- There are more non-technical issues with regulation on frequency allocation and usage. With the autonomy law, the local government tends to introduce their own policy to collect revenue from the use of resources including frequency.
- Regulations favor incumbents that still hold monopoly and control over long distance telecommunication infrastructure rights.
- Industry policy is not yet established and the current informal policy often excludes the small player. Regulators still favor big players in the supply chain.
- Government facilitation in the development of open source software for future MCI Centers.
- For the past two years, negotiations have been going on with proprietary software representative Microsoft Indonesia, but without any success. Currently, alternative Open source for Operating systems (Redhat 9.0, Suse 8.2) and Office application (Open Office) are used.

The Community
- The major benefit goes to students and marginal small businesses that can not afford to own PCs or Internet access. Warnets located near schools help students with their homework such as PC rental for making reports.
- After school hours, many students use the facility for entertainment such as online and multiplayer games.
- Many university students use the Warnet near their campus for their work and projects.
- The community can use the Warnet as an open online library and as a collaboration tools through e-mail. Although only 2 per cent of the population is wired, many people in the city use e-mail rather than fax and surface mail. Indonesia consists of 16,000 geographically dispersed islands. The Internet is an enabler tool to bridge this geographical distance.

Scalability/Replicability
MCI model used by APWKomitel involves only simple collaboration, public private partnership and facilitation from the association, using practical and simple technologies, to penetrate rural area and less developed parts of the country.

Limitations of the Model
- Continued dependency on government policy to empower APWKomitel as a business association. The membership is voluntary, so government facilitation can enhance efforts to introduce the MCI Center model to the community.

- Government facilitation can be in the form of socialization of model and the institution in the form of business association (APWKomitel) to other and remote areas in the archipelago.

- Connectivity is still an issue in rural areas. It is therefore required that the government provides good connectivity in these areas.

Website and Contact Information

APWKomitel
http://www.apwkomitel.org

Mr. Rudi Rusdiah, Chairman
cio@milenia.net

Mr. Mintakun Kunarto
mintakun@indo.net.id

Golden Plaza A37-A39, Jl RS Fatmawati No 15, Jakarta. Indonesia 12410
Tel: +6221-75900091 Fax: +6221-7507545

References

APWKomitel (Rudi Rusdiah), Case Study Presenter at ITU World Telecom 2003 Geneva, TDS-2 Session: Indonesian Case Study: Warnet - MCI Center

APWKomitel (Rudi Rusdiah), Paper Presenter at ITU World Telecom 2003, Geneva POL-8 Session: Indonesia Promoting ICT thru MCI (Community Internet Center) or Warnet

APWKomitel, Rudi Rusdiah, 2002 Directory Profile of Activity and Members
http://www.apwkomitel.org/

APWKomitel (Rudi Rusdiah) paper presented, 21-23 Nov 2001 ITU Workshop on "Internet in South East Asia", in Bangkok. http://www.itu.int/ITU-D/ict/cs/

APWKomitel (Rudi Rusdiah) paper presented at APEC Workshop "Transforming the Digital Divide into a Digital Opportunity", July 24-27, 2001, Chinese Taipei and "E-marketplace & Supply Chain Management," September 2002 in Pan Sari Pacific, Jakarta. Indonesia.

ITU, Geneva, March 2002, Kretek Internet: Indonesia Case Study

Rusdiah, Rudi, paper presented at ITU Telecom Asia 2002 (Hong Kong 4 December 2002), TDS-2 Benefits to Citizens & Society: Internet for Development. http://www.itu.int/asia2002/forum

Unesco, Workshop on "Telecenter (Combining traditional and new technology in ICT)", Kohtmale, Srilangka January 2001.

THAILAND

Thailand Canada Telecenter Project

Warren Wong; Dr. Jingjai Hanchanlash; Vasoontara Chatikavanij and David Barr

Project Summary

The Thailand Canada Telecentre Project (TCTP) was partly financed by the Canadian International Development Agency (CIDA) and implemented by Hickling Corporation, Canada; Loxley Public Company Limited, Thailand; and the TeleCommons Development Group, Canada over the April 2001 to June 2003 period. The primary objective of the TCTP feasibility study is to demonstrate that valuable Information and Communication Technologies (ICT) services can be delivered to people in the rural and remote areas in a financially sustainable manner. The intent of the Project is to promote "Universal Access" to ICT services in villages by locating several phones and computers with Internet access at a single location that is easily accessible to the community. This one location is often referred to as a "telecenter" (or more recently, as a "community information center"). Although individual households cannot afford the cost of a computer or even a telephone, use by the entire community has a better chance of generating enough revenue to support the shared facilities of a community information center (CIC).

At the end of the project, three of the six CICs had generated operating profits (revenue greater than all operating costs):

1) Hua Thanon Bann Mai Kao Kad CIC is owned and operated by a local firm called Bann Mai Kao Kad (BMKK) in the community of Hua Thanon Nakornsawan, and it accumulated profits of THB 19,575 (USD 470);

2) Mae Hong Son CIC is owned and operated by the Nawamintrachinee Mae Hong Son Industrial and Community Education College in the community of Chongkum Muang Mae Hong Son. It accumulated profits of THB 15,850 (USD 380);

3) Pong CIC is owned and operated by the Pong Community Library in the community of Pong Phayao, and it accumulated profits of THB 8,829 (USD 210).

These three CICs which are generating operating profits, exhibited the following characteristics:

- Strong and effective support from government (particularly from the Ministry of Education);
- Strong CIC managers and operators;
- Strong support from the community;
- Adopted private sector principles.

The major limitation, or Achilles heel, of the TCTP model is the lack of a supportive policy and regulatory environment. In the absence of a regulatory agency, such as the National Telecommunications Commission (NTC), the financial viability of CICs is dependent upon, for example, the Ministry of Education.

Socio-Economic Impacts

The purpose of the Thailand Canada Telecentre Project (TCTP) is to conduct a planning study and test the most promising concepts under actual field conditions for the delivery of ICT services in a financially sustainable manner in the rural and remote, as well as underserved and unserved, areas in Thailand. The intent of the Project is to promote "Universal Access" to ICT services in villages by locating several phones and computers with access at a single location that is easily accessible to the community.

The primary objective of TCTP is to demonstrate that valuable ICT services (e.g., education, health, government) can be delivered to people in the rural and remote areas in a financially sustainable manner. There are four secondary objectives, which are expected to demonstrate that the utilization of ICT services:

- can create new jobs in the rural areas that are status free and not marked by gender cues, particularly for the individuals operating the CICs;
- allows end-users to make informed choices, reduces their transaction costs, and enhances their economic and social activities and development;
- is an effective way of enhancing the Government of Thailand and international organization's development programs;
- in rural areas will help to promote the adoption of a supportive policy and regulatory environment.

The goal, or ultimate impact, is to convince the Government of Thailand that the establishment and operation of CICs is an efficient and effective mechanism for delivering valuable ICT services to people in rural and remote, areas of Thailand, where the majority of poor people reside.

Sustainability Model

The Thailand Canada Telecenter Project (TCTP) adopted "community driven and private sector operating principles" as the cornerstone of its sustainability model. The formulation of the model was guided by the work of the International Telecommunication Union (ITU) on communications for rural and remote areas.[1] The general approach of TCTP is to cover capital (or one-time) costs, such as phone services installation, computers, printer, modem, fax machine. The CICs are expected to cover operating (or recurring) costs, such as salaries, electricity. The exceptions are the basic monthly Internet and telephone charges that are covered by TCTP. However, after one year of operation, the CICs are expected to cover all operating costs including the basic monthly Internet and telephone charges.

The Project was implemented in three phases: a planning and establishment phase, from April 2001 to March 2002; followed by an operating and monitoring phase, from December 2001 to February 2003; and a wrap-up and lessons learned phase from March to June 2003.

Technology Infrastructure
TCTP's approach was to rely on the existing technology infrastructure. The basic technology configuration plan for each CIC consisted of four to five telephone lines, two to four computers, (dial up) Internet access, one printer, one fax machine, UPS (uninterrupted power supply), as well as desks and chairs. On the Communication Technology (CT) side, five of the CICs were connected by phone lines provided by the Telephone Organization of Thailand (TOT) while one CIC was connected by phone lines provided by the Thai Telephone and Telecommunication Company (TT&T). In regards to the Information Technology (IT) side, all six of the CICs were equipped with computers and printers that were 1) purchased locally and 2) could be maintained locally (to the best extent possible).

Partnerships
Two levels of partnerships were formed during the implementation of the project: internal and external. The internal project partnerships involved those organizations and stakeholders involved in the implementation of the Thailand Canada Telecenter Project. External project partnerships involved the establishment of a network to share experiences and lessons learned with other ongoing CIC pilot projects. This network was referred to as the Thai Telecenter Network.

Internal Project Partnerships
TCTP was partly financed by the Canadian International Development Agency's Industrial Cooperation Program. The balance of the financing was provided by the implementing organizations: Hickling Corporation, Canada; Loxley Public Company Limited, Thailand; and the TeleCommons Development Group (TDG), Canada. Hickling and Loxley acted as project managers, while the TDG[2] provided advice on participatory approaches to rural ICT development.

The Government of Thailand, and in particular, the Ministry of Education and the Ministry of Interior, were the main partners in the implementation of TCTP.

The Government is the partner in the top three CICs that are and continue to be financially sustainable (revenue greater than all operating costs):

- Hua Thanon Bann Mai Kao Kad is supported by the Or Bor Tor (municipal government) in Hua Thanon. The Hua Thanon Or Bor Tor is under the jurisdiction of the Department of Local Administration, Ministry of Interior;

- Mae Hong Son is supported by the Nawamintrachinee Mae Hong Son Industrial and Community Education College. The College is under the jurisdiction of the Department of Vocational Education, Ministry of Education;

- Pong, at the recommendation of the community consultations, is owned and operated by the Pong Community Library. The Pong Community Library is under the jurisdiction of the Department of Non Formal Education, Ministry of Education.

The Government of Thailand is not a partner in the bottom three CICs, which operated at a loss (revenue less than all operating costs).

External Project Partnerships
Our major partner, external to the project, has also been the Government of Thailand, specifically the National Electronics and Computer Technology Centre (NECTEC), National Science and Technology Development Agency, Ministry of Science Technology and Environment. NECTEC launched their pilot CIC project, which established four CICs, around the same time as TCTP was launched. As both projects were launched at roughly the same time, NECTEC actively participated in the TCTP project design workshop in May 2001. The project design workshop covered such items as international experience with CICs and views on "best practices", site selection criteria, ensuring community buy-in, and commercial sustainability.

Lessons from the Field
- Hua Thanon Bann Mai Kao Kad is a privately run CIC, with support from the local municipal government, or Or Bor Tor. This CIC is located in the community of Hua Thanon (central Thailand, near Nakorn Sawan). Based on the community consultations, this CIC was originally owned and operated by the Or Bor Tor within the government office. However, after three months of operation, the Hua Thanon Or Bor Tor decided that it was not an appropriate organization to run a commercially oriented venture and suggested transferring the CIC to Bann Mai Kao Kad, a local private sector firm, based in Hua Thanon. Bann Mai Kao Kad is in a more accessible location than the Or Bor Tor. Hua Thanon Bann Mai Kao Kad CIC began operations at the end of August 2002 and by the end of February 2003 it had accumulated an "operating profit" (revenue minus all operating costs) of THB 19,575 (USD 470). Gross revenue over the seven-month period was THB 36,292 (USD 860), and total operating costs amounted to THB 16,717 (USD 400).

- Mae Hong Son CIC is owned and operated by the Nawamintrachee Industrial and Community Education College in the community of Chongkum (north-west Thailand, near Mae Hong Son). Based on the community consultations, this CIC was originally owned and operated by an Or Bor Tor in Tambon Mae Ram. However, like the Or Bor Tor in Hua Thanon, after three months of operation, the Mae Ram Or Bor Tor decided that it too was not an appropriate organization to run a commercially oriented venture and agreed to transfer the CIC to the Nawamintrachee Industrial and Community Education College. The College's, and in turn the operating costs of the CIC, is supported by the Ministry of Education's Department of Vocational Education. Mae Hong Son CIC began operations in July 2002 and by the end of February 2003 it had accumulated an operating profit of THB 15,850 (USD 380). Gross revenue over the eight-month period was THB 83,406 (USD 1,990), and total operating costs amounted to THB 67,556 (USD 1,620).

- Pong CIC is owned and operated by the Pong Community Library in the community of Pong Phayao (northern Thailand, near Chiang Rai). Community support for their CIC was the strongest in Pong Phayao. The community donated five computers, two printers, one scanner, a telephone line, as well as five tables and chairs to their CIC. Pong community library's, and in turn the operating costs of the CIC, is supported by the Ministry of Education's Department of Non Formal Education. Pong CIC began operations in March 2002 and by the end of February 2003 it had accumulated an operating profit of THB 8,829 (USD 210). Gross revenue over the twelve-month operating period was THB 79,337 (USD 1,890), and total operating costs amounted to THB 70,508 (USD 1,680).

- Ban Mae CIC is owned and operated by the Women's Woodcarvers Association in the community of Ban Mae Sunpatong (northern Thailand, near Chiang Mai). Ban Mae CIC began operations in March 2002 and by the end of February 2003 it had accumulated an operating loss of THB 17,729 (USD 420). Gross revenue over the twelve-month period was THB 46,258 (USD 1,100), and total operating costs amounted to THB 63,987 (USD 1,520).

- Jakraj CIC is owned and operated by the Jakraj Population and Community Development Association (PDA) a non-government organization (NGO), in the community of Jakraj Koraj (northeast Thailand, near Koraj, or Nakhon Ratchasima). Jakraj CIC began operations in March 2002 and by the end of February 2003 it had accumulated an operating loss of THB 32,479 (USD 770). Gross revenue over the twelve-month period was THB 24,638 (USD 590), and total operating costs amounted to THB 57,117 (USD 1,360). This CIC is not located in an easily accessible location, and was a key factor behind its poor performance.

- Hang Hung CIC is owned and operated by the Hang Hung Women's Association in the community of Hang Hung Mae Moh (northern Thailand, near Lampang). It should be noted that Hang Hung CIC was jointly supported by TCTP and Chulalongkorn University. Chulalongkorn's objective differed from TCTP by focusing on providing health and environmental information services resulting from coal mining operations in the area rather than the financial sustainability focus of TCTP. Hang Hung CIC began operations in December 2001 and by the end of December 2002 it had accumulated an operating loss of THB 71,290 (USD 1,700). Gross revenue over the thirteen-month period was THB 41,983 (USD 1,000), and total operating costs amounted to THB 113,273 (USD 2,700).

The top three performing CICs (i.e., Hua Thanon BMKK, Mae Hong Son, and Pong Phayao) all of which generated operating profits, exhibited the following characteristics:

- Strong and Effective Support from Government
  ◦ Hua Thanon BMKK CIC had support from the Department of Local Administration, Ministry of Interior.
  ◦ Mae Hong Son CIC had support from the Department of Vocational Education, Ministry of Education.
  ◦ Pong Phayao CIC had support from the Department of Non Formal Education, Ministry of Education.

- *Strong CIC Managers and Operators*
  ◦ Pong CIC manager, Khun/Ms. Wilawan Chaimongkol, was awarded a contract in May/June 2003 for her CIC to provide computer training to government officials in three local offices.
  ◦ Mae Hong Son CIC manager, Arjan/ Mr. Mongkol Vanikorn, uses students to act as CIC operators, which provides the students with practical work experience.
  ◦ Hua Thanon CIC mangers, Khun/Ms. Jitra Meethong and Khun/Ms. Narumon Churdee, transferred their CIC at the local government office to a convenient and easily accessed location in the town. The CIC was set up to satisfy the large demand for computer training.

- *Strong Support from the Community*
  ◦ Pong donated 5 computers to their CIC.

- *Adopted Private Sector Principles*
  ◦ Mae Hong Son and Hua Thanon BMKK CICs pay their operators on a commission basis, as opposed to a salary.

- Notable Aspects
  - ◦ Mae Hong Son CIC is used by a local college to give its students hands on experience in running a business, while at the same time providing valuable service to the community.
  - ◦ Hua Thanon BMKK CIC is meeting the strong demand for computer training by children in the community; 80 per cent of the CIC's revenue is from computer training. The community considers computer literacy as a ticket to a better paying job.
  - ◦ Pong CIC provides community service while keeping an eye at the bottom line. The CIC accumulates a profit, and then provides computer training and usage services to poorer members for free which reduces performance to break even, they then repeat the cycle of profit generation followed by community service.

By comparison, the bottom three CICs - Ban Mae, Jakraj, Hang Hung - which have accumulated losses, exhibited the following characteristics:

- No Support from Government
  - ◦ Ban Mae was owned and operated by women's woodcarvers cooperative.
  - ◦ Jakraj was owned and operated by an NGO, the Population and Community Development Association (PDA).
  - ◦ Hang Hung was owned and operated by an NGO, a community association.

- Weak CIC Managers and Operators and Weak Organizations
  - ◦ Ban Mae cooperative and Jakraj PDA NGO both experienced internal organizational problems that also resulted in their CIC managers/ operators taking temporary leaves of absence.

- Not Integrated into the Community
  - ◦ The Jakraj CIC was not integrated into the community development activities of the PDA.

- Ignored Private Sector Principles
  - ◦ Hang Hung CIC subsidized their service. This CIC was jointly supported with Chulalongkorn University, which opted to cover the CIC manager/ operator salaries.

Financial Sustainability
The monthly profit/loss position of the top three CICs, the bottom three CICs, and the overall average for all six CICs over the one-year operating period of the project is shown in the "Achieving Cost Recovery" figure below. This figure

illustrates the rolling strategy that was used to ensure financial sustainability amongst all of the CICs.

Technology

There are two components to the technology: the telecommunications infra-structure and the information technology. The major difficulties were not so much the technology itself but the policy and regulatory environment pertaining to tele-communications and the high costs associated with information technology.

Communication Technology

The absence of a telecommunications regulatory agency is Thailand's "Achilles Heel", which inhibits the provision of financially sustainable ICT services in rural and remote areas of the country. Efforts to establish a telecom regulatory agency, known as the National Telecommunications Commission (NTC), have been seriously delayed.[3] The absence of an effective regulatory agency is the major factor inhibiting inward calling to rural and remote areas of Thailand. Our reco-nnaissance field survey and community consultations found that approximately 25-40 per cent of young adults (under 25 years) are living and working outside their village in an urban area such as Bangkok, or a foreign country. The desire to keep in touch with parents combined with their higher "urban" incomes is a major reason that inward calls were expected to be 3-4 times outward calls. This is consistent with the experience in other countries and studies conducted by international organizations, such as the International Telecommunication Union (ITU). Although several attempts were made to establish a revenue sharing arrangement between the telephone companies and the CICs, none were successful. Current policy is "sender keeps all", which is not conducive to, or supportive of, inward calling in rural and remote areas. Furthermore, phone numbers are not even posted on rural payphones, making it extremely difficult to call villages.

After regulatory issues, having the Internet connection dropped intermittently turned out to be a major annoyance for users of the CIC. The problem did not appear to be with the Internet Service Providers (ISPs) but rather the quality of the rural telecommunications infrastructure. In the absence of a regulatory agency, it is unlikely that this can be remedied in the immediate future.

Information Technology

Despite the continual drop in the cost of Information Technology (IT) over the last decade, its price remains too high relative to most rural incomes. Even when the community through a CIC shares the capital costs of IT, the cost is still prohibitive. As noted above, achieving financial sustainability (revenue greater than operating costs) is relatively easy, however, the sustainability challenge remains commercial sustainability (i.e., revenue greater than all costs, capital and operating). In an effort to reduce this cost barrier, Loxley adapted the "thin client-thick server solution" based on LINUX technology from India.

The Solution consists of 10-15 low-powered outdated PCs used as "thin clients" connecting to a more powerful server. Solution is cost effective way of providing 10-15 refurbished workstations compared to purchasing 10-15 new computers. Using processing power, memory, and disk storage on the thick server, users sitting at thin clients can run modern application software such as word processing, spreadsheet, presentation, Internet browsers, e-mail, instant messaging, etc. Thin client-thick server solution based on LINUX technology provides savings not only on hardware costs, but also on the software expenses. Both thin clients and thick server run LINUX operating system and utilize Open Source software applications thereby avoiding expensive licenses. At the same time, users have the additional advantages of stable and efficient environment of LINUX: centralized administration and management; centralized storage of data for easy back-up operation and flexible utilization of client PC-users can login from any client PC. It is also easier to download software upgrades to the server (one machine compared to 10-15 machines) and provide technical support at a distance. Depending on the number of workstations, the Solution is about 25-40 per cent of the cost of purchasing new and stand-alone computers.

Although cost is the major barrier, maintenance is a key factor underlying the IT operations side of the CIC. Although training was provided for CIC operators to conduct the "first line of defence" or simple maintenance, and even though there was a hot line (e.g., trouble shooting over the telephone), from time to time, actual site visits had to be undertaken by Loxley to solve a technical problem and/or effect repairs. The technical expertise required to solve technical problems and/ or repairs will reside in urban and generally not in rural and even less so in remote areas.

The Community

On December 11 and 12, 2002, NECTEC organized a "Thai Telecentre Workshop", with partial financial support from the World Bank. The workshop brought 50 CIC managers and operators from the five projects in the Thai Telecentre Network to Bangkok to share experiences and to consolidate lessons learned for the purpose of developing a framework for embarking on a largescale program that would roll out CICs in rural and remote, as well as underserved and unserved, areas of Thailand. When the CIC managers and operators were asked to identify what they could do on their own, if such a largescale CIC program were implemented, their response was:

- Employ Sound Business Practices: Prepare a business plan that includes marketing and promoting the CIC to the community.

- Adopt Participatory Management Approach: Involve the community in the management of the CIC through regular and frequent meetings, to provide a "feeling of community ownership".

- Achieve Financial Sustainability: "Nothing is free", and this applies to the CIC which must charge for its services in order to be sustainable.

- Stimulate Demand: As most members of the community will have never seen a computer, it is important to look for ways to create interest in the CIC; and to stimulate demand. Possible ways include: providing introductory computer training sessions at reduced or zero cost to new customers, provide more advanced training for customers who have already acquired some familiarity with using a computer, create a database of local activities and initiatives (e.g., community action plan, policies and decisions by government that affects the community), and develop web sites to advertise the community to potential tourists, the products of local firms, and so forth.

When the CIC managers and operators were asked to identify those areas where they would need external (outside the community) assistance, their response was:

- Improve the Infrastructure: the Internet connection is frequently terminated, which not only frustrates customers but increases the access costs.

- Provide training and technical support: the CIC managers and operators need to keep their computer skills up-to-date, particularly since they are training the community on how to use the computer, so refresher and advanced training is needed. Training should also be provided on how to solve simple technical problems. Technical support is required for major problems.

- Provide Financial Assistance to Get Started: the cost of computers is prohibitively high relative to the average income of the community, so financial assistance is needed to offset the high capital costs as well as assistance and advice to get started.

- Promote Thai Language Content: there are several initiatives such as ThaiTambon.com aimed at developing and promoting Thai language content. Such efforts should be continued and encouraged. In response to this suggestion, NECTEC has established a web site for the Thai Telecentre Network: www.Thaitelecenter.net, which also includes the proceedings from this workshop.

Scalability/Replicability

Suggestions for a largecale roll-out CIC program across all rural and underserved areas of Thailand were presented to His Excellency, Dr. Surapong Suebwonglee, Minister of Information and Communication Technologies (ICT) at the April 23, 2003 closing ceremony at Mae Hong Son CIC. The Project's recommendation to the Minister, should Thailand decide to embark on a largescale community CIC program, was to focus on the experience of the top three CICs (Hua Thanon, Mae Hong Son, Pong) which had: 1) support from a government agency; 2) support from the community; 3) strong and committed CIC manager, who is ideally supported by 1-2 good CIC operators; 4) good working partnership between government, the community and private sector; 5) subsidize capital/start-up costs, but look for ways to keep capital/equipment costs down, such as using Loxley's Octopus Connect Solution (Thin Client, Thick Server Solution); 6) where possible, minimize operating costs by locating the CIC in an existing facility as an additional service to an ongoing business or activity, such as a school, non-formal education centre, private business, etc.; 7) adopt private sector operating principles, even if it is owned by a not for profit organization, operate the CIC professionally as if it were a business.

Limitations of the Model

The major limitation, or "Achilles Heel", of the TCTP model is the lack of a supportive policy and regulatory environment, particularly for inward calling in the rural and remote areas. In an attempt to demonstrate the advantages and benefits of a supportive policy and regulatory framework, an agreement-in-principle was reached with a major communications company to provide wireless voice and data services. A major advantage of the wireless provider was that it relied on recent technology, which in turn meant that individual phone cards could be given to each member of the community.

Each phone card could be assigned a unique number and be equipped with voice messaging service to facilitate inward calls. Whenever an individual wished to make a phone call or check messages, s/he would insert the phone card into the cellular payphone to access their unique phone number/message service. It meant that each household could have a unique phone number without having the physical phone. Unfortunately, the current regulatory environment prevented the project from proceeding with this particular wireless communications provider.In the absence of a regulatory agency such as the National Telecommunications Commission (NTC), the financial viability of CICs are dependent upon government, such as the Ministry of Education, Ministry of Interior, and so forth.

Other Initiatives in the Country

As noted above, the Thai Telecentre Network coordinated by NECTEC, brought together the following five Community Information Centre Pilot Projects:

NECTEC: supported four CICs.

TCTP: supported five CICs plus one with Chulalongkorn University.

Chulalongkorn University: supported three CICs, plus one with TCTP.

CODI (Community Organization Development Institute): supported two CICs.

ThaiRuralNet: managed primarily by students from Thammasat University, supported two CICs.[4]

Website and Contact Information

Thailand Canada Telecentre Project (TCTP)
http://www.t-centre.com

Warren Wong, Principal, Hickling Arthurs Low (HAL) Corporation (TCTP Canadian Project Director)
Ottawa, Canada
wwong@hal.ca

Dr. Jingjai Hanchanlash, Exec. Vice President, Loxley Public Company Ltd. (TCTP Thai Project Director)
Bangkok, Thailand
jingjai@loxley.co.th

Vasoontara Chatikavanij, Director, Technical and Economic Cooperation Program, Loxley Public Company Limited (TCTP Project Manager)
Bangkok, Thailand
vasoonta@loxinfo.co.th

David Barr, P.Eng., Principal, DFB and Associates and Senior Associate, Hickling Arthurs Low (HAL) Corporation (TCTP Technical Advisor)
Ottawa, Canada
dave.barr@sympatico.ca

Notes

1. See International Telecommunication Union, Telecommunication Development Bureau, Recommendations: ITU-D Study Groups, particularly Question 4/2 on Communications for rural and remote areas, first study period (1995-1998), ITU: Geneva, 1998.

2. The TeleCommons Development Group (TDG) is currently part of Stantec Consulting Ltd., and formerly a division of ESG International.

3. Vasoontara Chatikavanij, "Information Technology/Electronic Business Status and Challenges" presented at The Regional Seminar on Information Technology Enabling Legal Frameworks for the Greater Mekong Sub-Region, for the United Nations (UN) Economic and Social Commission for Asia and the Pacific (ESCAP), September 29 to October 1, 2003.

4. ThaiRuralNet apparently has plans to support additional CICs.

HUNGARY

Hungarian Telecottages

Tom Wormald and Mátyás Gáspár
Telecottages Association

Project Summary

The telecottage in Hungary is a community and service organization that ensures access to, among other things, information and communications tools, information and services, and provides users professional and expert assistance. The telecottages in Hungary do not simply provide technology to people who might o-therwise not have access to it. Rather, the telecottage is viewed as a means by which local people may have access to those educational, informational and technological means by which they may address their own community's self-defined needs. Moreover, we see the building of a telecottage network, both nationally and internationally, as a means of realising a cooperative, interest guided infrastructure through which partnerships can be made and work leading to common goals. These include:

- the strengthening of civil life;
- improvement of public transparency and democracy;
- the growth of local social capital.

There are approximately 500 operating telecottages in Hungary. Each of these has on an average ten computers. A manager, who is assisted by a staff typically consisting largely of volunteers, runs each local telecottage. The manager must complete the approved training telecottage manager-training programme. Currently about 1000 people work in the telecottage network as their main profession. At least 2000-3000 local volunteers also help run services.

Socio-Economic Impacts

Bridging the Digital Divide

The most important task is the "bridging" of the digital divide. We view this as a process of simultaneous technological development and democratization; through giving people 'access' on a civil basis and offering them a broad range of services questions of social, as well as technological involvement are being addressed.

Public and communal accessibility efforts must address why many potential users do not have access to the potential benefits of information technologies.

We see the task of bridging the digital divide as primarily the responsibility of civil society. In Hungary many of the reasons behind the lack of uptake of information technology stem from the political changes that the country has undergone. A huge amount of economic investment was required to bring the necessary infrastructure up to a suitable level, and in certain rural areas this process is still continuing. The problem stems in part from the fact that in the years after the political changes in 1989, the government was unable/unwilling to take an active role in the development of computer use and the infrastructure needed for it.

Moreover, we are also convinced that through social and cultural provisions, communal accessibility efforts can help eradicate disparities in a far 'fairer' way. This is in part because through civil based assistance people have been able to take responsibility for their own 'connectivity' and have thus been able to work out the solution that best suits their own needs and abilities. Local people in their own interests also due to the fact that access points are embedded in the given community, operate it.

Building Community Access
When each individual telecottage is viewed as part of a strong network, it becomes clear that through a process of democratic representation of local needs on a broader stage, telecottages become access points for a huge range of services, firmly localising the demand for and application of these services within the specific social, economic and political dynamics of the given community. This is community access, the theoretical name for the practical activities undertaken by the telecottages in their everyday work. This concept also emphasises the need for cooperation between the government, business and civil sectors in communities and society as a whole, and seeks to reinforce this cooperation through participation and stimulation on a local level of the other important actors in society.

Community access thus differs in some crucial ways from public or Internet cafe based access, due to its civil and "value added" nature. This is the unique feature of the Hungarian telecottage association and, another of the chief reasons for its success thus far. The community access model at once eases the financial constraints on rural access, addresses the digital divide in a fair and people oriented way and also succeeds in strengthening civil society beyond all expectations. By giving communities responsibility for their own access, whilst developing a national and now international framework that allows them to lobby for and receive support from central government a powerful engine for change, from both bottom up and top down, is created.

Network Building
From the beginning it is important for the telecottages to create an association in order to move together onto a national stage, to take their places in the networks of existing relationships and to forge new partnerships of their own. Only in this

way can central and regional government officials, national and international organizations and ICT and other commercial and service companies be expected to be partners of the movement. We are currently preparing the next, crucial step in this process, the internationalisation of the movement. Later this year we will see the founding of EUTA, whose initial members will be the Russian, Polish, Yugoslav, Bulgarian, Slovakian and Estonian Telecottage Associations, as well as quite possibly the new Bosnian association. This kind of networking is an essential aspect of each individual telecottage's sustainability.

Through civil control, the movement's embeddedness in local society holds that the important purpose is to assure that telecottages serve the entire community in any 'sector,' and fulfil all needs, that it is not appropriated by any one individual or group in society, but that these work together with the telecottage network as a partner, so that the community can claim the results as its own. Characteristics of the provision of networked services are:

- the intersectoral multifunctionality of the telecottages;
- the economy of scale;
- orientation to local needs;
- the taking on public services supported by local and central government
- the relationships with local, regional and national business.

These characteristics of networked services are critical conditions of the operability and sustainability of the telecottages.

Sustainability Model

Telecottages operate in many types of institutions and legal entities (independent institution, library, community house, school, post office). The ideal - though not obligatory - organizational paradigm for Hungarian telecottages has the owner as a civil organization, the host as the local government, and the operator as a private company. Thus it is not classifiable in a single service branch or economic sector. Their service contracts reflect this, incorporating assignments, laws and obligations in an appropriate manner.

Each individual telecottage is an independent and largely self-sustaining civil organisation. They employ a wide variety of tactics to remain economically viable. Aside from modest charges for the use of the equipment and services, typical services provided by the telecottages are:

- publication of a local newspaper;
- website design and construction for local business;
- education and training;
- carrying out of local government tasks.

Training and education remain the single most important source of income for the telecottages; many act as training centres for ECDL (European Computer Driving Licence) courses and five telecottages also host ECDL examination centres. The other most common services are: school study and training, e-learning access points, entertainment, tele-workplace provision, employment services, official business consultation, social services and shopping.

The key actors of telecottage programmes are local devotees, who readily and skilfully work for the creation of telecottages, regularly making sacrifices for their work in order to realize their goals. Indeed the telecottage staff's own culture ensures the cohesion of the movement, which represents core values like solidarity, community, creativity, knowledge, information, openness, tolerance and humour. This human factor has been a defining characteristic of the telecottage movement since the very beginning and has been one of the most important factors in safeguarding the movement. Without this personal commitment to the success of individual telecottages and the movement as a whole, survival would probably not have been guaranteed.

The country is divided up into seven regions. Each of these contains approximately thirty-five telecottages, as well as a regional resource centre. This resource centre makes technological equipment available to telecottages and users that would otherwise be too expensive or complicated to place in individual telecottages. It is also a centre for mentoring activities, provision of education programmes and other services, and it provides the means for each telecottage to have a democratic voice in matters affecting the association on a national level. To sustain the movement's specialised activities, a professional core of 50-60 telecottage experts has come into existence. These serve as trainers, monitors and mentors in the network activities and work on the basis of the seven regions. The first representatives of new professions - community informatics, community managers - they help in the service provision inherent to the development and operation of the telecottage network.

Technology Infrastructure

The technological infrastructure of the telecottages varies from place to place. Different needs must be addressed in different areas, and the local nature of the telecottages means that they often undertake quite different activities and act in a broad range of ways. There are, however, a set of 'telecottage minimums' that must be fulfilled. These minimums are divided into three areas:

1) Service Minimums
   - Computer use, internet and email service provision;
   - Carrying out of tasks on the computer (data-entry, word-processing, printing, scanning, production of calling-cards, fliers and posters);
   - Computer games;
   - Photocopying, sending and receiving of faxes;
   - Provision of assistance with administrative issues;
   - Service provision for local NGOs, acting as 'civil centre';
   - Provision of public information, a brochure library, provision of information documents, acting as a local advertising and news centre;
   - Watching for prospective applications for local organisations, helping in

preparation of proposals;
- Organisation of training and education programs including those not on computers.

2) Technical Minimums:
- Internet connection;
- Telephone line;
- Computer system:
  - Minimum 3 for a population of 1500 or less;
  - Minimum 5 for a population of 1500 - 3000
  - Minimum 6 for a population of 3000 or more;
- Legally registered software necessary for provision of services;
- CD writer and reader, scanner, printer (A4 black and white), photocopier (A3 black and white), fax telephone, notice board.

3) Operational Minimums:
- Must be under civil control;
- At least one trained member of staff;
- At least two rooms, sink, toilet. This property must be ensured by a contract for at least 5 years;
- Suitable furniture;
- Publicly displayed service and price list;
- Must be open for a minimum of 20 hours per week, opening times must be publicly displayed;
- Main opening time must be between 14.00 and 16.00 on working days, other times are set according to local demand;
- Building and contents insurance;
- Publicly displayed postal and email address, telephone and fax number;
- Internal operating rules and registration.

Partnerships

Partnership is one of the most basic elements of the telecottages' existence. As mentioned above, the very notion of community access is implicitly concerned with cooperation between those sectors of society that are, particularly in a post socialist society, too often viewed as separate. This is the main reason why the goals of "bridging" the digital divide, and fostering civil society through the building of social partnerships are viewed as common and mutually supportive aims.

There are numerous examples of these partnerships. For example, at their present extent, the telecottages help access public services and in official matters. For example, those settlements with a population of 1000 or lesser usually have no mayor's office. This assistance includes maintenance of public records, dissemination of public information and coordination of a wide variety of local programmes, as well as the local implementation of central government initiatives. The telecottages are also increasingly merging with institutions such as local post offices or libraries in communities too small to sustain these independently.

From the beginning the aim of the telecottage movement has been to build partnerships with economic and social development goals in mind. These include addressing issues such as:

- employment;
- social position;
- retraining and skill acquisition;
- enterprise development;
- development of equal opportunities;
- quality of life;
- societal pressures;
- democracy;
- governmental transparency.

This partnership building gives people the means to achieve their own goals and seeking wherever possible to avoid the sometimes limiting and exclusionary nature of computer access.

Starting with small community resources (bottom-up) and proceeding to international, national and government support (top-down), programs are organized to complement each other, simultaneously following concrete local and national goals. An effective telecottage development strategy has been developed, based on training programmes for staff and volunteers. We are also involved in a consortium working to develop this as an entirely new kind of e-learning software which, if successful, will be used in other countries where new telecottage movements are being formed, and expanded to cover other professions such as that of community manager.

Government Partnerships

The telecottage movement has now been incorporated into the government's official strategy for developing information society in Hungary. More than 2000 "E-Hungary" access centers will be opened, serving as minimal access points offering 2 or 3 computers. The telecottage movement is the main partner in this program, approximately half of these points exist or are under-development telecottages, and many of the others may well develop into telecottages at a later stage.

Telecottage leaders have also taken an increasingly active role in local government bodies, and their role in political life is increasing. The participation of telecottage leaders in local political life has helped make the practice of governance - which too often operated in an autocratic fashion - become more community-oriented in those settlements where telecottages operate.

Through these partnerships local governmental and civil life has become increasingly bound together and both, through the means afforded by the telecottage, can express their strengths and needs more effectively. It is through this that the notion of "community manager" has come about. This is a person trained in the specific skills needed to liaise effectively between the different groups in a micro-level society. From next year students at Hungary's biggest college will be able to obtain qualifications in this vocational skill.

We are also establishing an ever-wider contract-based partnership with government entities; in addition to the programs we already provide (e.g. work-related, rural development, social, youth, informatics, and civil society programs). For example, the network was heavily involved in the campaign to get people voting in the referendum on EU accession, and many telecottages are working as EU information centres in their local communities. Numerous agricultural programmes have also been initiated on a national basis. In each case individual telecottages are contracted through the national association, by the government ministry in question, to provide a certain service in their community.

Private Sector

Telecottages have also taken an active role in building links between local communities and the business world. The national association has active links with companies such as Microsoft, Vodafone and Intel. Telecottages can open a gateway to new markets that companies - particularly larger nationals or multi-nationals - would otherwise be unable to exploit. Crucially, they provide a kind of "buffer-zone" for the inhabitants of these communities; introducing them to Internet commerce and helping them understand the way that multi-national telecommunications and software companies operate.

On a local level, many telecottages - among them the original in Csákberény - serve as local business centres where entrepreneurs can network, seek advice, hold meetings and use facilities. Telecottages seek to maintain excellent links with business in the region and can provide more 'buying power' for the community.

This kind of social assistance is central to the telecottage association's mission. It has created increasing numbers of professional bodies dealing with specific groups in society or issues affecting citizens, for example public utilities, the youth, the unemployed or retired people. It continuously handles, develops and represents new services, often contracting these out to local entrepreneurs and businesses. In many places computer or management training is provided in tandem with introductions to these services, so that people can experience the possibilities of the information society in a practical and demand-driven fashion.

With this kind of introduction to e-commerce and business activity, as well as with the organization of an infrastructural network and technological services in mind, we have established a business-partner cooperation, which is setting up the private service provider network of the telecottages. According to this partnership, businesses pay for the rights to operate through the national network. This has had a significant impact on the take-up rates for e-commerce services ranging from as e-banking to online theatre ticket purchase.

Lessons from the Field

The main lesson learned is that 'home' and 'community' access do not exclude each other, but can instead be viewed as complementary alternatives. It has been clearly demonstrated in Hungary that Telecottages assist in the expansion of home computer and Internet penetration in general. A perceptible rise in computer and home-internet use in those settlements where telecottages have been established has been observed. A significant rise in demand for the kinds of services provided on the internet has been observed, as has participation in education and learning programmes. It is clear to us that community accessibility has both increased and helped satisfy latent demand in rural parts of the country. It has also led to a marked improvement in the quality of civil life; in almost every case there are significantly more NGOs operating in those communities where a telecottage is to be found than in those where one is not.

Limitations of the Model

The main limitation of the telecottage as it operates in Hungary is, unfortunately, also its main source of strength: its civil basis. This has meant that a fight for survival and sustainability has characterised the first ten years of the movement's existence. If a means cannot be found to address this situation, it may be that the individual telecottages will start to disappear, especially considering how many of them rely on the sacrifices of committed individuals to survive. The main issue that must be addressed relate to the lack of a culture of donation in Hungary.

The lack of a real technological infrastructure is another shortcoming of the model. Many telecottages are difficult to contact because e-mail addresses and phone numbers change. At present there is no central server that supplies all the telecottages with e-mail access, for example. Telestart, a business partner is addressing this problem but this process is a long one.

The loose nature of the network can also often seem like a shortcoming. Many telecottages seek to take an active role in the association's affairs, however many prefer to keep to themselves. However we continue to see ourselves as a support organisation and we prefer that the telecottages remain independent and thus are better able to address local needs.

Other Initiatives in the Country

Sulinet: Helping students and teachers gain access to the information society.

Library-based Access: Provision of computers and Internet access in libraries.

E-Hungary: Government programme to provide access on a national basis.

Post office - Telecottage Partnership: Alliance of post offices and telecottages in communities too small to sustain one or the other.

Website and Contact Information

Teleházak Háza
http://www.telehaz.hu

Tom Wormald
Alkotmány u. 15 Fsz 1/a 1054, Budapest, Hungary

CHILE

Community Telecenters

Pedro Hepp and Rodrigo Garrido
Instituto de Informática Educativa (Universidad de la Frontera)

Project Summary

In Chile, thirty-two Community Telecenters and Infocenters form the Community Information Network (Red de Información Comunitaria), created in 1997. Coordinated under the auspices of the Institute for Educational Informatics (Instituto de Informática Educativa, Universidad de la Frontera), the telecenters are strategically located in areas that have the lowest level of human development and the highest concentration of indigenous population of La Araucanía Region.

The services provided through the Community Telecenters are oriented towards bridging two kinds of divides: 1) Digital - lack of access to information and communication technologies and 2) Cognitive - lack of knowledge in how to make use of information resources. The Telecenters are managed by local members of the community and the activities and training programs offered on them target women, indigenous communities, the unemployed, seniors, social leaders, the handicapped and also, local micro entrepreneurs.

Socio-Economic Impacts

The socio-economic impacts of Community Telecenters could be described as:

- Increasing human capital by offering access and training programs in ICT;
- Strengthening the social fabric;
- Increasing self-esteem of people participating in the ICT programs who after overcoming the technological shock (el shock tecnológico) become frequent users of the Community Telecenters;
- Providing access to ICTs in areas where access is limited;
- Facilitating access to online information to improve decisionmaking;
- Opening new possibilities for local businesses to flourish;
- Modernizing the management of small and medium enterprises (SMEs) through ICT training programs offered at the Community Telecenters;

- Strengthening business opportunities for SMEs through the use of ICT. The use of ICTs opens unparalleled possibilities for SMEs to diversify their activities more efficiently and attracting more resources for their businesses.

Sustainability Model

The sustainability model of Chile's Community Telecenters is based on three pillars:

1) Social, which is structured along two components:

- Training of Telecenters' managers in the use of ICT and in the appropriation of different strategies to administer the telecenters and to participate in other community work;

- Community Participation in every activity related to the telecenters. Specifically, developing participatory research practices that link the community with the Telecenter's management team. The main purpose of this component is to generate the social fabric that supports and manages the Community Telecenters.

2) Economic, which refers to the activities that contribute to the financial sustainability of the Community Telecenters. The economic pillar of the model is designed along two lines:

- Provision of services (Internet access, photocopying, printing) for a fee;

- The selling of products such as diskettes and CDs. These two sources of revenue combined, increase the possibilities for a Community Telecenter to become sustainable.

3) Technological, which refers to the framework that will ensure the optimum technical functioning of the Community Telecenters. For this purpose two processes have been developed:

- Technical support to prevent or repair malfunctions of the equipment. A technical team from the Instituto de Informática Educativa (IIE)[1] performs field visits and online monitoring of the Community Telecenters;

- Technical training of Community Telecenters' managers to develop the necessary skills to diagnose technical problems and to either generate local solutions to overcome them or to look for support with the technical team at the IIE.

The initial investment for setting up a Community Telecenter is USD 15,000, which includes: computer equipment, database, networking, power supply and electric wiring to support the increase in energy demand, furniture, and stationary. This initial capital comes from three different sources:

- *The Local Municipality*, which provides the telecenter with the physical space, connectivity and the telecenter operator;

- *Chilean Government* (Regional and Federal), which provides the equipment and makes informational resources available for the telecenter. The investment required for technological equipment comes, in part, from the subsidies available through the Telecommunications Development Fund (FTD2, Fondo de Desarrollo de Telecomunicaciones 2), and from donations of recycled equipment by not-for-profit organizations, such as TodoChil@anter;[2]
- *Institute for Educational Informatics*, which provides technical assistance regarding the implementation of different models to operate the telecenters.

On average, the monthly operational cost of a Community Telecenter is USD 550 (See Figure 1 below for costs breakdown) and the revenues generated by the telecenter itself cover 39 per cent of the total cost (USD 230) and a third of the utilities expenses (water, electricity, gas).

Figure 1. Distribution of Costs of a Community Telecenter (per month)

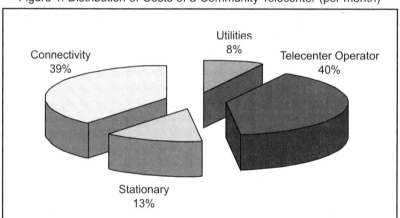

Technology Infrastructure
It has been observed that a typical Community Telecenter is equipped with 2-18 computers, Laser and Bubble Ink Printers, Photocopy machine, Fax and Scanner and Handicapped Kit (Magic Touch, Mouse Kid Trac+). In terms of connectivity, Community Telecenters use a variety of modes - Cable, RDSI, dedicated and analog lines 56/64/128 KBPS modems - depending on the availability in the area.

Partnerships
Partnerships have played a major role in the realization of Community Telecenters. Chilean government, non-government, private sectors, and multisectorial agencies are some of the partnership pillars described below:

Government

The Chilean government has been the most valuable partner in the deployment of Community Telecenters. Some of the government departments and agencies are mentioned below:

- Ministry of Economy and Mining;
- Undersecretary of Telecommunications;
- Department of Libraries, Archives and Museums;
- National Institute for the Youth;
- Service for Technical Cooperation;
- Institute for Provisional Normalization;
- Solidarity and Social Investment Fund;
- National Foundation for overcoming poverty;
- Corporation for productivity encouragement;
- La Araucania Regional Government;
- Municipalities Association of La Araucania region;
- Municipalities of La Araucania Region (27 or 83.3 per cent of the municipalities participate in the program);
- Municipalities Association of Nahuelbuta.

Non-Governmental Organizations

- Association of Mapuches Communities "Lonko Leftraru" (Lumaco);
- Trafkin;
- Ekhos I+C Consultants;
- Gente Expresa.

Private Sector

- CorpAraucania;
- Temuco Chamber of Commerce.

Multisectorial

- Coordination of Infocentros (Chilean Government);
- Regional Office for Information and Communication Technologies of Araucania (MRTIC-A)[3.]

Lessons from the Field

Financial Sustainability

Community Participation is the most important ingredient to achieve financial sustainability. The community where the telecenter is established is the most appropriate source of information regarding the mechanisms to foster sustainability, from developing strategic alliances to determining the type of services, fees and products that better suit local needs.

Technology
- There must be a careful process regarding the selection of equipment provided to each Community Telecenter. Not only in terms of choosing appropriate technology considering community demand but also in terms of the quality and warranty that each provider offers.

- The equipment must be simple and include restoration software that enables easy solutions for certain technical malfunctions.

The Community
- Community involvement in the design of the strategic plan to implement the Community Telecenter is crucial not only to procure financial sustainability, but most importantly, to offer services and different use tailored to local needs. This strategic plan must consider the concrete problems that affect the community and the ways in which the telecenter can become a mechanism through which alternative solutions can be found.

- Learn about local cultural practices of the communities in order to develop a localized use of information and communication technologies that is respectful of traditions.

- Develop a heterogeneous curriculum as a base for the ICT training programs. This curriculum must be founded on the understanding that people have different learning needs.

Scalability/Replicability
Management
- Creating an entity (Community Information Network) that coordinates the management, training activities, evaluation, monitoring, technical support and operation of the Community Telecenters is crucial in order to ensure the scalability of the program and to increase the chances for achieving financial sustainability.

- Finding members of the local communities to operate and manage the telecenters ensures that the activities and training programs offered are responsive to local needs.

- Development of evaluation methods to monitor telecenter activities and performance involving different actors from the community.

Knowledge Transfer
- Generation of training processes for telecenters' managers that include from technical support, to community intervention and diffusion. Leveraging from the expertise that managers acquire through these training programs allows

them to become technological agents in their communities and fosters the autonomy of the telecenter.

- Implementation of appropriate pedagogical methodologies that foster effective processes of technological appropriation by the communities. The main pillars of the Community Telecenters' model are: trust, participation, leverage from cultural capital of the communities and incremental learning.

Generation And Strengthening Of Social Networks
- Identification of existent social networks in the communities - NGOs, governmental social programs, SMEs etc. - that can be linked to the activities of the Community Telecenters, either as users of the services offered or as providers of new ones.

- Development of the Community Information Network providing a space where telecenters' operators can exchange information, knowledge and experiences.

Limitations of the Model
Community Empowerment
There is no "one-model-fits-all" strategy to promote community empowerment through the use of the telecenters. The process of developing community social capital is not standard; rather, it depends on the social and organizational dynamics embedded in each community.

Technological Constrains
- High connectivity costs in Chile limit the scalability of Community Telecenters to areas where access is available. There are some alternative solutions to the connectivity problem but the quality still remains poor.

- There is a need to develop a structure that enables the efficient provision of technical support to the Community Telecenters.

Financial
- High dependency on the subsidies provided by the Telecommunications Development Fund (Fondo de Desarrollo de Telecomunicaciones) for the implementation and operation of the Community Telecenters.

Other Initiatives in the Country
Red de Enlaces Abierta a la Comunidad: a national strategy designed and managed by the Ministry of Education designed to expand ICT access to a wider segment of the population by establishing Infocenters - Schools (Infocentros - Escuelas) and to bridge the cognitive divide through the creation of ICT training programs. http://www.enlacesycomunidad.cl

BiblioRedes Abre tu Mundo: managed by the Department of Libraries, Archives and Museums and financed by the Gates Foundation and the Chilean Government. This initiative was established to provide computer equipment to municipal public libraries (Bibliotecas Publicas Municipales) and to develop ICT training programs. http://www.biblioredes.cl.

Maule Activa: implemented in El Maule region to provide ICT access and support to micro and small enterprises. This initiative is similar to the Community Information Network. http://www.mauleactiva.cl.

Website and Contact Information

Community Telecenters - Community Information Network
http://www.redcomunitaria.cl

Mr. Pedro Hepp and Mr. Rodrigo Garrido
info@redcomunitaria.cl

Notes

1. Institute for Informatics and Education (Universidad de la Frontera). http://www.iie.ufro.cl

2. Initiative headed by the Chilean President's Wife with the objective of empowering disadvantage communities through the provision and access to information and communication technologies.

3. Mesa Regional de Tecnologias de Informacion y Comunicacion Araucania (MRTIC-A).

EL SALVADOR

Infocentros

World Resources Institute*
Washington, D.C. (USA)

Project Summary

Infocentros is the product of a 1998 joint El Salvador-World Bank national consultation on the information society called Conectandonos Al Futuro (Connecting to the Future).[1] The consultation engaged experts and citizens from all segments of Salvadorian society in working groups, teleconferences, and face-to-face meetings to identify methods to develop El Salvador's rudimentary Internet infrastructure. The goal was to improve Internet access in a country suffering from a gaping digital divide. As of 1999, only 40,000 Salvadorians, some 0.7 per cent of the population, were using the Internet.[2] This extremely low penetration rate was to a large extent the result of access costs that, at USD 30 to USD 40 per month, equaled 20 per cent to 45 per cent of El Salvador's average minimum monthly wage. Moreover, because the country's fixed telephone infrastructure is so limited (only 20 per cent of urban residents and 2 per cent of rural residents own phones), home dial-up Internet access is unavailable to most citizens at any price.

As a non-profit entity, Infocentros was able to negotiate generous financing from the Salvadorian government. The recent privatization of the state telecommunications company (ANTEL) and the sale of licenses to telecom operators gave El Salvador a financial windfall that it was encouraged to re-invest in information technology. With the support of the country's Finance Minister, the government granted Infocentros a 10-year, USD 10 million interest-free loan with a four-year grace period. In exchange for these terms, Infocentros agreed to use the funds to create a network of 100 telecenters within a two-year period, along with relevant content and applications identified during the Conectandonos consultation as critical to the country's Internet development.

The IA business strategy is built around franchising: of the 100 telecenters planned by the end of 2002, only 10 will be operated by IA itself as regional "mother" centers.[3] Franchises will cost about USD 80,000 and are expected to be

*This case study was adapted from an earlier publication and it is reproduced here with permission from WRI: Kheladi, Yacine (2001) "What Works. The Infocentros Telecentre Model". World Resources Insitute, Digital Dividend. Washington D.C.

profitable within 27 months. However, IA will launch each center and get it operating well before handing it over to the franchise partner; franchise revenues will be re-invested in additional centers and new services. Telecenters will typically have 20 computers and include open access and training areas.

Infocentros hopes that its network of Internet centers will reach 2 million middle- and low-income Salvadorians, or 30 per cent of the country's population. To reach nearly a third of the country, Infocentros plans to minimize Internet user costs, provide access where it is not currently available, transform the cultural perception of the Internet as inaccessible and complex, and stimulate demand for Internet services by creating content and applications that are relevant to the needs of Salvadorians.

Socio-Economic Impacts

- Development of nationwide IT infrastructure to provide low cost access by building a network of physical and virtual facilities.

- Generation of human capacity that fosters cultural transformation in the Salvadorian society.

Sustainability Model

Although formally a non-profit, Infocentros is headed by a CEO and will build, operate, and franchise telecenters throughout El Salvador. The IA business strategy is built around franchising: of the 100 telecenters planned by the end of 2002, only 10 will be operated by IA itself as regional "mother" centers. Franchises cost about USD 80,000 and are expected to be profitable within 27 months. However, IA launches each center and begins operations well before handing it over to the franchise partner; franchise revenues will be re-invested in additional centers and new services.

The Infocentros business model, with its rapid deployment of franchises to reach scale, enables the enterprise to negotiate favorable contracts for equipment and services from a wide range of vendors. IA also has been very entrepreneurial; negotiating deals with private companies to offer discounted Internet access to groups of employees or clients and agreements with several government agencies to create e-government portals. To increase telecenter usage during evenings and weekends, partnerships are being developed with schools and small businesses that wish to offer computer and Internet training to their students, faculty, and staff. To extend Internet access throughout El Salvador and reduce the need for physical plant, IA is planning to create virtual telecenters located within existing institutions, such as medical centers and central courthouses. And to help perpetuate its entrepreneurial spirit, IA maintains a three-person new business development group charged with assessing new opportunities quickly. Nonetheless, long-term profitability is not assured. As many Internet startups have found, building market share and creating content can be costly. Currently, for example, 90 per cent of IA telecenter users are paying discounted student rates.

Infocentros assists its franchisees by supplying management support, training, technical assistance, network marketing, and other services to help ensure that telecenters remain profitable. But it also uses an enterprise-wide Intranet to share new business ideas across the telecenter network and to compare the monthly performance of each telecenter, providing strong incentives for telecenter managers; managers who do not perform are replaced.

Because of the focus on local content and training, human capacity development is a major outcome of the Infocentros approach. At the telecenter level, Infocentros trains its own rapidly growing staff and offers one-to-one assistance to customers unfamiliar with computers or the Internet. Through alliances with government and business, IA also seeks to teach a large segment of the population how to use information technology to increase skills, create jobs and raise incomes, and overcome social problems. For example, Infocentros is negotiating an 8-hour Internet training course for all Salvadorian high school students, in partnership with the Education Ministry. IA is also developing financial applications for small and micro businesses and still other applications for farmers, doctors, and government officials. IA plans to offer free Web page hosting for the 470,000 small businesses that, in El Salvador, constitute 99 per cent of private enterprises.

Infocentros received the first payment of its loan at the end of February 2000. The initial months were dedicated to planning, organizational development, recruitment, technical design, identification of content and applications, franchise model development, and the preparation of procedures and manuals. Infocentros management reported that they spent an especially long time developing manuals so that they could serve as long-range business guides for the franchises.

The first five telecenters, including the one contiguous to Infocentros' main offices, were opened between October and November 2000 in Auachapan, San Miguel, Santa Ana, Soyanpango, and San Benito.[4] They operated as pilot centers to test the business model and to evaluate capacity use rates, the optimal mix of services offered, organizational and management procedures, income levels of users and price structures, and to iron out technical glitches. After three months of operation, Infocentros disengaged from the finances of these five telecenters. Since April 2001, they have not received any additional cash from Infocentros.

Technology Infrastructure
Telecenters will typically have 20 computers and include open access and training areas. Infocentros will also provide or catalyze the creation of local content, computer training services, and e-commerce infrastructure, in order to make Internet access an effective development tool. It is this content, such as courseware or business applications built around computers and Internet access that is central to the IA business model. Relevant local content generates usage and additional revenue sources for telecenters, as well as significant social benefits for the country.

Partnerships

Infocentros officials believe that ubiquitous IT will facilitate individual empowerment and social transformation, and that developing human capacity is core to achieving this goal. To accomplish this, Infocentros is developing numerous alliances with Salvadorian businesses, NGOs, and government agencies.

For example, Infocentros has entered into an agreement with Costa Rica-based Aura.com to provide online Microsoft Office software training, and is negotiating with Oracle, Cisco, and Adobe for similar training products. In the future, Infocentros plans to offer its own online training modules, but for now finds working with existing products more efficient. Infocentros is also developing financial applications for small and micro businesses and applications for farmers, doctors, and government officials.

Infocentros also plans a variety of activities to educate Salvadorians not only in how to use the Internet, but also in why information technology is essential to their economic future. One step involves designing specific information technology products for target groups most likely to benefit from Internet access, such as academics, professionals, technicians, businesses, government officials, and NGOs. Infocentros has established content development agreements with the Salvadorian government to implement a portal for government services, with the Ministry of Agriculture for a portal on agricultural services, with the Netherlands cooperation agency HIVOS for culture and art programming, with Banco Multisectorial de Inversiones for financial services, and with a Salvadorian business school for a cyber-school project.

Lessons from the Field

Research was conducted in 2001 so the data presented herein reflects the performance of Infocentros of the mentioned period. Currently, the World Resource Institute is planning the second phase of the research.

Financial Sustainability

- Infocentros has developed models to assess the financial feasibility of five different types of facilities, from small "economic telecenters" with 10 public computers to standard facilities with 20 computers, with services varying by facility type. The total initial fixed investment required per facility equals approximately USD 33,512.

- Total startup costs range from approximately USD 54,000 for a low-end operation with 10 PCs to USD 71,000 for a larger facility with 20 computers and all ancillary services. The least expensive facility is just 25 per cent cheaper than the larger, full-service business.

- Infocentros' model calculations determined that a telecenter with 20 PCs, operating at a realistic 45 per cent of capacity, can be economically sustainable. With fewer than 15 computers, the Infocentro franchise is not financially sustainable at reasonable occupancy and use rates. However, the business plan anticipates that with alliances and partnerships up and running, usage will in fact exceed 45 per cent and consequently increase profits.

- Each Infocentro must meet monthly revenue targets to achieve profitability. A monthly revenue stream of USD 7,800 will just cover costs, but income of USD 15,000 monthly is considered a good level of performance.

- In terms of the actual performance of the five initial telecenters for the period November 2000 to March 2001, the facilities had sustained income growth. In only one case, at the center in Auchapán, had there been a small diminution in revenues. Infocentros replaced the facility manager and anticipates resumed growth. In the next few months, four of the five reached the break-even target of USD 7,800. The fact that the San Miguel Infocentro reached this level of revenues relatively quickly was attributed by an Infocentros supervisor to the local manager's ability to identify and market services within local social networks.

Scalability/Replicability

A key aspect of the Infocentros model is the cultivation of multiple revenue streams. In addition to access fees, which are kept low, Infocentros receives substantial revenues from providing training and it operates telecenters as incubators of local businesses that, when successful, share a portion of their revenue with Infocentros. Thus Infocentros departs substantially from the conventional, access-oriented telecenter model, and for this reason may be more scalable and replicable.

Limitations of the Model

The Infocentros model places high demands on its managers. They must not only run daily operations, but also help innovate and incubate new businesses that use the infrastructure. This is a significant challenge, in El Salvador or elsewhere.

Website and Contact Information

Infocentros
http://www.infocentros.org.sv/

World Resource Institute
www.wri.org/

Notes

1. http://www.conectando.org.sv/English/index.htm.

2. International Telecommunications Union, 2001. Telecommunications Indicators. http://www.itu.org.

3. Five telecenters were operational during this case study. The IA business plan projected 18 months for these initial telecenters to become financially self-sufficient, but they achieved it in six months.

Twenty-five additional telecenters are were expected to open by July 2001, and over 5 years the number is was expected to reach 500, although some will be smaller. But as of today only 50 are operational.

4. Another 15 had opened by mid-June, 2001.

PERU

Cabinas Públicas de Internet

Ana María Fernández-Maldonado
Delft University of Technology

Project Summary
Peru stands out in the ICT map of the world thanks to the widespread presence of cabinas públicas de Internet, which constitute the main way of access to Internet of the Peruvian population. More than 85 per cent of Internet users get access through them. Cabinas are simple neighborhood businesses that rent computer connected to the Internet to local customers at affordable prices, especially to those who do not have home access.

The first *cabina* was created in 1995 as an initiative of the Peruvian Scientific Network (Red Cientifica Peruana: RCP), the first Internet service provider in Peru. Since 1998, *cabinas* have spread swiftly in middle and low-income districts of Lima, the capital city of Peru, and soon after in other cities, as individual initiatives of thousands of local entrepreneurs that are providing a service that is in high demand among local customers: cheap Internet access.

Not being the fruit of a centralized organization, the cabinas' organizational model has evolved and adapted itself to different circumstances. Originally, RCP conceived the cabinas as a way to achieve universal access in a country as Peru, where most people do not have sufficient means for home connectivity. The first cabina was located in Lima in the RCP offices. To become a user there was a registration charge and a monthly fee of USD 15 for 20 hours of use of Internet. The cabina was only operational during weekdays and office hours.

In the following years, while RCP was opening new Internet nodes in other cities of Peru, a cabina was sometimes installed by RCP in the recently connected city, and run by universities, local governments or other local institutions. RCP made promotion of this model in international forums and conferences and tried to sell it as a franchise, but with little success at national level. In Lima only three more cabinas were implemented by other ISPs relying in RCP network, and another by an NGO. Due to problems of financial sustainability, RCP gradually evolved from a non-profit consortium of research and educational institutions joined with the goal to provide Internet to the Peruvian population, towards a commercial firm.

The circumstances changed in mid-1998 when the telecommunications sector was opened up to free competition, after four years of monopoly of Telefónica del Peru. The presence of new competitors drastically reduced the prices of dedicated lines. New semi-informal businesses emerged soon after in different areas of the city, generally in commercial places or close to educational institutions. They called themselves cabinas públicas de Internet, a name that was familiar to the population thanks to the wide promotional campaigns previously launched by RCP. However, they had no links with RCP and their organizational scheme was completely different from the RCP model. The new cabinas model was similar to the model of commercial cybercafés and as such much more convenient to the users: they emerged in places of high demand, the computers were rented for the hour, and the businesses were open until late and in the weekend. More important, the fees were much more affordable as computers could be rented for an hour, half an hour, or fifteen minutes. The new model of cabinas soon became extremely popular.

During 1999 and 2000 there was a huge growth in the number of cabinas in Lima. Since then, the main growth has been in the other cities of Peru. During this period, the cabinas spread from commercial areas to middle and low-income neighborhoods of the city, becoming a familiar facility at neighborhood level. This outstanding growth was promoted by a massive local demand, attracted by the continuous reduction of prices. This reduction of final prices was possible thanks to competition at two levels: among providers of the dedicated lines; and among cabinas to secure more clients.

The continued success of this last model is mainly based on the high demand of the population, the capacity and flexibility of the cabinas entrepreneurs to adapt their business to the type of demand of local customers.

Socio-Economic Impacts

The most evident socio-economic effects of the presence of cabinas in Peru are:

- The democratization and extension of access to the Internet to the lower income sectors of the population, who otherwise would not be able to get connectivity;
- The use of computers and the Internet by school and university students in cabinas has become common. According to evaluation studies, this is improving the quality of education;
- Users are much better connected with their families and relatives that live in other provinces or abroad. Social networks, so important for the livelihood of the poor are now extending themselves outside the locality;
- Cabinas are making possible the use of Internet by micro and informal enterprises for different business purposes;

- In poor and informal neighborhoods, which lack standard urban facilities, cabinas are fulfilling the role of libraries, study places, post offices, recreation facilities and youth centers;

- Cabinas are nourishing the growth of a new generation of ICT-literates and ICT-professionals. Children and young people are learning to use computers from each other, and in some cases teaching their own parents;

- ICTs and access to the Internet are seen as a medium to improve life chances by most people and as such something to strive for;

- Peruvians are simply proud of their cabinas, which they consider something "typically" Peruvian.

Sustainability Model

Cabinas are completely commercial and independent small businesses that are established with the purpose of giving revenues to the owners. As they do not enjoy any financial support they have to be sustainable since the first day of operation. This obliges the owners to open a cabina in a place of high demand for the service, therefore to be knowledgeable of the market. Owners are generally knowledgeable of the area where they operate, since they are local residents. This knowledge is of essence to provide those services that are in higher demand in order to achieve the financial sustainability of the business and to adapt the prices to the type of demand of local clients.

Cabinas are generally family enterprises run by entrepreneurs that have little money to invest. For this reason owners try to minimize the initial costs. These include the installation costs of a dedicated line and the internal network, the computer hardware, peripherals and software, the furniture costs, the renting of the space and the license of the local municipality to run the business. Besides the installation costs, the monthly fixed costs include the electricity bill, the rent of the dedicated line, the rent of the location and sometimes advertising. It may include the salary of the administrator(s), in the case it is not the owner.

Owners of the business are generally the administrators. If the owner has no affinity or familiarity with computers one or two young people, generally working in turns due to the long working hours, assist him. The administrators (or the assistants) need to have skills in computer networking, maintenance and repair. They also need to have experience with the different software programs since they assist the clients when they have problems or special requirements.

There are several enterprises specialized in installing cabinas as a whole package, but to lower the costs the owners generally take this task in own hands, hiring technicians in the black market. Regarding hardware, it is usual to buy computers assembled locally, with parts imported from China, Taiwan or Korea, which saves installation costs. Regarding software, most cabinas buy low-cost software programs reproduced without license by local dealers.

When the cabina is in activity, there is generally a high level of competition to attract clients with other *cabinas* working in the neighborhood. Cabinas' owners tackle this by trying to lower the costs as much as possible, making promotions (cheaper prices in the morning or in the night hours, or one free hour for every ten hours of use, etc.), and in some cases advertising their services at local level.

The prices in Lima are generally 2 Peruvian soles (USD 0.57) for the hour in middle income areas and 1.50 soles (USD 0.43) in lower income neighborhoods. In other cities of Peru they charge 1.50 or 1 sol (USD 0.30) for the hour. Thanks to these low prices, much lower than home access, and to the better connectivity of cabinas in comparison with home access, cabinas are extremely popular and used even by people with home access.

Technology Infrastructure

Each cabina is equipped with 10 to 12 Windows-based PC computers, on average, but some have up to 30. The computers are mainly of the Pentium III type, equipped with MS Office, Internet browser, and instant messaging software. All computers are connected to a printer. Some computers have, in addition, more sophisticated equipment such as CD and/or DVD burners, digital video cameras for videoconferencing, scanners, joysticks and microphones. In some cases one or more computers have a faster connection, so there is a special tariff to use them. Other services include as photocopies, fax, selling disks and CDs. They also generally sell cold drinks and sweets.

The connection to the Internet is made with dedicated lines that are provided by different ISPs. A dedicated line is the best choice for the connection to Internet backbones as it is a connection from point to point. As there is no intermediary node, this type of connection is faster, with fewer errors and more reliable. The dedicated lines can have 64 Kbps, 128 Kbps, 256 Kbps, 512 Kbps, 1Mbps or 2 Mbps of bandwidth, but the most used are the lower speeds of 64 (for 12 computers) or 128 Kbps (for 25 computers). They can be landlines or wireless lines.

Main Stakeholders

Cabinas have emerged as individual commercial initiatives without initial support from the government or the private sector. However, due to their prevalent success they are increasingly attracting the interest of both. NGOs have not been interested in cabinas because they only work for profit. NGOs have focused on the telecentres model, which involves providing Internet services with a social orientation.

Government

Even if there is a fund, FITEL, created to bring telecommunications connectivity to rural areas and isolated villages of Peru, the government approach to universal access in cities has been basically regulating competition in the telecommunications sector. It is only quite recently that the government has begun to pay attention to cabinas. This has been because the visible interest of the population in cabinas. Government officials are now divulging the advantages of the cabinas model in international forums and congresses.

A successful online forum on "Internet Cabinas: opportunities for all" was organized in December 2002 by the National Council of Science and Technology (Consejo Nacional de Ciencia y Tecnología - CONCYTEC) with the purpose to discuss with *cabinas* owners, administrators, users and other stake-holders the main problems and possibilities of the cabinas.

Recently, the government has approved a legislation to regulate the functioning of cabinas. According to it, all cabinas must have at least two computers to be used by children. At the same time, all computers should have filters to avoid that children be exposed to adult content.

Other public institutions that have shown clear interest in the cabinas are:

- National Institute for Telecommunications Training (INICTEL);

- The Peruvian Telecommunications Regulatory Body (OSIPTEL);

- Commission for the Promotion of Small and Medium Enterprises (Prompyme). This institution has designed a cabina network: Cabipymes, the members of which have been trained to promote the use of Internet by SMEs;

- The Service of Tax Administration (SAT) has a program CabiSat, to promote the electronic payment of taxes through a network of cabinas.

Private Sector
Almost since the origins of the cabinas, traditional and online newspapers and portals have paid attention to their development and published lists of where people can find them. Some of these firms have found a way to take advantage of the possibilities of the cabinas. There are also new firms that have been established to serve the needs of the *cabinas* owners.

- *El Comercio*: *El Comercio* portal created EC-Cab as a new concept linking the portal with cabinas. The cabinas affiliated to the portal get some benefits and free services to improve their business in exchange for using the portal in all computers of the cabina. There are hundreds of cabinas affiliated to EC-Cab in many cities of Peru.

- *Terra Networks*: Terra Networks, a subsidiary of Telefonica, created Terra Cabinas, which sponsors cabinas by providing logistic support and reducing the costs of the dedicated line in retribution for the promotion of Terra's portal. The amount of the reduction depends on the number of hits that the Terra portal gets originated from the affiliated cabina. There are hundreds of cabinas affiliated to Terra Cabinas in many cities of Peru.

- *RCP*: The initiator of the cabinas, with special section on cabinas in its portal. It is a very complete overview of the history, problems, possibilities, cases, etc. It also gives a basic introduction of how to install a new cabina and provide a listing of cabinas, providers, associations, research and an online forum.

- *Adonde*: A Peruvian online portal that maintains a listing of cabinas and an online forum. After RCP, it is the second most consulted directory of cabinas.
- *Revista Info Cab*: This is a magazine specialized in cabinas, distributed to 2500 cabinas in Metropolitan Lima. They organized a Congress for owners and administrators of Cabinas, INFOCABINAS 2003, held from the 9th to the 11th of April 2003, which attracted 1500 visitors.
- *Peru Mundo Internet*: Another firm that promotes the use of cabinas for business purposes. It has organized three National Cabinas Meetings in 2001, 2002 and 2003 and two Fairs (Feria ExpoCabinas) with products for cabinas the last two years.

Associations
- *Cabinas Peru*: A non-profit association of owners that aims to share problems, technical knowledge, projects and initiatives (http://www.cabinasperu.org/).
- *ASPESI*: Peruvian Association of Internet Services - For-profit institution that gathers cabinas' owners and administrators and which offers a series of services to cabinas. They have designed a new cabinas typology: la oficina virtual (the virtual office), with the purpose to serve micro and small entrepreneurs.

Lessons from the Field
The success of the cabinas in Peru has promoted a number of studies to evaluate their effects in the user population. The main findings give some light about the main users and main uses.

Main Users and Uses
The users are very young, and there is a high proportion of school and university students and people with tertiary education. There are also a relatively high proportion of users coming from lower-income groups, since high income groups enjoy home connections.

Communication (e-mail and chat), training, entertainment and surfing the web are the most popular activities undertaken in cabinas. Children and young people visit the cabinas to play online games with other young people in other cabinas. Chat is extremely popular with the youth, an activity that is performed at a Latin American scale. School students attend the cabinas to make their homework and school projects. University students search the web looking for sources for their academic work. Other popular uses include downloading music, adult entertainment and looking for different types of information.

A visit to the cabinas will show that education is a great part of the activities undertaken in cabinas. They are generally very crowded when schools and universities are working. Another significant function of the cabinas is entertainment. Recent surveys on recreation activities of the general population show that cabinas have become the preferred place for recreation since 2002.

Users express their satisfaction with the cabinas to access the Internet. Among the reasons users give for their preference to cabinas are the speed of navigation (better than home connection), the service (they are helped when they encounter technical or software problems), the privacy (cabinas generally have private cubicles), the equipment, the low prices and the location of the cabinas (most users visit cabinas at walking distance from their home).

Main Effects in Society
People with relatives outside the country use e-mail and Voice through Internet to communicate with their loved ones (almost 10 per cent of the Peruvian population lives abroad). The amount of remittances of Peruvian living abroad has grown explosively in the recent years thanks to the increased communication.

The existence of cabinas and their popularity has promoted the awareness that they can be a bridge between the government and citizens (as in Cabipymes, CabiSat, Mi Vivienda Fund, e-government initiatives), as well as a source of revenues for businesses (ECCab, Terra Cabinas, Info Cab, etc.).

They have also promoted the willingness of government officials to provide some services electronically. Examples of current online government activities are e-procurement procedures, customs procedures, payment of traffic fines, payment of municipal taxes, etc.

The existence of cabinas has promoted the emergence of a dynamic sector to provide services and training to the *cabinas* owners and users. The interest of the general population in the topic is outstanding. Meetings, Fairs, Congresses and Forums attract thousands of visitors.

Scalability/Replicability
The cabinas model is an urban model, which might be replicable in cities that offer similar features. Similar types of businesses have also been observed in other cities of the Andean region as in Ecuador and Bolivia, although with less significance than in Peru. The main elements of the cabinas model include:

- Affordable infrastructure: Affordable telecommunications prices for dedicated lines to access the Internet are indispensable. For-profit enterprises need to achieve financial sustainability and profitability since the very beginning. Without affordable connections there is no possibility to make business;

- Local knowledge and skills: To open a cabina and run it successfully requires owners with entrepreneurship spirit, a good knowledge of the local market, some management and technical skills and willingness to work with relatively low returns as the prices go down;

- Scale: Cabinas are simple family businesses and as such they are not special individually. Their value resides in many of them offering computer and Internet services to people without home access. The presence of several cabinas in the same area promotes competition between them, which in turn causes the reduction of the final prices;

- Demand-orientation: Studies show that since the emergence of cabinas, their services and prices have been adapting to the local demand. Those cabinas that were unable to do it have lost the competition struggle and closed the business.

Limitations of the Model

- Sustainability problems in the long run: Most cabinas businesses work with economic practices that are characteristic of the informal sector. This means that they prefer to charge a lower price sacrificing the quality of the service. The revenues are, therefore, not very high. To increase earnings, the cabinas owners try to increase the number of users, attracting them with promotions.

- Due to the low returns, owners do not invest in the future of the business. This problem is made worse with the fact that most cabinas owners do not have enough training or experience on how to run a business, so they do not consider the costs of depreciation and maintenance of the equipment in their fixed business costs;

- Links with the informal sector: Since to keep costs low many cabinas use products produced and commercialized by the informal sector, they cannot get the status of 'formal businesses'. This is why the intents to associate the cabinas in networks by the government, private sector or associations have a limited success. The semi-informal condition of the business hinders the full acceptance of some *cabinas* by official instances and keeps them in an uncertain situation;

- Technical connectivity can become a problem in *cabinas* during peak hours. Dedicated lines are much more efficient than home connections if used properly. However, if too many persons are connecting at the same time, the speed lowers depending on the number of users and type of activity.

Useful Websites: (in Spanish)

Cabinas Virtual Forum and Publications
http://socinfo.concytec.gob.pe/foro_cabinas/default.htm

RCP
http://cabinas.rcp.net.pe/

El Comercio Cabinas
http://www.elcomercioperu.com.pe/ECCab/

Revista InfoCab
http://www.infocab.net/

Peru Mundo Internet
http://www.perumundointernet.com/

Conclusion

Akhtar Badshah
Digital Partners

The challenges are obviously enormous in the effective use of ICT to improve the lives of the world's poor. Nevertheless, the insight provided by the contributing authors and the highlighted case studies demonstrate that innovative solutions are achievable. It is becoming equally obvious that, by meeting the challenges, the benefits to the world community will be great.

Governments, realizing that they cannot develop the solutions alone, are turning to the private sector and civil society organizations to help develop solutions that are effective, financially viable, and sustainable. The case studies emphasize the point that, ultimately, all sectors have to collectively take action and become responsible for creating an environment that encourages economic growth, social equity and stability, and cultural vitality.

The articles and case studies in this volume, as well as reseach being conducted by Digital Partners, demonstrate that various entities are experimenting all over the world with the use of information kiosks to provide a basket of services valuable to poor communities. They show that many are succeeding in spite of unreliable energy sources and connectivity, lack of public-policy support, and inadequate financial resources. The promoters have demonstrated remarkable entrepreneurial skills. Working with limited resources, they have engaged and utilized the skills and knowledge from different sectors and applied highly evolved organizational and managerial tools of the private sector. Because of these innovators, Information Kiosks designed to serve poorer communities, once thought of as a quixotic effort at best, are now integral to an overall global development strategy.

Schware's article points out that private sector kiosks are spreading much faster and in many parts of the developing world. He emphasizes that, with the right government incentives, these kiosks can become viable channels for the distribution of services that can support development goals. The case studies further support Schware's position and make it clear that the active participation of the private sector will be required to meet the information needs of world's underserved billions living in poor and marginal communities. We conclude that partnerships will develop increasingly between civil society, which understands the needs of these billions, and the private sector, which has the technology and skills needed to develop sustainable solutions for these needs.

The "network of places" concept, promoted by Sherry, Salvador and Ilahiane, shows the Information Kiosks that have managed to integrate effectively into existing networks are more apt to be successful. Further, they also point out that these networks pose both an opportunity and challenge to multinational corporations hoping to provide services through networks of Information Kiosks. The private sector is being required to develop new methods and mechanisms for the effective partnership development needed to reach and serve unfamiliar needs and communities.

Possibilities

Whether initiated by the government, private sector, NGOs, multilateral organizations, or individuals, most of the projects discussed recognized the need to collaborate with other sectors. Drishtee's model is based on effective partnership, first and foremost, with the District Collector's office to ensure that e-government services will be provided. The Thailand Canada Telecenter Project depends on an extensive network of partners ranging from the Government of Thailand to private companies, educational institutions and community center managers. In its effort to reduce poverty in some of the poorest regions in China, the Chinese Ministry of Science and Technology (MOST) is collaborating with the United Nations Development Program (UNDP) to establish ICT Centers in 5 provinces. The Telecottages Program in Hungary has 500 operating telecottages built on a tripartite model by involving the community, the business and the government to ensure economic and social development of the community. The success of the Songhai Network of Telecenters in Benin has depended on the partnerships developed between NGOs, schools and local neighborhood associations to ensure that the services offered are of value to the local population.

The authors make it clear that while partnerships and collaborations may be essential to success they are not sufficient for success. The innovations they discuss demonstrate how other key variables can be integrated to ensure efficiency, effectiveness and long-term viability:

- **Projects can share the burden of responsibilities traditionally held by the government alone.** Private sector involvement can often reduce costs and improve service quality and efficiency. Local organizations can also provide essential insight and innovation. A franchised model of kiosks operators shows promise where private operators and the business community are taking the risk rather than the government. Drishtee is an example of a franchised model. The Peruvian Cabinas initial model was a private sector driven approach by Peruvian Scientific Network (RCP). In Benin the local community associations are driving the development of the Songhai Network of Telecenters, whereas in Thailand the private sector is working in partnership with the government in its effort to provide Internet access to the community.

- **Projects can guide future development and influence national policy.** The n-Logue project in India is an effort to develop alternative communication model - wireless local loop - influencing the shift in national thinking that is leading to telecommunication reform for universal access. The long-term goal of the Chinese Ministry of Science and Technology Project is lobbying the Chinese government on national policy changes to cross-subsidize universal access without which most projects will not become financial sustainable. The most successful effort to-date that has had national impact is the Telecottage Movement in Hungary that is now incorporated into the national government's official strategy for developing an information society in Hungary.

- **Projects can tap community involvement.** Working with the larger community to develop a sustainable program has been the goal of several of the projects that we have studied. Kusakabe in his paper states that there are four key functions to build local capacity: effective community organization to support the kiosks; efficient and innovative kiosk managers; telecom service providers; and Kiosk support institutions to provide technical, business and logistical support to kiosk managers. APWKomitel MCI Center (Warnet) in Indonesia is an example of a grassroots approach empowering existing SME and Warnet, which are already in place and operating in the market and society.

- **Projects can develop innovative solutions to financial sustainability.** Several projects have a self-sustaining commercial focus as the driving factor - Drishtee (India), Cabinas (Peru), Warnet (Indonesia), n-Logue (India), Telecottages (Hungary), are all based on a business model. According to Amin, one way to structure a business driven kiosk model is as a franchise and many of the successful efforts analyzed have adopted this approach. Financial sustainability is the key to a successful and scalable model and many of the cases show that they are trying to achieve this.

- **Projects can challenge the traditional use of technology and even serve as incubators of new products and services.** Local wireless loop and rapidly developing WiFi technology are seen as the next frontier to the accelerating the development of information kiosks. Jensen in his paper shows that at the telecommunication infrastructure and access will usually involve both fixed and mobile solutions using wired, satellite, and wireless connectivity along with a mix of low cost access devices. Projects such as n-Logue - and Warnet use local wireless loop for last mile connections, and the Songhai Telecenters use VSAT connections, many of the other projects are tapping into the exiting phone lines or high-bandwidth connections.

- **Projects can effectively exploit networking among the stakeholders to achieve sustainability.** Networking among various stakeholders and between the IK is often key to successful deployment. Stoll in his article shows that building networks of cooperation among NGOs, governments and private sector leads to facilitating efficient exchange of information and resources and fosters coordination within the development community. He further, illustrates the advantages of a network form of organization with lessons from Somos@Telecentros (the Network of Telecenters in Latin America and the Caribbean) underscores the need for having a open relationship between self-interest and common goals in order to exert the power of networking. The Infocentros project in El Salvador is has effectively utilized its network for negotiating better deals from the government and the private carriers.

A Continuum of Possibilities - From Philanthropy to Social Investment
No one disputes that the face of philanthropy has changed over the years. Historically, a few colossal foundations, established by retiring industrialists, contributed to projects that aligned with the interests of their often family-driven board's. Today, philanthropy has become increasingly decentralized and donors want a greater sense of interaction and influence with the grassroots initiatives they support.

There are more endowments today, many resulting from the technology fortunes of the last two decades. Most are in the millions rather than billions and are influenced by their younger, more business and tech savvy contributors. Collectively, they are shaping a new philanthropy where limited funds are being highly leveraged and funneled into the most efficient and effective development programs, creating the opportunity to provide greater benefit with each philanthropic dollar.

The increased interest by these donors in measurable results is creating the opportunity to develop new, transparent, and reliable tools to measure results. Traditional measures, such as the ratio of operations to total budget, are no longer adequate to evaluate the more complex philanthropic initiatives involving multiple collaborators and a myriad of services.

A significant opportunity lies in the potential impact of these changes on the development community. In order, to learn from the trials and experiences of others a system for measuring success and failures needs to be utilized. As is the case with many things in life, while effort and deployed resources are admirable, they do not equate to success, nor is there a linear correlation to impact. Feedback is an essential tool for building solid organizational models and motivating teams.

The venture capital market in the US would collapse if incremental progress was not measured between seed funding and going public. Venture capitalists constantly monitor revenue growth, gross margins, and other key indicators to evaluate if a shift in strategy, management, product offerings, customer acquisition strategy, etc. needs to occur. This level of scrutiny is needed in development efforts as well. The Development sector has heavily relied on the inputs but not enough on the impact. Anecdotes alone will not provide the required information needed to refine or modify projects at regular or needed intervals during the course of their mandate.

There is not enough reliable information for us to effectively measure and compare the various information kiosks efforts. Most currently available information is more promotional than analytical. Wisner in her article lays out a framework for measuring impact and highlights that such an effort is challenging from a number of perspectives. She argues that kiosks represent a non-traditional business model - some kiosks are for-profit ventures, while others are non-profit or partially funded by governments or by donors making comparative measurements difficult. However, the work that needs to be done is to go beyond the standard ROI measurement to a combination of ROI and SROI (Social Returns on Investment). Further research, as Roman and Colle's article show, needs to be undertaken in a comparative and multidisciplinary fashion that will allow us to evaluate a whole range of for-profit and non-profit ventures. At Digital Partners we have just begun to develop the tools that will allow for:

- Ethnographic research to understand the impact of information kiosks on people and the improvement in their lives.

- Social Return on Investment measurements to understand the community-wide economic impact.

- Return on Investment measurements that analyze the financial sustainability of the project and measuring the ability of the project to generate revenue.

As Wisner states "only by having a multi-dimensional set of performance measures that reflect the impact of the kiosks from the viewpoints of multiple stakeholders that a determination can be made about the value created by the ICT kiosk projects", such a study is badly needed and we trust that this book will inspire further development of these analytical tools.

The Road Ahead

The road ahead looks quite promising given the vigorous worldwide experimentation as highlighted by the case studies and the analyses of the contributing authors. The cases and articles show that the models of information kiosks are fast evolving. From mere places of access to the Internet, information kiosks are becoming full-scale community service centers such as Hewlett Packard's i-Village in Kuppam, India.

Information kiosk can also serve as centers of technological innovation and product and service development of value to underserved communities. The El Encuentro Project in Chile is an example where kiosks are fast becoming places of innovation in developing new technology and using information technology in far more innovative ways.

The phase of experimentation is ending. The potential for information kiosks to serve the needs of poor communities is clear. Building blocks to success have been identified. Leadership is needed now to turn opportunity into reality. As we deliberate in Geneva at the World Summit on Information Society, we would like to point out that:

- **Innovation** is evolving at a dramatic rate in developing economies, largely driven by the people and trusted organizations serving the underserved. Today, the question is not whether people living under $1 a day need ICT, but what is the appropriate use of ICT and what are the services needed to raise their income potential. Improved methods of encouraging grassroots innovation and entrepreneurial enterprise must be developed.

- **Government and Regulatory Policy** is generally conservative maintaining the status quo. History, tradition and even prejudice can be subtle and powerful hindrances to the potential of ICT to empower the underserved. Bold and enlightened action is required.

- **Effective Partnerships** are critical but often difficult to develop, especially when they are between sectors that do not have traditional ties. ICT and its impact on the global economy are causing governments, private enterprise, multilateral development organizations, academics, and NGO's to develop new means of understanding and collaboration. Partnerships at the local level are increasing important as ICT serves to devolve power from the center, opening new opportunities to serve the needs of more of the world's people.

- **Networking** has been highlighted by several authors as being a driver especially the effective utilization of existing social and professional networks so that there is a leverage effect. Further, networks are not only social but consist of support structures, financial networks, and network of places.

In conclusion, we would like to leave the reader with five key messages:

1) Information and Communication Technology can play a fundamental role in the economic and social empowerment of poor people all over the world.

2) As the world becomes more connected, inaction by governments to leverage this opportunity will be increasingly criticized. New ICT infrastructures must

consider non traditional opportunities and customers. Policies and regulations must be revised to encourage grass roots innovation, creative partnerships, and new investments in traditionally bypassed communities.

3) Effective social investment requires:
   - Innovative Funding Mechanisms
   - Mobilizing Core Competencies
   - Partnerships
   - Community Capacity Building

4) There can be no "digital dividend" unless business leaders are willing to see beyond today's bottom line and look to the bottom of the economic pyramid and encourage more of the world's people to contribute to and benefit from the global economy.

5) The community information kiosk is becoming a force for positive change in poorer communities. Government leaders can play an invaluable role by supporting the development of effective partnerships among the sectors. To do this, the "inner circle" must be widened to include the stakeholders who have been on the front lines in the use of ICT for development.

About the Authors

Deepak Amin is currently Senior Vice-President at Streamserve, heading its next generation web services products division. Prior to Streamserve, Deepak founded vJungle, Inc, a web services integration and deployment platform company. vJungle was acquired by StreamServe in 2002. Prior to that Deepak started a software services company, Indicus based in Mumbai, India. Deepak also worked at Microsoft for many years as a technical lead in Microsoft Works and Windows95 Networking teams and the Internet Browser team. He is the co-author of the HTTP-based IrDA standard that enables communication between devices over infra-red ports. Deepak received his Bachelor of Technology in Computer Science from Indian Institute of Technology, Bombay and Master of Science from University of Rhode Island. Deepak is a regular speaker at technology and development conferences.

Akhtar A. Badshah is the CEO and President of Digital Partners, a Seattle, Washington-based non-profit organization, where he has been responsible for establishing the organization and building its core programs. He is also an Affiliate Professor at the College of Architecture and Urban Planning, University of Washington. Dr. Badshah has over 20 years of experience as a practitioner, educator, researcher, and development expert. He has worked on projects in the United States, Asia and the Middle East and consulted with The Asia Society, Environment Canada, Pfizer Inc., Graham Foundation, UNDP, USAID, World Resources Institute, World Bank, and other international development organizations. He is the author of *Our Urban Future: New Paradigms for Equity and Sustainability*, (London: Zed Books, 1996). Dr. Badshah is very active in the Seattle area community and serves on various local committees. He is the Co-President of the PTO of his local school; serves on the MIT Alumni Committee for Puget Sound; and is a member of The Indus Entrepreneurs (TiE), Seattle Chapter.

David F. Barr is a Principal with DFB and Associates (a Canadian telecommunications consulting firm focusing on rural areas of developing countries), and the Technical Advisor on the Thailand Canada Telecentre Project (TCTP). He has over 40 years experience as a telecommunications engineer, including 32 years with Bell Canada. Since 1990, he has consulted in telecommunications for the rural and remote areas of developing countries, specifically focused on the development of national policy, regulatory, financing and operational arrangements which encourage and support the provision and continuity of telecommunication services in rural areas. Mr. Barr led the work in Study Group 2 of the International Telecommunication Union Development Sector (ITU-D), as Rapporteur for the Question on "Communications for rural and remote areas", in the 1994 to 1998 study period, which developed five Recommendations, addressing: I) technology options; ii) rural development planning; iii) universal access via telecenters; iv) appropriate regulatory arrangements; and v) sources of finance.

Vasoontara Chatikavanij is Director, Technical and Economic Cooperation Program, Loxley Public Company Limited (major Thai conglomerate), and Project Manager of the Thailand Canada Telecentre Project (TCTP). She has experience with an Internet Service Provider, Data Hosting, Data Sync Gateway for Personal Digital Assistant (PDA), e-business process automation, e-commerce and payment online, EDI, and advertising online/offline. Ms. Vasoontara Chatikavanij was one of the architects of the "thick server thin client solution" developed by Loxley. She holds a MBA in area of International Business and Marketing from SASIN Graduate Institute of Business Administration of Chulalongkorn University (http://www.sasin.edu/) a joint academic endeavor of Kellogg School of Management of Northwestern University and the Wharton School of the University of Pennsylvania.

Royal Colle has been on the faculty of Cornell University for 37 years, focusing especially on communication for social change and development. In 2002, he received a lifetime achievement award from the International Communication Association. He has served as a development communication consultant for the World Bank, the Food and Agriculture Organization, the World Health Organization, and the U. S. Agency for International Development. Most recently, Mr. Colle has been active in studying and writing about the telecenter movement in developing nations, as well as assisting in telecenter project planning in India and Mexico.

Ana María Fernández-Maldonado is Research Associate in the Spatial Planning Chair of the Section of Urbanism of the Faculty of Architecture at Delft University of Technology in the Netherlands. She is involved in research on the relationship between Information and Communication Technologies (ICTs) and the contemporary city since 1997. Since that date she has coordinated a Design Studio for the students of the Faculty addressed to that topic. She has published in different scientific journals on topics related to the Internet in developing countries. She is presently finishing her PhD research on ICT transformations in Latin American metropolises.

Jose Maria Figueres is the Chairman of the United Nations ICT Task Force and the Managing Director of the Centre for the Global Agenda, World Economic Forum and former President of Costa Rica. From 1988 to 1990, he was the Minister of Foreign Trade and Minister of Agriculture. Mr. Figueres earned a Bachelor's degree in Industrial Engineering at the US Military Academy at West Point and a Masters in Public Administration from the Kennedy School of Law and Government at Harvard University.

Richard Fuchs is Director, of Information and Communication Technologies for Development. A Sociologist, he established North America's first system of rural telecenters and online services beginning in 1988 as the CEO of a Crown Corporation in Newfoundland called Enterprise Network Inc. He also served as a Commissioner with the Newfoundland Economic Recovery Commission and, from 1996-2000 operated his own company, Futureworks, which won the International Trade Exporters Award from Minister Pettigrew in 2000. In January 2001, Mr. Fuchs joined IDRC as its first Director of Information and Communication Technologies for Development.

Maria Garrido is a PhD Candidate in the Department of Communication at the University of Washington and a Research Associate at Digital Partners, a Seattle, Washington-based non-profit organization. Her research explores the role of information technology in fostering economic development in low-income communities with a focus in Latin America. She has published research on how grassroots organizations make use of new media as a tool to mobilize and create networks of support on a global scale (Cyberactivism: Online activism in Theory and Practice, Rutledge 2003). She earned her Bachelor's degree in International Relations at the Universidad Iberoamericana in Mexico City, and a Masters in International Relations at the University of Chicago.

Rodrigo Garrido holds a Masters Degree in Technology for Education and Works as the Director of the Community Information Network at the Instituto de Informática Educativa of Universidad de La Frontera. He is a permanent member of the board that coordinates the government Infocentros in Chile and acts as an adviser to the Ministry of Education in Chile on the design and implementation of the "Red Enlaces Abierta a la Comunidad" project.

Mátyás Gáspár is currently president of the Hungarian Telecottage Association, a post he has held since 1995. He has worked in a variety of other fields during this time, chiefly concerned with public management and government community relations. He is the author of several books including *Local Government Management, Build a Telecottage!*, and *Telecottages and Telework in Hungary*.

Allen Hammond is Vice President for Innovation and Special Projects at the World Resources Institute, a non-profit, non-partisan policy research institute located in Washington, D.C. His responsibilities include institute?wide leadership in Internet strategy and digital technologies and development of new initiatives. He also directs WRI's Digital Dividends project and consults on ICT-for- development with foundations, development agencies, and a number of major corporations. His book, *Which World?: Scenarios for the 21st Century*, focused on the long-term sustainability issues facing the world. Dr. Hammond holds degrees from Stanford University and Harvard University in engineering and applied mathematics. Prior to joining WRI, he helped to edit the international journal Science and went on to found and edit several national publications,

Jingjai Hanchanlash is Chairman, Loxley Pacific Company (major. Thai conglomerate); Secretary General, Development Cooperation Foundation (DCF); and Project Director (Thailand) of the Thailand Canada Telecentre Project (TCTP). Dr. Jingjai Hanchanlash has nine years experience with a government agency dealing with aid coordination, 23 years with the International Development Research Centre (Canadian research funding agency on international development issues) of which 17 years were spent as the Regional Director for Asia, and six years in the private sector with Loxley Public Co. He was formerly Chairman, Telecommunication, IT and E-Commerce Commission, International Chamber of Commerce; and Director, Thai Chamber of Commerce. He is currently administering a Good Governance program through Development Cooperation Foundation (DCF), which is funded by a CAD 1.5 million CIDA grant to Thailand.

Pedro Hepp is a civil engineer with a doctorate in computer science. Between the period of 1993-1997 he acted as the National Coordinator for the Educational Network Enlaces. He directed the Insititto de Informatica Educativa at the Universidad de La Frontera until 2001. He is currently a consultant in areas of Educational Informatics and new technologies and education for a variety of international organizations, among them the World Bank. Currently, he is working as an advisor tothe Ministry of Education in Chile in the area of the politics of technology for education.

Hsain Ilahiane is assistant professor of anthropology at Iowa State University. He has served on the faculty since receiving his PhD from the University of Arizona in 1998. Dr. Ilahiane's primary research focuses on natural and cultural resource management, ethnicity and social mobility, and technological and cultural change. A Moroccan by birth (of Berber descent), Dr. Ilahiane has most recently been involved in studying the uses of mobile technology in economic, social and cultural development in his native country

Mike Jensen is a South African independent consultant with experience in over 35 countries in Africa assisting in the establishment of information and commu-

.nications systems over the last 15 years. He provides advice to international development agencies, the private sector, NGOs and governments in the formulation, management and evaluation of their Internet projects. Mr. Jensen is a trustee of the African IT Education Trust, a board member of the South African Internet service provider for NGOs - SangoNet - and was a member of the African Conference of Ministers' High Level Working Group which developed the African Information Society Initiative (AISI) in 1996.

Dr. Ashok Jhunjhunwala is a Professor at the Electrical Engineering Department, IIT Madras, and heads the Telecommunications and Computer Networks (TeNeT) Group there. He graduated from IIT Kanpur, and received his MS and Ph.D. from the University of Maine, USA. He joined the faculty of IIT Madras in 1981 and was Head of the Electrical Engineering Department from August 1998 to July 2001. He was a founder of the TeNeT Group at IIT Madras - a team of telecommunications faculty members from IITM committed to the development of the education and the telecommunications sector in India. He was awarded the Padmashri in 2002 for distinguished service in Science, Engineering and Telecommunications. His other awards include Vikram Sarabai Research Award-1997, Shanti Swarup Bhatnagar Award-1998, Millennium Medal by CSIR-2000 and the H.K.Firodia Award-2002.

Sarbuland Khan is the Director of the Division for ECOSOC Support and Coordination of the United Nations Department of Economic and Social Affairs. Mr. Khan directed the preparation of the Ministerial meeting of the Economic and Social Council on ICT for development and has been responsible for its follow-up in the context of servicing the Secretary-General's Advisory Group on ICT and the establishment of the United Nations ICT Task Force. Mr. Khan has held numerous positions in the United Nations for the past twenty years. Prior to joining the United Nations, he was the Director for Economic Coordination in the Ministry of Foreign Affairs of Pakistan. Mr. Khan holds a Masters degree in economics.

William J. Kramer is a Senior Fellow at the World Resources Institute, where he also serves as Deputy Director of the Digital Dividends program. Mr. Kramer founded The Knowledge Initiative, Inc., a non-profit organization working on issues of knowledge and development. His work in the non-profit arena follows a 30-year career as an entrepreneur in the book industry and in other arenas. He founded, and remains president of, Kramerbooks & afterwords, the original bookstore/café, in Washington, D.C. He was more recently a principal in several companies that served colleges and universities with web-based applications for campuses, including e-procurement, digital printing and publishing, and course management tools. As a consultant, Mr. Kramer has worked with global companies, NGOs, and think tanks. He has served on numerous boards for local, regional, and national organizations.

Motoo Kusakabe is the Senior Counselor to the President of the European Bank for Reconstruction and Development, and the founder of E-Community Link (a non-profit organization to bridge the Digital Divide). He retired from the World Bank's Vice-President for Resource Mobilization and Co-financing in January of this year and spent half a year at Stanford University as a visiting scholar. He joined the World Bank in 1997. Mr. Kusakabe has been responsible for mobilizing concessional resources for the Bank's operations for poor countries. He led the Bank's initiative to promote global partnership programs as the Chair of the Council of Development Grant Facility, and has been instrumental in drumming up support for the ICT and Development, community-driven initiatives and has promoted partnership with NGOs and foundations. He initiated the Global/Local Connectivity Workshop in December 2000, and promoted the Community Telecenters in the World Bank. Before joining the World Bank, he worked for the European Bank for Reconstruction and Development as Country Director for Uzbekistan and Kazakhstan and held other operational positions there. Mr. Kusakabe held key positions at the Japanese Ministry of Finance including Deputy Commissioner of National Tax Administration and Deputy Director-General of Banking Bureau in charge of financial sector reform. He has a M.A.in Mathematics from the University of Tokyo and M.Phil in economics from Yale University.

Morenike Ladikpo is the Research Officer for the Acacia Initiative (Communities and the Information Society in Africa) and the Connectivity Africa (a new initiative) of Canada's International Development Research Centre (IDRC). Prior to joining IDRC, she helped set up three Songhai telecenters in rural Benin Republic. She also worked with a web development agency in Paris, France.

Bruno Lanvin joined the World Bank in September 2000 as E-commerce and E-governance Advisor. Before that, he was Head of E-commerce in UNCTAD (United Nations Conference on Trade and Development) in Geneva (1996-2000). Since 1979, he has held various positions in the United Nations in New York and Geneva, covering international trade, telecommunications and technology issues. A French national, he holds an MA in Mathematics and Physics, an MBA from HEC (Paris) and a PhD in economics from La Sorbonne (Paris).

Osama Manzar is the Founder and Secretary of Digital Empowerment Foundation, Founder and Editor-in-Chief of Inomy.com; India. As an ICT expert, Mr. Manzar is a widely quoted IT entrepreneur, editor, columnist, and new media specialist. He has authored "The Internet Economy of India", and was awarded a joint Chevening/Young Indian IT Professional Programme 2002 Scholarship by the Foreign and Commonwealth Office to attend the Advanced IT Management Programme at Manchester Business School. He is an ICT4D Advisor to Development Gateway Foundation and is cofounder and board member of 4Cplus, a software company in New Delhi.

Jonathan Peizer is currently CTO of the Open Society Institute where he developed and managed that organization's Internet Program as well as its IT area. Mr. Peizer has worked in both the for-profit and non-profit world in a variety of technology related positions with, for example, Citicorp and the Soros Foundations. He is founder of for-profit business as well as a non-profit software development NGO for the civil sector called Aspiration. Mr. Peizer has written numerous articles on non-profit's use of ICT as well as ICT and development issues. He has over two decades of work in technology related activities and has performed work in approximately 75 countries. He is currently focusing his efforts on the strategic use of technology by the civil sector while managing OSI's Internet Policy and ICT Toolsets Portfolio through the Information Program.

Francisco J. Proenza is an Economist with the Investment Centre of the Food and Agriculture Organization of the United Nations. He has extensive international experience, mainly in Latin America and the Caribbean and in Africa, in the design of investment projects for multinational agencies. He holds a PhD in Food and Resource Economics from the University of Florida. His recent work focuses on the application of information and communication technologies to help combat poverty.

Raul Roman is a doctoral candidate at the Communication Department of Cornell University. His research focuses on the impact of information and communication systems on socioeconomic development in disadvantaged communities of the developing world. He has conducted research on rural telecenters in South Africa and India and is currently working on a project to evaluate the use and impact of electronic agricultural research resources in research centers and universities of Asia, Africa, and Latin America.

Rudy Rusdiah is the founder and chairman of the nonprofit APWKOMITEL (Association of Community Internet Center), which has more than 200 warnets (cyber cafes). The mission of this organization is to empower the community with Internet access anywhere. Previously he worked as a Director of Micronics Internusa PT, distributor and reseller for DELL Computers. He acted as a member of the Steering Committee Indonesian National IT Framework (NITF). He got his BE in Electrical Engineering from Carleton University in Ottawa, Canada and MBA from Indonesian University.

Tony Salvador received his Bachelor of Arts degree in Experimental Psychology from Franklin & Marshall College in Lancaster, Pennsylvania. He went on to earn a Ph.D. in Human Factors and Experimental Psychology at Tufts University in Boston. Mr. Salvador was born in Newton, New Jersey, and lives in Portland, Oregon

Robert Schware is Lead Informatics Specialist in the World Bank's Global ICT Department. He was the Task Manager of the Bank Group's Information and Communications Sector Strategy Paper. He has nineteen years of experience in Bank operations working on telecommunication reform and information techno-logy-related projects in East and South Asia, Africa, the Caribbean, and the Middle East. Before joining the World Bank, Dr. Schware consulted for UNIDO, the UN Software Technology Institute in Macau, UNRISD, and USAID. He con-ducted some of the first field work in the use and effectiveness of microelectronic techno-logy applications in rural development projects in the Middle East and Africa. He has authored and co-authored several books and papers on informa-tion techno-logy including, an Internet Toolkit Manual for Policy Makers in Africa, Information Technology and National Trade Facilitation Guide to Best Practice, and Rural Applications of ICT in India.

John Sherry was born in Portland, Oregon. He received a Bachelor of Science degree in Computer Science from the University or Portland in 1985. He holds a Ph.D. degree in Anthropology from the University of Arizona. Mr. Sherry joined Intel's People and Practices Research Group in 1996.

Klaus Stoll studied theology in Germany and the UK and has been active in the ICT's for development sector for over 15 years. In 1997 he co-founded Fundacion Chasquinet in Quito, Ecuador. The main aim of Chasquinet (www.chasquinet.org) is to promote the strategic use and development of the Internet in the social sectors of developing countries through research, education and enhanced co-mmunication. His personal goal is to further develop, in co-operation with other relevant organizations and individuals, the policies, strategies and tools that are very much needed in order to use the available information technologies as a effective means for just development.

Njideka Ugwuegbu is the Executive Director of Youth for Technology Foundation (YTF), an international non-profit organization in Nigeria, West Africa and in Washington. Ms. Ugwuegbu's vision for Nigeria is one that brings the benefits of information and communication technology to rural communities with a particular focos on the youth. Ms. Ugwuegbu graduated with honors from the University of Massachusetts, Amherst where she studied Finance and International Business. She also has an advanced degree from the Haarlem Business School in Holland. She is currently a Reuters Digital Vision Fellow at Stanford University. Ms. Ugwuegbu serves in an advisory capacity to several African and international non-profit organizations.

Paul Ulrich is currently an independent consultant. Over the past 18 years, he has worked for the private sector, NGOs, and donor agencies in economic, busi-ness, and strategy consulting in 56 countries. With proficiency in multiple foreign languages, expertise in strategic applications of information and communication technologies, and skills in macroeconomics, finance, and econometrics, he most enjoys using cross-disciplinary approaches to applying ICT for developmental objectives. Mr. Ulrich has an undergraduate degree from Yale and graduate degrees in public administration and development economics from Harvard and Stanford.

Priscilla S. Wisner is an Assistant Professor of Global Business at Thunderbird, The American Graduate School of International Management. Dr. Wisner teaches cost management, performance measurement and managerial decision making to MBA and executive education students. Dr. Wisner's research focuses on the implementation of strategy in organizations, concentrating primarily on management control and performance measurement tools. Her most recent research examines and discusses the drivers, management control systems, and impacts of implementing corporate responsibility strategies. Dr. Wisner has over fifteen year's experience in consulting with corporations regarding financial systems implementation, process and product costing, and performance measurement systems. Fluent in Spanish, she has conducted classes in Argentina, Columbia, and Mexico. Prior to joining Thunderbird, Dr. Wisner earned a Ph.D. at the University of Tennessee and an MBA degree from Cornell University.

Warren Wong is a Principal with Hickling Arthurs Low (HAL) Corporation (Canadian management consulting firm specializing in science and technology), and the Project Director (Canada) of the Thailand Canada Telecentre Project (TCTP). He has over 20 years experience in the international development field, focusing on science and technology (S&T) and information and communication technologies (ICT), as a management consultant with HAL and as a program officer with the International Development Research Centre (Canadian research funding agency on international development issues). Major international assignments include: three-year World Bank funded Technical Assistance and Training Program (TATP) on information and communication technologies for small and medium enterprises in Indonesia; five-year CIDA-funded information technology project in Vietnam; and five-year ADB-funded project to develop a social impact monitoring system in Papua New Guinea.

Tom Wormald is a PhD student in Social Anthropology at the University of Manchester, UK, due to complete in January 2005. He is currently on an extended two year fieldwork assignment in Budapest, where he is working as a volunteer at the Hungarian Telecottage Association. He also works part-time at the Soros Foundation, Hungary.

APPENDIX

Resources on ICT Initiatives for Development

Interim Report of Research Conducted by Digital Partners
Seattle, Washington (USA)

ICT Kiosks: A Comparative Study

The Information and Communication Technology (ICT) Kiosk has been widely promoted as the silver bullet to address the "digital divide" confronting rural and poor communities throughout the world. Many models and hundreds of initiatives have been launched through the investment of hundreds of millions of dollars.

In spite of this enthusiasm, little is known about the comparative effectiveness of different models or the essential components of a successful ICT Kiosk initiative. Nevertheless, significant resources continue to be invested in various kiosk models by governments and development institutions in the apparent hope that "if we build it, they will come."

Digital Partners has undertaken a straightforward, six-month research project to discern best practices among various models to guide its investments in this field. The results will be made widely available to the development community in an effort to support the design and deployment of effective and sustainable ICT initiatives working to benefit poorer communities. Research was begun in late April of 2003, however the preliminary findings included in this interim report are intriguing and will shape continued efforts. This investigation is not limited to any specific region and readers are invited to contribute to this research by writing to info@digitalpartners. Please be sure to include "Kiosk Research" in the subject line.

Research Outline
Research projects to date have generally focused on documenting "what" is being done by various noteworthy kiosk initiatives. The intent of this effort is to better understand "how" issues critical to the success of an ICT-kiosk initiative are resolved.

Research Categories
- Content/Services
- Deployment Mechanism
- Economic and Social Impact
- Management
- Replicability
- Sustainability
- Technology

Methodology
- Literature review (including available research papers, relevant websites, recognition awards, etc.)
- Consolidation of models
- Categorization of models
- General findings by region
- Selection of projects within categories for more in-depth investigation
- Refinement of research questions based on overview research
- Conduct interviews and surveys
- In-depth research on selected models by research coordinator and practitioners
- Profiles of selected "best practices" within research categories and of model projects

General Findings by Region
Disclaimer: Specific information about individual projects has been sourced primarily from web-based information, which is often "promotional" in nature. The findings of this interim report will inform further in-depth research on specific projects in India, Latin America, and Africa.

Africa
- Government support of private/public partnerships is critical;

- Market forces alone can't bring the service to rural areas because they are not as profitable as urban ones;

- Local ICT champions are the last link in the chain to stimulate awareness and interest among community leaders to join the ICT revolution.

Sustainability in Terms of Infrastructure and Equipment:

- Unreliability of electricity and telecom connectivity, frustration in service and decrease in use of ICT centers;

- Community ICT centers also need to develop technical capacity to operate communication equipment to maintain a stable service;

- Identification of the best media for delivery of information and communication for the target community. Clients of Timbuktu Telecentre in Mali preferred radio, television, newspapers, telephone and letters. Combination of traditional and new media (Africa Sustainability document page 16);

- If the ICT center is conceived as development agent, simple information and communication functions will not make it sustainable. Need to be relevant for community practices;

- Nakaseke Telecentre has been quiet effective in making local content in agriculture and Indigenous Knowledge (IK) and a lot of experience has been generated in the area. Local Luganda language;

- Need to anticipate trends in usage of ICT, create services and 'cultivate' customers. Need for ICT centers to assess usage pattern once the Telecenter is in place to adjust to changes in community habits;

- Another interesting aspect of infrastructure is the use of mobile devices: It seems that Ghana has the higher percentage of users.

Financial Sustainability for ICT Centers

- An interesting strategy used in South Africa Galesca Telecenter hired 7 agents prior to building it to raise awareness in the community and surveyed needs and interests of people;

- Mamelodi Telecentre in South Africa designed a community directory and offers space for small businesses to advertise at a modest price;

- The staff of the Community ICT centers must prepare to deal with competition in the provision of ICT services.

India

- India is further ahead compared to other countries or regions in the development and use of ICT kiosk models;

- Many of the projects are profit driven. It seems that in India the tiered franchised business model is the most common or at least the projects that are using this model are the most visible;

- Government e-initiatives in India seem stronger than in any other country. India is taking the lead in e-governance initiatives compared with Latin America and Asia;

- The most ambitious ICT kiosk franchise effort has been launched by [S. Kumars.com Ltd.] in India. If it is successful it will have a considerable impact on low-income people. It provides for the installation of an estimated 50,000 kiosks starting with 1,000 in 2001. For a total investment of US$ 4,545, each franchisee is being offered a complete package of services (LA Report, 2000: 47);

- Who supports and maintains the equipment in these centers? This is an issue that few of the big projects address and it could definitely hamper the sustainability of the ICT Kiosks, particularly the ones located in rural areas where there is a lack of connectivity and infrastructure (telecom and electricity is poor);

- Many initiatives by NGOs and other organizations provide access to government services and have developed with initial support from the government. The uncertainty about the future role of government my come to hinder investments from other sectors;

- Greatest number of Local ICT promoters. Most likely the result of technical training in India not found anywhere else in the developing world. It would be very interesting to develop a social network between the local leaders in India that are advocating ICT for development and possible promoters in Latin America to share Indian experiences and lessons that this continent can learned from;

- Some of the projects have had limited success because of lack of advertising within the community. People in the villages some time are not aware of the services that ICT Kiosks can bring to them. May be for the model one key issue to consider is promotion before the Kiosks is build and during the process.

Latin America

- Commercialization of ICT centers can dilute or overwhelm the initial focus on social return. For example, in Peru the progressive RCP initiative has moved away from developing ICT centers since Telefonica has entered the market. Universal access initiatives may be considered as "relevance" is demonstrated;

- Multi-service models work better; it is easier to design business models that combine income generation with access to the poor;

- Commercial ICT centers developed by private sector are healthy businesses but they don't often succeed in reaching the poor. "Universal access" initiatives by governments could foster their spread to rural areas;

- Commercial ICT centers or cyber cafés very common in Latin America (150 Mexico, 700 Argentina, 520 Peru) but mostly serve low-income people in URBAN centers. There is a need to transfer this model to RURAL settings;

- State-centered initiatives can be successful but if decision-making is centralized within the hands of the government, this will discourage participation of private funding and NGO's;

- Hard to assess the most common Telecenter model in LA. It seems that the most sustainable have been the commercial type. The NGOs and School ICT centers however are the ones with higher impact for the rural poor;

- Partnerships are crucial à Need to develop a networking strategy between NGO, Government and International Organizations;

- Need to foster initiatives to network the ICT centers themselves for example: somos@telecentros.org to share information, experiences and possibilities for replicating models;

- There are many interesting government-led initiatives in Latin America taking shape right now, the most renowned: El Salvador Infocentros project;

- Latin America is lagging behind other regions in terms of ICT initiatives. Some critics point to the lack of local leaders, top-down control, rather than support of entrepreneurial experimentation.

ICT Initiatives in the Region

- IDRC Pan-American Initiative (Similar to Pan-Africa and Pan-Asia) provide funds, research for ICT in development;

- In Peru Telecom Company has created the fund FITEL to foster connectivity in rural areas (490 ICT centers planned by 2000);

- In Mexico the e-Mexico initiative, very comprehensive project to connect Mexico. Digital Community Centers are part of the pilot project in partnership with Microsoft and Telefonos de Mexico;

- In Colombia à Ministry of Communications Social program COMPARTEL plans to install Internet Community Access Centers (175) 2001-2002. Partnership with Telefonica and Gilat and second phase open to many other firms;

- El Salvador *Conectandonos al futuro* initiative by the Government with support from the World Bank. June 1999. Infocentros project became part of this after Mexico and Peru's experiences.

AFRICA Information Kiosks (Selected Case Studies)

Name of Project	Country	Funding sources	Areas	Sustainability Model	Services Provided	ICT/Software use	Operation	Geog. Location
1. Sonatel Telecenters	Senegal	SONATEL (National Telecom Operator)	Connectivity and Access	FEE for use but they give email accounts for free	Fax, printing, phone, Internet but is only 1% of telecenter income	8 computers, two printers, a scanner, a photocopier, a VCR/ TV, a video camera, and a projector	Networked 9,000 around country	Rural and Urban areas
2. Bindura Telecenters	Zimbabwe	Zimbabwe Ministry of Education-World Bank sponsored-World Links	IT Literacy Economic Development Access	Free training for teachers and studentsFee for adult training and access in evening	Training for students and teachers on DAYAdult training and access in evening (PAY FEE) crucial for Sustainability Training;	Microsoft '95/98 software, 10 networked computers, server Windows NT software), printer, modem, dial-up connection.	Networked 13 in different villages	Rural areas mostly
3. ACACIA Iniactive	Africa	International Development Research Center	An initiative by the IDRC aimed at providing developing nations, particularly in Africa, to take advantage of the potential that ICT offer to empower African communities and to give them voice in the Information Society. Please see website for further details: http://www.idrc.ca/acacia					Remote villages
4. Universal Service Agency Telecenters	South Africa	Government Funding during startup phase.	Affordable Universal Access for disadvantage communities	No information on sustainability model	Connecivity and Access	Four computers, phone lines, a printer, a copier and a TVSome of them offer IT training for a fee (Cyber Labs project)	Networked 63 Centers created	Remote areas

AFRICA Information Kiosks (Selected Case Studies)

Name of Project	Country	Funding Sources	Areas	Sustainability Model	Services Provided	ICT/Software use	Operation	Geog Location
5. Tel@Bureau	Niger	International Agency-Philanthropy Services	Creation of Radio Broadcast stations that can also serve as Telecenters	Non-for-profit No further information. Connectivity through phones	Information for economic development	World Space digital receiver, PC, MultimediaPower by solar energy	Networked	Rural Villages
6. Africa Online e-touch	Kenya Ghana Uganda Namibia	Private Investment	Access and Connectivity	For Profit but Africa Online provides email accounts for free	Email, Internet access	No information about technology	Networked	Primarily Urban Centers
7. Sudan Infotech	Sudan	International Agency	Computer Training Education Empowerment of Disabled Empowerment of Women Job Training	Non-for-profit No further information on sustainability model	Provision of computer training to primary, secondary and vocational schools in Southern Sudan	No information about technology	N/A	Southern Sudan with plans to expand to refugee camps in Northern Uganda
8. Nakaseke Telecenter	Uganda	ITU-Government of Uganda IDRC- Training	Access and connectivity to rural areas Content in Local Language Indigenous Knowledge	There is no information about the business model or the pricing scheme	Access to telephones, facsimile machines and computing facilities, including Internet access. It also offers training, technical support	No information about technology	Stand-alone	Remote rural village

ASIA Information Kiosks (Selected Case Studies)

Name of Project	Country	Funding sources	Areas	Sustainability Model	Services Provided	ICT/Software use	Operation	Geog. Location
1. Jhai Foundation Internet Learning Centers	Cambodia	Schools online org JHAI Foundation	Computer literacy and access Agriculture	FREE: Training for schools FEE: For after hours service	Computer training for schools In future, internet services	10 PC/facility LAN, Printer, scanner, digital camera LINUX based	Networked there are only 2	Rural Remote Areas
2. E-Bario	Malaysia (Sarawak)	- IDRC Malaysian Inst. Microelectronics	IT literacy in schools Communication and web site development	Free	Email, internet, word proc	VSAT/10PCs	Stand Alone	Rural Remote Areas
3. Internet Information Centers	Mongolia	Mongolian Government SOROS Foundation	Fee for service Kiosks are in supermarkets, stores and banks Fee for service	Fee Charged to users	Email, internet, word and training	4-6 PCs/ VSAT Fully equipped	Networked	Scattered Population (Nomads)

EASTERN EUROPE Information Kiosks (Selected Case Studies)

Name of Project	Country	Funding sources	Areas	Sustainability Model	Services Provided	ICT/Software use	Operation	Geog. Location
1. Estonian Telecottages (1996)	Estonia	Government, Swedish and Finish Telecenter Association, Small entrepreneurs Open Estonia Foundation	Rural connectivity Business IT Training	FREE FEE (Different business models)	Communication access services Complex needs such as consulting	PCs, printers, phones, multimedia (in some)	50 Telecenters Networked	Rural areas were priority but now they are installed all over

INDIA Information Kiosks (Selected Case Studies)

Name of Project	Country	Funding	Area	Sustainability Model	Service Provided	Operations	ICT/ Software	Geog location
5. FOOD (NGO)	India (Chennai)	FOOD DRC Philanthropy Services	Access, commercial information, Herb Cultivation	Fee for service	Email, internet, data-bases NGO capacity building	Land line and 4 PCs Wireless radio modem	Stand Alone	Rural Remote Area
6. TARAhaat Dr. Ashok Khosla	India (Delhi)	Development Alternatives Group		For profit Fee for use Franchises	E-Government E-commerce (Taravan) Credit (Taracard) Email, Internet access IT Training	PCs connected through fixed lines and there are plans to use VSAT		Uttar Pradesh, Madhya Pradesh and Punjab
7. Community Learning Centers (CLC)	India (Karnataka)	Azim Prejim Foundation Philanthropy Services Government		FREE:- CLCs built in public schools integrating ICT with education PROFIT - before and after school hours open to public for a fee.	ICT Training Education for children Different services: e-mail, e-governance, private classes, summer classes for youth etc.	4-8 PCs/ Modem MS Office in some they have multimedia (camera, mic. etc but not in all)		Rural Villages in Karnataka
8. SARI Contact à Joseph Tomas	India (Tamil Nadu)	Private Funding: n-Logue IIT Madras MIT-Harvard		For Profit Revenue from three sources: IT and computer training, Off line services (job typing, Audio-video) Internet Based	Information and access to com-munications. Email, health information, education, entertain-ment, agriculture etc. Tamil Office tools	Connectivity: corDECT Wireless Access Centers: Antenna and network interface, Telephone hand-sets, PCs, Power supplies, Software suite including Tamil office tools.		Remote rural/ poor areas of Madurai District

INDIA Information Kiosks (Selected Case Studies)

Name of Project	Country	Funding	Area	Sustainability Model	Service Provided	Operations	ICT/ Software	Geog location
1. eChoupal Part of this initiative: soyachoupal aquachoupal plantersnet.com	India	India Tobacco Company Ltd	Agricultural Information Reduce transaction costs- Enhance farm productivity	Kiosks managed by local farmers No further information on sustainability model	Access ready info in their local language on the weather & market prices, disseminate knowledge on scientific farm practices & risk management	Solar	Networked	650 kiosks across four states (Madhya Pradesh, Karnataka, Andhra Pradesh and Uttar Pradesh).
2. Chiraag Internet Kiosks Contact à Joseph Tomas	India (Tamil-Nadul)	Private Investment	Computer training E-Governance Rural Telephony	For profitFee for use of service	Training, government procedures, telephony email		Networked	Tamil Nadu
3. Tripura e-government kiosks (CIC) Contact à Sri J K Sinha	India (Tripura)	Government Funding	E-governance Telephony	Fee for service Not sure if simple access to email and Internet is free	Email, government processes, education		Networked	North Eastern region
4. Village Information Shops	India (Pondicherry)	Swaminatan Foundation IDRC Canadian Government	Access, training, developmentWomen empowerment	No information on sustainability model	Email, internet, spreadsheets, databases, audio, graphics		Networked 10 telecenters	Pondicherry and Tamil Nadu

INDIA Information Kiosks (Selected Case Studies)

Name of Project	Country	Funding	Area	Sustainability Model	Service Provided	Operations	ICT/Software	Geog location
9.- Akshaya Project	India (Kerala)	Government Funding	IT Literacy and different services for local citizens/Generation of employment	For Profit No further information on sustainability model	Information, training, e-government related services, content generated in local language.	Connectivity: No info Access Centers: 5 PCs mandatory with MS Office 98 or Linux, Web Cam, Printer, Modem)		Objective is to connect the entire state of Kerala
10.- Agritech Telecenters	India (Andrah Pradesh)	Samaikya Agritech P. Ltd	The centers provide agricultural support services to farmers on a commercial basis	For profit	Farmers register with centers and pay a fee per growing season (two or three seasons per year) of Rs.150 (about US$3) per acre/crop	No information about technology		AndrahPradesh

LATIN AMERICA Information Kiosks (Selected Case Studies)

Name of Project	Country	Funding sources	Areas	Sustainability Model	Services Provided	ICT/Software use	Operation	Geog. Location
1. Telecenters Cuba Joven Club de Computacion y Electronica	Cuba	Cuban Government - USAID-	Computer Training, Access	Service free Not sure if training is also free	IT training, Email, Internet Access	Land lines Modems	Networked	300 ICT Kiosks
2.- Amic@s Community Learning Centers	Paraguay	Paraguayan government - Digital Partners	Economic development and education	Fee for Internet Access service	IT Training, Email, Internet Access	PCs, dial up connection and Software	Networked	Urban low-income areas in Asuncion
3. Committee to Democratize Information Technology (CDI)	Brazil	- Private Funding - CDI Foundation Private Investment	Computer Training, Access	Free Not sure if training for everybody is free	Computer and software Training. Email, Internet Access	PCs, Software, dial up connection (not available in all CDIs)	Networked	Rural and Urban poor
4. Todito	Mexico	IDRC	E-Commerce Financial Services	Fee for serviceKiosks are in supermarkets, stores and banks	Communication and money transferred services	PC, ATM Machines, Fax/ phone and in some printers.	Networked	Started in the US-Mexican border now expanding South
5. Coinodo (NIUs)	Colombia	Colombian Government (COMPARTEL)	Training and Communications Emphasis on Women	Fee for service	Training, access to email, internet	No information about technology	Networked	Areas around Bogotá
6. e-Mexico Digital Community Centers	Mexico	Very interesting but in incubation stage. Deal signed between government and Microsoft to build DGC in remote areas in Mexico to give people free access to Internet. Seemingly Microsoft will contribute with the software but no further specifications regarding connectivity and technology for access.						

LATIN AMERICA Information Kiosks (Selected Case Studies)

Name of Project	Country	Funding sources	Areas	Sustainability Model	Services Provided	ICT/Software use	Operation	Geog. Location
7. Educ.ar	Argentina	- Government - Private - Philanthropy	Education	Based on 3 pillars: - Connectivity Plan - Portal - Capacity Building	Internet access and computer equipment to 40,000 schools by 2004. Internet Portal www.educ.ar to train more than half a million teachers in		Networked	Nation-wide strategy
8. El Encuentro	Chile	Corporacion El Encuentro	Economic Development IT Literacy/Support for SMEs	Technological Social Franchise	Computer Training, Internet Access, Consulting for SMEs.	PCs, Software, modems for Internet Connection.	Networked	Low-income areas in Santiago (the capital)
9. Multipurpose Community Centers	Honduras	Private and Government dona-tions	IT Literacy Economic Development Access	Fee for service No information on sustainability model	Computer Training. Internet Access, Development of Web Portals, Phone Service	In Each Center: 10 PCs connected with dedicated line-sPrinter.	N/A	2 Rural Villages: Santa Lucia-Valle de los Angeles
10. PRODEM Promotion and Development of Enterprise	Bolivia	International Telecomm. Union (ITU) Private Investment	Economic Development Women Empowerment	Commercial Bank that targets SMEs in and low -income communities	Micro financial ser-vices in urban and rural areas of the country	SMART CARDS. ATMs with 3 optional languages: Quechua, Aymara	Networked of ATMs all over the country	Rural and Urban Areas

Glossary of Terms

B2B	Business to Business
CONCYTEC	Peruvian National Council of Science and Technology (Consejo Nacional de Ciencia y Tecnologia del Peru)
CTCs	Community Technology Centers (Centros Tecnologicos Comunitarios)
ECDL	European Computer Driven License
EU	European Union
EUTA	European Union of Telecottage Associations
Fitel	Peruvain Telecommunications Investment Fund (Fondo de Inversion para las Telecomunicaciones)
GESAC	Governo Eletrônico - Serviço de Atendimento ao Cidadão (Brazil)
GSM	Global System for Mobile Communication
ICT	Information and Communication Technologies
IDRC	International Development Research Center
IIE	Instituto de Informatica Educativa, Universidad de la Frontera (Chile)
IIT	Indian Institute of Technology, Madras (India)
IK or IKs	Information Kiosks
INICTEL	Peruvian National Institute for Telecommunications Training
ISRO	Indian Space Research Organization
ITID	Information and Communications Technology for International Development
MDIC	Ministério do Desenvolvimento, Indústria e Comércio Exterior (Brazil)
MDIC	Ministry of Development, Industry and Foreign Trade (Brazil)
MOST	Chinese Ministry of Science and Technology
NGO	Non-Governmental Organizations
OFDM	Orthogonal Frequency Division Multiplexing
OSIPTEL	The Peruvian Telecommunications Regulatory Body
PHS	Personal Handifone System
POP	Point of Presence
RCP	Peruvian Scientific Network (Red Cientifica Peruana)
SEBRAE	Serviço de Apoio às Micro e Pequenas Empresas (Brazil)
SERCOTEC	Servicio de Cooperacion Tecnica (Chile)
SHG	Self-help Groups
SLA	Service License Agreement
SME or SMEs	Small and Medium Enterprises
SMS	Short Messaging Service
SPG	Social, Private and Governmental sectors
Subtel	Subsecretaría de Telecomunicaciones de Chile
UN ICT Task Force	United Nations Information and Communications Technology Task Force
UNDP	United Nations Development Program
UNESCO	United Nations Educational, Scientific and Cultural Organization
UTRC	University Training and Research Centers
UWB	Ultra-Wide Band
VCD	Video Compact Disk
VIC	Village Information Centers
VIK	Village Information Kiosks
VSAT	Very Small Aperture Terminal
WAP	Wireless Application Protocol
Wi-Fi	Wireless Fidelity
WLAN	Wireless Local Area Network